OXFORD WORLD'S CLASSICS

———

AUTHORS IN CONTEXT

General Editor: PATRICIA INGHAM, University of Oxford
Historical Adviser: BOYD HILTON, University of Cambridge

GEORGE ELIOT

AUTHORS IN CONTEXT examines the work of major writers in relation to their own time and to the present day. The series provides detailed coverage of the values and debates that colour the writing of particular authors and considers their novels, plays, and poetry against this background. Set in their social, cultural, and political contexts, classic books take on new meaning for modern readers. And since readers, like writers, have their own contexts, the series considers how critical interpretations have altered over time, and how films, sequels, and other popular adaptations relate to the new age in which they are produced.

TIM DOLIN is a Research Fellow at Curtin University of Technology, Western Australia. He is the author of *Mistress of the House: Women of Property in the Victorian Novel* (1997) and co-editor (with Peter Widdowson) of *Thomas Hardy and Contemporary Literary Studies* (2004). He has written several articles on Victorian fiction, edited novels by Thomas Hardy and Charlotte Brontë, and is presently working on a study of mass-market fiction and the development of Australian culture between 1880 and 1950.

D1082705

CVCA Royal Library
4687 Wyoga Lake Road
Stow, OH 44224-1011

OXFORD WORLD'S CLASSICS

*For over 100 years Oxford World's Classics have brought
readers closer to the world's great literature. Now with over 700
titles—from the 4,000-year-old myths of Mesopotamia to the
twentieth century's greatest novels—the series makes available
lesser-known as well as celebrated writing.*

*The pocket-sized hardbacks of the early years contained
introductions by Virginia Woolf, T. S. Eliot, Graham Greene,
and other literary figures which enriched the experience of reading.
Today the series is recognized for its fine scholarship and
reliability in texts that span world literature, drama and poetry,
religion, philosophy and politics. Each edition includes perceptive
commentary and essential background information to meet the
changing needs of readers.*

OXFORD WORLD'S CLASSICS

TIM DOLIN

George Eliot

OXFORD
UNIVERSITY PRESS

823.8
Eli

T 27830

OXFORD
UNIVERSITY PRESS

Great Clarendon Street, Oxford OX2 6DP

Oxford University Press is a department of the University of Oxford.
It furthers the University's objective of excellence in research, scholarship,
and education by publishing worldwide in

Oxford New York

Auckland Bangkok Buenos Aires Cape Town Chennai
Dar es Salaam Delhi Hong Kong Istanbul Karachi Kolkata
Kuala Lumpur Madrid Melbourne Mexico City Mumbai Nairobi
São Paulo Shanghai Taipei Tokyo Toronto

Oxford is a registered trade mark of Oxford University Press
in the UK and in certain other countries

Published in the United States
by Oxford University Press Inc., New York

© Tim Dolin 2005

The moral rights of the author have been asserted

Database right Oxford University Press (maker)

All rights reserved. No part of this publication may be reproduced,
stored in a retrieval system, or transmitted, in any form or by any means,
without the prior permission in writing of Oxford University Press,
or as expressly permitted by law, or under terms agreed with the appropriate
reprographics rights organizations. Enquiries concerning reproduction
outside the scope of the above should be sent to the Rights Department,
Oxford University Press, at the address above

You must not circulate this book in any other binding or cover
and you must impose this same condition on any acquirer

British Library Cataloguing in Publication Data

Data available

Library of Congress Cataloging in Publication Data

Data available

ISBN 0–19–284047–9

1

Typeset by RefineCatch Limited, Bungay, Suffolk
Printed in Great Britain by
Clays Ltd, St Ives plc

CVCA Royal Library
4687 Wyoga Lake Road
Stow, OH 44224-1011

CONTENTS

LIST OF ILLUSTRATIONS

A CHRONOLOGY OF GEORGE ELIOT

Life	*Cultural and Historical Background*
1819	Born, 22 November, at South Farm, Arbury, nr Nuneaton, Warwickshire, the youngest of the 3 children of Robert Evans and his second wife Christiana Pearson. Christened Mary Anne Evans, 29 November.	Birth of Victoria. Scott, *The Bride of Lammermoor* Scott, *Ivanhoe*
1820	Evans family moves to Griff House, Arbury, where Robert Evans is agent for Francis Newdigate's estate.	Death of George III; accession of George IV. Keats, *Lamia, . . . and other Poems* Shelley, *Prometheus Unbound*
1824–7	Boarder at Miss Lathom's School in nearby Attleborough, with her sister Chrissey.	
1828–32	At Mrs Wallington's boarding-school, Nuneaton, where she becomes friendly with Miss Lewis, the principal governess and a strong evangelical.	1829: Catholic Emancipation Act. 1830: Death of George IV; accession of William IV. Tennyson, *Poems, Chiefly Lyrical* 1830–3: Charles Lyell, *Principles of Geology*
1832–5	At the Miss Franklins' School, Coventry, run by the daughters of a Baptist minister. Leaves school finally at Christmas.	1832: First Reform Act. 1833: First Factory Act. 1835: David Friedrich Strauss, *Das Leben Jesu*
1836	Mother dies 3 February. After Chrissey marries, in May 1837, GE takes charge of her father's household. Learns Italian and Greek from a Coventry teacher, and reads Greek and Latin with the headmaster of Coventry Grammar School. Changes her name to Mary Ann.	

	Life	*Cultural and Historical Background*
1837–9	Reads widely, especially in theology, the history of religion, and in Romanticism, including Wordsworth, Coleridge, Southey, and Scott (her favourite novelist).	1837: Death of William IV; accession of Victoria. Carlyle, *The French Revolution* Dickens, *Pickwick Papers* 1838: Anti Corn Law League founded; London–Birmingham railway opened. 1839: Chartists demand suffrage. Charles Hennell, *An Inquiry into the Origins of Christianity*
1840	Her first publication, a religious poem, appears in the *Christian Observer* in January.	Penny Post established; Victoria marries Prince Albert.
1841	Brother, Isaac, marries and takes over the house at Griff. GE moves with father to Coventry. Introduced to Charles Bray and his wife Caroline (Cara), Coventry freethinkers, through whom she makes contact with Charles Hennell. Reads Hennell's *Inquiry* and finds her religious faith challenged.	Robert Peel becomes Prime Minister. Carlyle, *Heroes and Hero Worship*
1842	Refuses to attend church with her father, January–May, but finally agrees to accompany him at the end of what she calls their 'Holy War'. Meets and begins corresponding with Charles Hennell's sister Sara.	Chartist riots; child and female underground labour becomes illegal; Act for inspection of asylums. Browning, *Dramatic Lyrics* Comte, *Cours de philosophie positive* Macaulay, *Lays of Ancient Rome* Tennyson, *Poems*
1843	In November visits Dr Brabant of Devizes, father of Charles Hennell's wife who had undertaken a translation of Strauss's *Das Leben Jesu* but, on marrying, discontinued it.	Thames Tunnel opened. Carlyle, *Past and Present* Ruskin, *Modern Painters* begins publication Wordsworth, *Poems*
1844	Takes over the translation of *Das Leben Jesu*.	Robert Chambers, *Vestiges of Creation* (published anonymously)
1845	In March declines a proposal of marriage. Meets Harriet Martineau. In October visits Scotland with the Brays, and visits Scott's home, Abbotsford.	Newman received into the Catholic Church; Irish potato crop fails. Disraeli, *Sybil; or, The Two Nations*

	Life	*Cultural and Historical Background*
1846	*The Life of Jesus* published in 3 vols. in June after much labour and many complaints of being 'Strauss-sick'.	Repeal of the Corn Laws; Irish famine. Ruskin, *Modern Painters* II
1847	Nurses her father.	James Simpson discovers the anaesthetic properties of chloroform. 'Currer Bell', *Jane Eyre* 'Ellis Bell', *Wuthering Heights* Thackeray, *Vanity Fair* Dickens, *Dombey and Son*
1848	Meets Emerson; reads Sand and Scott. Nurses her father.	Revolutions in Europe; Disraeli becomes leader of the Tory party in the House of Commons. Elizabeth Gaskell, *Mary Barton*
1849	Reviews J. A. Froude's *Nemesis of Faith* favourably for the Coventry *Herald*. Begins translation of Spinoza's *Tractatus theologico-politicus*. Father dies on 31 May. In June leaves for France, Italy, and Switzerland with the Brays; winters alone in Geneva. Begins *Journal*.	Cholera epidemic in England; Bedford College for Women founded. Henry Mayhew's 'London Labour and the London Poor' articles begin publication in the *Morning Chronicle*
1850	Returns, unhappily, to Coventry and lives with the Brays for seven months. Adopts the French spelling of her name, Marian, in preference to Mary Ann. Decides to earn her living by writing. Lodges with John Chapman in London for two weeks in November.	Death of Wordsworth. *The Prelude* published posthumously Spencer, *Social Statics* Dickens, *David Copperfield*
1851	Reviews Mackay's *The Progress of the Intellect* for the January no. of Chapman's *Westminster Review* and moves to Chapman's home, 142 Strand, but in March is driven away by the jealousy of his wife and mistress. Returns in September to become, in all but name, the editor of the *Westminster Review*.	Great Exhibition opens at the Crystal Palace.

Life	*Cultural and Historical Background*
1852	Friendship with Herbert Spencer leads to rumours of an engagement. Through him she meets George Henry Lewes, arts editor of the *Leader*.	Death of the Duke of Wellington, 14 September; Kings Cross station completed.
1853	Heavily involved with the *Westminster Review*. Reads Gaskell's *Ruth*, Brontë's *Villette*, Goethe, Schiller, Lessing, and Hegel. Resigns editorship of *Westminster Review* at the end of the year.	Harriet Martineau's translation of Comte's *Positive Philosophy* Dickens, *Bleak House* Charlotte Brontë, *Villette* Elizabeth Gaskell, *Ruth* and *Cranford*
1854	Her translation of Ludwig Feuerbach's radical critique of orthodox belief, *The Essence of Christianity* is published in July. In the same month she travels to Germany with Lewes, first visiting Weimar then wintering in Berlin, causing scandal back in Britain. Lewes unable to obtain a divorce because he had condoned his wife's adultery. Assists Lewes in the research and writing of his biography of Goethe and in November begins a translation of Spinoza's *Ethics* (unpublished until 1981).	Crimean War begins.
1855	Returns to England in March and sets up house with Lewes in Richmond. Writes regularly for the *Leader* and *Westminster Review*. In November Lewes's *Life and Works of Goethe* is published to general and lasting acclaim.	Gaskell, *North and South* Turgenev, *Russian Life*, trans. James D. Meiklejohn
1856	Visits Ilfracombe, May–June, for Lewes's research into marine biology (later published as *Sea-Side Studies*, 1858), then Tenby in Wales, July–early August where she conceives the idea of writing 'The Sad	Crimean War ends 29 April; public celebrations of the peace with Russia are held across Britain on 29 May. Meredith, *The Shaving of Shagpat*

Life	*Cultural and Historical Background*
Fortunes of the Reverend Amos Barton'. Begins writing in September, and the story is accepted by *Blackwood's Edinburgh Magazine*. Her review of Riehl's *The Natural History of German Life* appears in the *Westminster Review* in July, and 'Silly Novels by Lady Novelists' in October. Begins writing 'Mr Gilfil's Love-Story' on Christmas Day.	

1857   In January Part I of 'Amos Barton' appears in *Blackwood's* and her last major article in the *Westminster Review*. Assumes the pseudonym 'George Eliot'. In March travels with Lewes to Scilly Isles where she completes 'Mr Gilfil's Love-Story' for the June issue of *Blackwood's*. Tells her brother, Isaac, about her relationship and he insists her family break off all communication with her. 'Janet's Repentance' finished 30 May on Jersey, where GE and Lewes stay until late July. Begins writing *Adam Bede* in October.

Indian Mutiny.
Flaubert, *Madame Bovary*
Gaskell, *The Life of Charlotte Brontë*
Dickens, *Little Dorrit*

1858   *Scenes of Clerical Life* published in 2 vols. in January. Dickens writes praising the book, and convinced the author must be a woman. In April GE and Lewes travel via Nuremburg to Munich, remaining there until 6 July when they make their way via Salzburg, Vienna, and Prague to Dresden. Work on *Adam Bede* proceeds quickly. They return to England in September, and the novel is completed on 16 November

Government of India Act transferring British power over India from the East India Co. to the Crown; Burton and Speke discover source of the Nile; Bessie Parkes and Barbara Bodichon found the *English Woman's Journal* which campaigns for married women's property rights and higher education for women.

	Life	*Cultural and Historical Background*
1859	*Adam Bede* published in 3 vols. in February to critical acclaim; 16,000 copies sold in the first year. In February they settle at Holly Lodge, Wandsworth, where GE forms a close friendship with the positivists, Mr and Mrs Richard Congreve. Sister Chrissey dies of consumption in March. Work on *The Mill on the Floss* is slow, and she breaks off to write 'The Lifted Veil' (finished in April and published in *Blackwood's* in July). In July, under pressure, the secrecy of the pseudonym is relinquished. Dickens visits in November and invites her to contribute to *All the Year Round*.	Charles Darwin, *The Origin of Species* J. S. Mill, *On Liberty* Tennyson, *Idylls of the King* *Macmillan's Magazine* launched in November
1860	*The Mill on the Floss* finished on 22 March and published in 3 vols. on 4 April. GE and Lewes leave for a holiday in Italy where, in May, GE conceives the idea for a historical novel based on the life of Savonarola. They return to England via Switzerland, bringing Lewes's eldest son Charles back with them. GE writes 'Brother Jacob'; begins *Silas Marner*. With Charles they move house twice, settling in December at 16 Blandford Square, off Regent's Park.	Unification of Italy. *Cornhill Magazine* founded
1861	*Silas Marner* published in April; they revisit Florence where GE collects more material, and she begins writing *Romola* in October.	American Civil War begins.
1862	Smith, Elder offer the unprecedented sum of £10,000 for *Romola* (GE eventually accepts £7,000)	

Life   *Cultural and Historical Background*

which begins serialization in
the *Cornhill Magazine* in July.
As part of her research for the
book reads Elizabeth Barrett
Browning's *Casa Guidi
Windows*.

1863   *Romola* published in 3 vols. in   Thackeray dies suddenly on Christmas
        July and finishes serialization   Eve; over 1,000 people attend the
        in the *Cornhill* in August: 'I   funeral.
        began it as a young woman,—   Elizabeth Gaskell, *Sylvia's Lovers*
        I finished it an old woman.' In
        August they move to The
        Priory, Regent's Park, the
        house associated with
        GE's most famous years.

1864   They visit Italy in May. In   Dickens, *Our Mutual Friend* begins
        June GE begins research for   publication
        The Spanish Gypsy, a tragic
        play in blank verse. Starts
        writing in October. Reading
        includes Newman's *Apologia
        pro Vita Sua*.

1865   Work on *The Spanish Gypsy*   Abraham Lincoln assassinated,
        proves so stressful that Lewes   14 April; American Civil War ends in
        insists she abandon it in   May; death of Palmerston in October;
        February. Begins *Felix Holt* in   Russell succeeds him as leader of the
        March. Lewes becomes editor   House of Commons.
        of the *Fortnightly Review* and   *Fortnightly Review* founded
        GE contributes a review of   Walter Bagehot, *The English
        Lecky.   Constitution* serialized
                                            Lecky, *History of . . . Rationalism in
                                            Europe*

1866   *Felix Holt* completed in May   Russell's 1st Reform Bill defeated; in
        and published in 3 vols. in June   April Gladstone tells the House: 'You
        but sales disappoint. They   cannot fight against the future. Time is
        visit the Low Countries and   on our side'; rioting in Hyde Park on
        Germany, and in August GE   23 July after the resignation of Russell's
        resumes work on *The Spanish   ministry; Austria and Prussia at war.
        Gypsy*. In December they set
        off for the South of France.

1867   In January they extend their   2nd Reform Bill introduced by
        trip to Spain so that GE can   Disraeli; 20 May John Stuart Mill
        collect material. On 22   moves to amend the new Reform Bill to
        February they visit gipsies   include women.
        living in holes in the   Turgenev, *Fathers and Sons*, trans.
        mountains above Granada.   E. Schuyler
        Return on 16 March.

Life	*Cultural and Historical Background*
1868	Gives £50 'from the author of *Romola*' to the foundation of what became Girton College, Cambridge. *The Spanish Gypsy* finished 29 April and published in June.	Browning, *The Ring and the Book* begins publication
1869	Writes 'Address to Working Men, by Felix Holt', for publication in *Blackwood's* in January. Writes some short poems early in the year. March and April in Italy. In Rome GE meets the stockbroker John Walter Cross for the first time. Henry James visits in May. GE intermittently researches a long poem to be called 'Timoleon', but abandons the project in September. Begins writing 'Middlemarch' (the Featherstone–Vincy part) in August. Lewes's second son, Thornton (Thornie), returns from Natal in May with spinal tuberculosis and dies in October. GE writes the poems eventually published as *The Legend of Jubal and Other Poems* (1874).	Hitchin College opens in May (becomes Girton College in 1873). J. S. Mill, *The Subjection of Women* Arnold, *Culture and Anarchy* (book form)
1870	Puts aside 'Middlemarch' in despair, and in December begins a new story, 'Miss Brooke', which develops rapidly. Corresponds with Harriet Beecher Stowe. Combines the two narratives early in the year to create the first section of *Middlemarch*, to be published in 8 parts.	Franco-Prussian War begins; death of Dickens; Married Women's Property Act; Elementary Education Act.
1871	Book I of *Middlemarch* published in December.	Franco-Prussian War ends.
1872	'Simmering towards a new book', November. Final part of *Middlemarch* published in December; the whole published in 4 vols.	Le Fanu, *In a Glass Darkly*

	Life	Cultural and Historical Background
1873	Begins 'Sketches towards Daniel Deronda', January. July–August visits France and Germany to research the novel. *The Legend of Jubal and Other Poems* published.	Pater, *Studies in the History of the Renaissance*
1874	*Poems* published, including the 'Brother and Sister sonnets'. Suffers a first attack of kidney stone in February. Begins writing *Daniel Deronda* in the late autumn, but progress is slow due to ill health. Vol. I of Lewes's *Problems of Life and Mind* published in November.	Disraeli becomes Prime Minister. Hardy, *Far from the Madding Crowd*
1875	Writing *Daniel Deronda*. Vol. II of Lewes's *Problems of Life and Mind* published.	Death of Kingsley. Trollope, *The Way We Live Now*
1876	*Daniel Deronda* begins publication in 8 parts in February, the last part appearing in September. Richard Wagner and his wife visit in May. June–September travelling in France, Germany, Switzerland. In December they buy The Heights at Witley in Surrey as a summer residence.	Alexander Graham Bell patents the telephone. James, *Roderick Hudson*
1878	Writes *Impressions of Theophrastus Such*. Lewes dies on 30 November. GE refuses to see anyone for several weeks and occupies herself in completing and preparing the last two volumes of his major philosophical work, *Problems of Life and Mind*, for the press.	London University becomes the first to offer degrees to women. Gilbert and Sullivan, *HMS Pinafore*
1879	Agrees to see Cross in February, and helps him to learn Italian. *Impressions of Theophrastus Such* published in May. Gives £5,000 to fund a Studentship in Physiology at Cambridge in Lewes's name, the first Student being	Ibsen, *A Doll's House* James, *Daisy Miller*

Life	*Cultural and Historical Background*
appointed in October. For legal reasons changes her name by deed poll to Mary Ann Evans Lewes.	

| 1880 | In April agrees to marry Cross. Married on 6 May, upon which her brother Isaac writes to congratulate her after 23 years of estrangement. Honeymoons in France and Italy, principally Venice, returning to England via Austria and Germany in late July. Moves to 4 Cheyne Walk on 3 December. Catches cold at a concert and dies on 22 December aged 61, her death probably in part the result of kidney disease. Buried in Highgate Cemetery on 29 December. | Elementary education becomes compulsory in England and Wales; Parnell demands Home Rule for Ireland. Tennyson, *Ballads and Other Poems* Gissing, *Workers in the Dawn* |

ABBREVIATIONS

Biography	Gordon S. Haight, *George Eliot: A Biography* (Oxford: Oxford University Press, 1968)
CH	David Carroll (ed.), *George Eliot: The Critical Heritage* (London: Routledge and Kegan Paul, 1971)
Essays	Thomas Pinney (ed.), *Essays of George Eliot* (London: Routledge and Kegan Paul, 1963)
Journals	Margaret Harris and Judith Johnston (eds.), *The Journals of George Eliot* (Cambridge: Cambridge University Press, 1998)
Life	J. W. Cross, *George Eliot's Life as Related in her Letters and Journals*, 2nd edn. (Edinburgh: Blackwood's, 1885)
Letters	Gordon S. Haight (ed.), *The George Eliot Letters*, 9 vols. (New Haven: Yale University Press, 1954–78)

CHAPTER I

THE INSURGENT AND THE SIBYL: THE LIFE OF GEORGE ELIOT

VITA SACKVILLE-WEST once described George Eliot as 'one of those authors of whom it is almost impossible to think without instantly recalling their physical appearance'.[1] There has always been intense curiosity about Eliot's appearance, in part because of her striking ugliness:

To begin with she is magnificently ugly [the young Henry James wrote to his father in 1869]—deliciously hideous. She has a low forehead, a dull grey eye, a vast pendulous nose, a huge mouth, full of uneven teeth and a chin and jaw-bone *qui n'en finissent pas*. . . . Now in this vast ugliness resides a most powerful beauty which, in a very few minutes steals forth and charms the mind, so that you end as I ended, in falling in love with her. Yes behold me literally in love with this great horse-faced blue-stocking. I don't know in what the charm lies, but it is thoroughly potent. An admirable physiognomy—a delightful expression, a voice soft and rich as that of a counselling angel—a mingled sagacity and sweetness—a broad hint of a great underlying world of reserve, knowledge, pride and power—a great feminine dignity and character in these massively plain features—a hundred conflicting shades of consciousness and simpleness—shyness and frankness—graciousness and remote indifference—these are some of the more definite elements of her personality.[2]

Few surviving images of Eliot express either her magnificent ugliness or powerful beauty. The formal portraits in oil and chalk discreetly foreshorten her long, equine face and hooked nose, tending rather to a common blandness than a common likeness (see pp. 3 and 22). The scant photographs—Eliot was extremely sensitive about photographs of her, and suppressed them wherever she could—are not flattering, but nor are they particularly revealing.[3] They leave us perplexed, not as James was by the 'hundred conflicting shades' of personality, but by the apparent contradictoriness of that personality. Here is a writer whom we feel we know intimately in some way, but who is at the same time opaque and impenetrable.

Similarly, all attempts to bring George Eliot alive, even in the best biographies, stumble, as James does, over this enigma of a woman who is at once so approachable and so resistant to approach, so gracious and so remotely indifferent, so knowable and so inscrutable. Of course, as Eliot herself observed in *Daniel Deronda*:

Attempts at description are stupid: who can all at once describe a human being? even when he is presented to us we only begin that knowledge of his appearance which must be completed by innumerable impressions under differing circumstances. We recognize the alphabet; we are not sure of the language. (chapter 11)

Eliot's biographers—with the notable exception of her surviving husband of only eight months, John Walter Cross, who wrote a staid, reverential Victorian 'life and letters' biography—have struggled to make sense of the paradoxes and contradictions thrown up by her life and work. The George Eliot they have produced is a strangely uncomfortable compound of two antithetical characters: variously the insurgent and the sibyl, the rebellious woman and the respectable woman, the radical intellectual and artist who was also profoundly conservative in social and political matters.

The image of the 'insurgent' had its origins in a memoir written in 1885 by William Hale White, author of *The Autobiography of Mark Rutherford* (1881). The intention of this memoir, published in the *Athenaeum*, was to challenge Cross's 'official' biography of Eliot, which had just come out. Cross's well-meaning act of homage portrayed Eliot as an eminent Victorian—humourless, ponderously wise, dully respectable and conventional. Hale White remembered quite a different person:

She was really one of the most sceptical, unusual creatures I ever knew, and it was this side of her character which to me was the most attractive. She told me that it was worthwhile to undertake all the labour of learning French if it resulted in nothing more than reading one book—Rousseau's *Confessions*. That saying was perfectly symbolical of her, and reveals more completely what she was, at any rate in 1851–54, than page after page of attempt on my part at critical analysis. I can see her now, with her hair over her shoulders, the easy chair half sideways to the fire, her feet over the arms, and a proof in her hands, in that dark room at the back of No. 142. (*Biography*, p. 123)

Hers was an 'entirely unconventional life', Hale White concluded,

Portrait of George Eliot by Frederic Burton, 1865

and Cross's biography had done her a grave disservice by removing her 'from the class—the great and noble church, if I may so call it—of the Insurgents' (*Biography*, p. 123).

In a spiteful memoir published in 1899, the novelist Eliza Lynn Linton described Eliot in exactly the same terms, but alleged she had lived an inauthentic life 'in her endeavour to harmonise two irreconcilables—to be at once conventional and insurgent'.[4] Linton's view is severely distorted by envy and mischief-making (and it is fair to say that Hale White's view is distorted by his distant, nostalgic affection for the young woman at 142 Strand). But if we are to understand and appreciate the nature of Eliot's achievement as the greatest novelist of ideas in English, and the greatest novelist of the Victorian period, it is necessary to examine at the outset these 'two irreconcilables', which have a bearing on every aspect of her life and work. What Linton means by 'conventionality' is more complex and far-reaching than it first seems. Eliot's life, she implies, but for one spectacularly unconventional event—or the more so because of that one event—was in reality highly conventional, even strenuously respectable. That respectability was reflected in the fact that Eliot, banished from society for living with a married man, strove in everything she did and wrote to be accepted back; which, in the end, is exactly what happened. She became, Linton declared scornfully, 'so consciously "George Eliot"—so interpenetrated head and heel, inside and out, with the sense of her importance as the great novelist and profound thinker of her generation'.[5] A monument of the establishment, Eliot's greatness was indistinguishable from her deep-seated respectability and conventionality.

Conventionality also implies conservatism, and the paradox Linton presents is closely related to the paradox of Eliot's 'conservative-reforming intellect' ('Amos Barton'). Basil Willey argued in 1949 that her whole life united 'advancing intellect and backward-yearning affections'—her head took her in one direction and her heart in another—and, ever since, we have grappled with feelings of uneasiness towards political opinions and social views that seem out of step with someone otherwise so progressive.[6] For there is no avoiding it: Eliot's richest insights come out of political and social convictions that are deeply conservative, anti-democratic, and avowedly anti-feminist. Eliot was no bohemian, and there is no evidence that her politics were ever radical, even when she presided over the most important periodical of intellectual dissent in mid-Victorian Britain. Yet who among the Victorian novelists was more trenchantly critical of the oppressiveness of social structures? Who more eloquent about the curtailment of women's lives? Eliot's conservatism was, paradoxically, integral to her social critique, of a piece with her intellectual radicalism, and the foundation of her artistic enterprise—it is what made her, and still makes her, a great novelist.

The life of George Eliot cannot therefore be reduced to the narrative of an insurgent who abandoned God, renounced marriage, and embraced progressive views only to be transformed by fame and mid-Victorian prosperity into a politically conservative and socially reactionary voice of the establishment. Her unorthodoxy was intellectual, her conservatism sentient: and both were deeply rooted in the clear-thinking, plain-speaking environment of her childhood and youth in the English Midlands. She grew up around successful men, and rejoiced in the steady secure rhythms of rural working life; she also struggled against the stifling oppressiveness of those men, who briskly dismissed the pretensions of an intellectual young woman. This countryside of her upbringing came to represent for Eliot the spirit of England itself. As the eccentric narrator of her last book, *Impressions of Theophrastus Such*, recalls, the 'midland plains' were a paradigm of English 'national life':

Is there any country which shows at once as much stability and as much susceptibility to change as ours? Our national life is like that scenery which I early learned to love, not subject to great convulsions, but easily showing more or less delicate (sometimes melancholy) effects from minor changes. ('Looking Backward')

Eliot's was not a personality susceptible to the great convulsions of the age; the social, political, religious, technological, and scientific revolutions of her lifetime she absorbed into the immense continuities of the past. This is Eliot's characteristic milieu—the provincial landed estates and small towns where the stable rhythms of common life endure in the face of profound social changes—and her fiction traces the 'more or less delicate (sometimes melancholy) effects' of these changes under these particular conditions.

Mary Anne Evans, as she was first named, was born on 22 November 1819 at South Farm on the 7,000-acre Arbury estate situated between Nuneaton and Coventry in Warwickshire, in the

English Midlands. Her father, Robert Evans, was manager of the estate and land agent for its incumbent, Francis Parker Newdigate. He had been brought in from Derbyshire in 1806 when his employer, then plain Francis Parker, inherited Arbury and the Newdigate name and arms from the childless Sir Roger Newdigate. Evans was a carpenter by trade, but his thorough knowledge of timber as well as his wide practical skills, business acumen, and exceptional integrity had brought him to Parker's notice as a young man, and he rose steadily from farm bailiff to land agent, and even ultimately managed several neighbouring estates in addition to Arbury, as well as being frequently called in to arbitrate in disputes and value land and timber. He was described by his daughter as having

raised himself from being an artizan to be a man whose extensive knowledge in very varied practical departments made his services valued through several counties. He had large knowledge of building, of mines, of plantation, of various branches of valuation and measurement—of all that is essential to the management of large estates. He was held by those competent to judge as *unique* amongst land agents for his manifold knowledge and experience, which enabled him to save the special fees usually paid by landowners for special opinions on the different questions incident to the proprietorship of land. (*Letters*, iii. 168)

He was the kind of man who, several decades later, would become a representative figure in the mid-Victorian middle-class ethos: physically strong, skilled, down-to-earth, socially ambitious, trustworthy, thrifty, self-helpful. Indeed, Evans himself contributed something to that myth, as the model for aspects of the characters of Adam Bede, Felix Holt, and Caleb Garth (in *Middlemarch*).

Evans's first wife, Harriet Poynton, died a few years after they arrived in Warwickshire, and in 1813 he married again, this time above his class. Christiana Pearson was the daughter of a local yeoman (a small property freeholder), 'a woman with an unusual amount of natural force—a shrewd practical person, with a considerable dash of the Mrs. Poyser vein in her' (*Life*, p. 7). Her three sisters, all married and all living nearby, were the originals for the redoubtable Dodson sisters in *The Mill on the Floss*. But for all the 'force' of her nature the second Mrs Evans remains a shadowy figure, barely mentioned in George Eliot's letters and journals. Mary Anne was the youngest of her children, stepsister to Robert (born 1802) and Frances (known as Fanny, born 1805), and sister to Christiana (or Chrissey, born 1814), and Isaac (born 1816). When she was just a few months old, in 1820, the family moved from South Farm to Griff, a substantial brick house just off the Coventry Road near the intersection of the road to Arbury Hall, where they lived for twenty years.

The rich Midlands countryside around Griff was vitally import-ant to the development of George Eliot's imagination. 'It is interest-ing', she wrote towards the end of her life, '. . . to know whether a writer was born in a central or border district—a condition which always has a strongly determining influence' (*Letters*, vi. 163). One of her chief aims, indeed, was to make her readers see the poetry of this flat unpoetic region, and experience the 'things that make the gamut of joy in landscape to midland-bred souls—the things they toddled among, or perhaps learned by heart standing between their father's knees,' as she did, 'while he drove leisurely' *(Middlemarch*, chapter 12). This was not a landscape of manor houses and parks, or picturesque farmsteads and villages. In the Introduction to *Felix Holt, the Radical*, Eliot describes it rather as that unique region of the English countryside where two extremes, of agriculture and industry, past and present, intermingle, and where the traveller may pass 'rapidly from one phase of English life to another: after looking down on a village dingy with coal-dust, noisy with the shaking of looms, he might skirt a parish all of fields, high hedges, and deep-rutted lanes'. Arbury was a modern working agricultural and indus-trial-commercial estate in the middle of the weaving districts. Griff House and its farm offices, from which Evans ran the estate's farm-ing and timber businesses and oversaw estate building and repairs, were just a mile from the Griff Colliery. Coal was the most important source of income for the estate; indeed, the canal which ran by Griff linked Arbury directly to the great industrial cities of the Midlands. Chief among Robert Evans's duties were management of the mine and its shipping operations, and of the villagers who worked in the pits and on the canal.

In 1824 Mary Anne attended a dame school across the road from Griff with her brother Isaac, whom she passionately adored, as Maggie adores Tom Tulliver. Late that year, however, when Isaac went off to Foleshill to begin his schooling in earnest (and where he would begin to grow away from his sister as Tom does), Mary Anne was sent to join Chrissey at Miss Lathom's boarding school a couple of miles away at Attleborough. She was only 5 years old, and later confessed to suffering from cold and night-terrors there, which may have contributed to her intermittently poor health and susceptibility to attacks of anxiety. But this was no Dickensian charity school, and Mary Anne's miseries were allayed by her father's frequent visits and weekends at home. These years are memorialized, not as they were for Charlotte Brontë, for example, by want and death, but by the deep happiness of her home life.

In the course of a few years, Mary Anne and Chrissey were moved to Mrs Wallington's boarding school in Nuneaton. There Mary Anne met Maria Lewis, head governess at the school, who became the first of her regular correspondents and close friends. The earliest preserved George Eliot letter is addressed to Lewis, and most of the first seventy-odd surviving letters are written to her. Their friendship lasted nearly thirteen years, until the end of 1841 (although there was no final break until early in 1847). An Irishwoman, Lewis was also an evangelical, a member of that branch of the established Church of England which grew out of the Evangelical Revival in the eighteenth century and was a powerful catalyst for Church reform in the early 1800s, bringing Wesleyan ideals of personal spiritual conversion and the examined life to mainstream Anglican congregations. The year of Mary Anne's arrival at the school, 1828, was the year the revival came to Nuneaton in force, in the controversial figure of John Jones, who had just been installed as perpetual curate of the Chapel of Ease in outlying Stockingford. Like the Reverend Mr Tryan in 'Janet's Repentance', who is based on Eliot's memories of this charismatic curate, Jones alienated local Churchmen and Chapel preachers alike by attracting Dissenters to his services. It is not clear exactly when Mary Anne came under the influence of Maria Lewis's austere evangelical piety, but Robert Evans's journal reports that she accompanied the Evanses to Chilvers Coton church (the Shepperton Church of *Scenes of Clerical Life*) on Mary Anne's tenth birthday, in 1830. In any case Mary Anne was soon 'earnestly endeavouring to shape this anomalous English-Christian life of ours into some consistency with the spirit and simple verbal tenor of the New Testament' (*Letters*, iii. 174).

Her development in this direction was encouraged by her removal to the school of Rebecca and Mary Franklin in Coventry in 1832.

The Franklins were Baptists, and further cultivated the girl's seriousness and piety. They also provided her with the rudiments of a wide-ranging education, however, especially in literature. She read Pascal, Shakespeare, and the English poets (even Byron), as well as popular miscellanies of literature such as the *Keepsake* and those (to some Dissenters) most dangerous forms of writing, novels: by Sir Walter Scott (who died in 1832, and whom George Eliot came to worship); and the younger generation of his followers and popular imitators in historical romance, especially Edward Bulwer-Lytton and G. P. R. James. Mary Anne even began a romance of her own at this time, fragments of which are interspersed in her notebook with religious verses. Under the Miss Franklins she also further refined her speech, erasing any elements of Midlands dialect and pronunciation left after Maria Lewis had begun the task. In time, Mary Anne would develop a speaking voice that became an integral part of George Eliot's mystique. The Franklin sisters also encouraged the stiffly formal diction in which Maria Lewis had inducted Mary Anne; it would be some time before she would develop the vigorous prose that came to characterize her published writing.

Mary Anne stayed at the Miss Franklins' school until the end of 1835, when she was called home to help Chrissey nurse her mother, who was dying of breast cancer, and her father, who was bedridden with a severe attack of kidney stones. Robert Evans soon recovered, but on 3 February 1836, after months of suffering, Mrs Evans died. Mary Anne was 15 years old, and her formal schooling was over. For the next thirteen years, until her father's death in 1849, her education was to be continued at home, largely by her own efforts, and with the help of language and music tutors. She and Chrissey shared duties until the latter married in 1837; thereafter Mary Ann, who changed the spelling of her name at this time, took over the role of her father's sole housekeeper, and later his nurse during his final illnesses. Her evangelical piety intensified then into a grim, doctrinaire, self-hating Calvinism, as she faced the sadness and bitterness of her mother's death and its long dreary aftermath, despairing, as she would later become constitutionally prone to do, of ever being able to achieve anything.

The early letters to Maria Lewis and Martha (or Patty) Jackson, Mary Ann's friend from the Franklins' school, are curious and revealing documents, stiff in their puritan conventionalism and

tireless in their performance of piety. Their self-ironies are muted or
absent, but they are not insincere letters, and show very clearly
George Eliot's later great gift of entering sympathetically into the
world-view of her correspondents, and taking up their ways of thinking and speaking. Evangelicalism was a world-view she shared
enthusiastically with her friends, to be sure, but it is difficult in these
letters to distinguish Mary Ann's voice from the collective voice of
the trio (this is most obvious when, under the influence of the
'language of flowers' craze, they address each other as 'Veronica' and
'Clematis'). Yet at the same time many of the elements of these letters—the wary surveillance of her own egotism, present here as
puritan moral self-examination; the periods of black despair; the
kindliness and considerateness—are important elements in the
making of George Eliot.

Mary Ann's fanaticism reached its apogee in 1838. That year she
visited London with Isaac, refused to go to the theatre with him, and
purchased as a souvenir of the trip Josephus' *History of the Jews*.
She denied herself the pleasures of music and novels, but learned to
displace them into such approved 'serious' pleasures as biography.
Instead of Scott, she read Lockhart's *Life of Scott*; instead of G. P. R.
James, she read his *Life and Times of Louis Quatorze*, confessing to
Martha Jackson that 'I devour it as a romance'.[7] At the same time her
reading was widening. In 1839 she read Carlyle's *Chartism*, rhetorical
elements of which entered her letters, and Wordsworth. She also
read 'scraps of poetry picked up from Shakespeare, Cowper,
Wordsworth, and Milton, newspaper topics, morsels of Addison and
Bacon, Latin verbs, geometry entomology and chemistry, reviews
and metaphysics, all arrested and petrified and smothered by the fast
thickening every day accession of actual events, relative anxieties,
and household cares and vexations' (*Letters*, i. 29). Mary Ann was
also continuing her intensive self-education, reading in religious history (at this time she was preparing a detailed chart of ecclesiastical
history), theology, and controversy. For the first time, too, in 1839,
she admitted to Maria Lewis: 'I am powerfully attracted in a certain
direction but when I am about to settle there, counter assertions
shake me from my position' (*Letters*, i. 25). By 1840 her fanatical
evangelicalism had begun to subside; soon her faith would be shaken
to pieces. That year Isaac was planning his marriage, and it was
agreed that he would move to Griff and take over the 67-year-old

Robert Evans's duties as Newdigate's agent. Mary Ann and her father would begin the search for a new house. It was, as Cross describes it, 'a change almost amounting to a revolution in Miss Evans's life' (*Life*, p. 40).

On 17 March 1841 they moved to a house in Foleshill Road on the rural outskirts of Coventry. Mary Ann had been apprehensive, even fearful, about the change, and at first she felt isolated and depressed, although she soon made contact with a friend of Rebecca Franklin's, Mary Sibree, and joined her new next-door neighbour, Mrs Elizabeth Pears, in local charitable activities. Coventry was in the heart of the ribbon-weaving districts, and Mrs Pears's husband and brother were both prosperous ribbon manufacturers. On 2 November 1841, she introduced Mary Ann to her brother, Charles Bray, and his wife Caroline (Cara), at their home, Rosehill, about a mile away from Foleshill on the Radford Road. This meeting would change her life. A large house set among expansive gardens over-looking Coventry, Rosehill was a congenial meeting place for independent, progressive thinkers, not only from the Midlands but from London and further afield (its visitors included Thackeray, Emerson, Herbert Spencer, and Harriet Martineau). Here the Brays cultivated what Charles was to describe as a 'free-and-easy mental atmosphere, harmonizing with the absence of all pretension and conventionality', where talk flowed 'unrestrained' and there was a rich 'interchange of ideas, varied and peculiar according to the character and mood of the talkers and thinkers assembled there'. Everyone 'who came to Coventry with a queer mission, or a crotchet, or was supposed to be a "little cracked" ', he wrote in his memoirs, 'was sent up to Rosehill'.[8]

The Brays were also Unitarians, members of the Dissenting sect that included some of the most influential manufacturing families of the north and Midlands; a sect that tended to radicalism and reform-ism in politics, and rationalism in thought (regarding reason as the chief source and test of knowledge). Cara was staunchly Unitarian, but Charles, born a Methodist, had been attracted chiefly by the rationalist and reformist traditions of Unitarianism. He was a more enthusiastic apostle of the popular new 'science' of phrenology, a form of physiological determinism advanced by George Combe, in which bumps on the skull were 'read' according to coded areas to reveal mental and moral capacities. Bray was also an Owenite socialist (not a Marxist but a follower of Robert Owen, another regular Rosehill visitor, whose life was dedicated to the ideal of class cooperation and the establishment of socialist communities). In his idiosyncratic *Philosophy of Necessity* (1844), he argued that because the mind was subject to fixed laws, and because everything was determined by a necessary chain of causation, the improvement of social conditions through active intervention in that chain of causation was an urgent responsibility. He himself worked assiduously to that end, agitating for working-class reform and education, proposing co-operative schemes, and writing pamphlets. Whether or not his political idealism affected his business prospects during the downturn in the ribbon trade in the 1850s is unclear, but he went out of business in 1856 and was forced to sell Rosehill.

It was not the political radicalism of Charles Bray and Mary Hennell that revolutionized Mary Ann Evans's thinking, however, but Bray's iconoclastic rationalism in matters of religious faith. On 13 November 1841, shortly after her first visit to Rosehill, Mary Ann wrote tantalizingly to Maria Lewis: 'My whole soul has been engrossed in the most interesting of all enquiries for the last few days, and to what result my thoughts may lead I know not—possibly to one that will startle you, but my only desire is to know the truth, my only fear to cling to error' (*Letters*, i. 120–1). She was referring to *An Inquiry Concerning the Origin of Christianity* (1838), a book researched and written by Cara's brother Charles Hennell (1809–50) at his sister's particular request, which Mary Ann may have read even before she met the Brays. Cara's faith had been deeply shaken by her husband's rationalism, and she had asked Charles, also a devout Unitarian, to collect evidence from the Bible confirming the truth of 'the principal miraculous facts supposed to lie at the foundation of Christianity': the Virgin birth, the miracles of Jesus, the ascension, and the resurrection.[9] Hennell concluded from his scholarly study of the Four Gospels, however, that 'the true account of the life of Jesus Christ, and of the spread of his religion, would be found to contain no deviation from the known laws of nature'.[10] Nor was the possibility of a future life supported by biblical evidence. Significantly, though, Hennell's inquiry did not lead him, as one might expect, to atheism or agnosticism. As a Unitarian he already accepted the non-divinity of Christ, and neither his faith nor Cara's was much shaken by his findings. Paradoxically the *Inquiry* freed him from dogmatic, literal readings of Scripture, and opened him to Christianity as a vital moral system—a 'natural religion'—for the here and now.

Nor did the irrepressibly heretical Charles Bray consider himself an atheist or even an agnostic. He appears never to have grappled with religious doubt, in fact, simply discounting the existence of evil—a happy consequence, perhaps, of a privileged social position and a life without struggle. For Mary Ann, however, financially dependent on her ageing father, faced with a humdrum existence and an empty future, and finding her faith, and the deep knowledge of theology and philosophy that supported it, withering under the bright glare of rationalist analysis, life was turning into a deadly struggle. Like the Brays and Hennells, she could not reconcile faith and reason, but for her there was only one possible consequence of accepting Hennell's conclusions. On 2 January 1842, for the first time in her life, she told her father that she would not be accompanying him to church. Robert Evans suspected that his daughter, under the harmful influence of the Rosehill circle, had turned Unitarian. Shocked and angered, he fell into 'blank silence and cold reserve' (*Letters*, i. 125). Two months later, on 28 February, she was forced by his hostile silence to write to him, pleading that she was 'one who has no one to speak for her' (*Letters*, i. 130), and trying to explain her actions:

I regard [the Scriptures] as histories consisting of mingled truth and fiction, and while I admire and cherish much of what I believe to have been the moral teaching of Jesus himself, I consider the system of doctrines built upon the facts of his life and drawn as to its materials from Jewish notions to be most dishonourable to God and most pernicious in its influence on individual and social happiness. . . . Such being my very strong convictions, it cannot be a question with any mind of strict integrity, whatever judgment may be passed on their truth, that I could not without vile hypocrisy and a miserable truckling to the smile of the world for the sake of my supposed interests, profess to join in worship which I wholly disapprove. This and *this alone* I will not do even for your sake— anything else however painful I would cheerfully brave to give you a moment's joy. (*Letters*, i. 128–9)

Lest her father should suspect, too, that she was motivated by an unseemly spirit of rebellion against his respectability (Bray was considered 'a leader of mobs' who would introduce her 'to Chartists and

Radicals' (*Letters*, i. 157)), or that she had sunk into the moral laxity of free-thought, she added: 'I am really sincere . . . my only desire is to walk in that path of rectitude which however rugged is the only path to peace.' She insisted, however, that 'the prospect of contempt and rejection shall not make me swerve from my determination so much as a hair's breadth until I feel that I *ought* to do so' (*Letters*, i. 129). In letters to others she reiterates this redoubled determination to act as she must according to a sense of *duty*, revealing that already, at the first moment of her religious crisis, she had found a way of moving beyond Christianity to the position of moral seriousness she would continue to hold all her life. This letter contains the seeds of what she 'pronounced, with terrible earnestness' at Cambridge years later, on 'the words *God, Immortality, Duty*,—. . . how inconceivable was the *first*, how unbelievable the *second*, and yet how peremptory and absolute the *third*'.[11]

By 3 March, however, Robert Evans was still so hurt, angry, and humiliated that he resolved to give up the lease on Foleshill and send Mary Ann away altogether. Isaac, however, objected that his father was being too severe (or too hasty) and he suggested that his sister come back to Griff for a time, whilst Mrs Pears and Rebecca Franklin tried to persuade Evans not to let the house. In the event Mary Ann did retreat to Griff on 23 March, but was back at Foleshill with her father, though still unreconciled, on 30 April. At last they reached an uneasy truce, agreeing that he would tolerate her agnosticism if she at least attended church for the sake of appearances, which she duly did on 15 May 1842.

In July, Mary Ann was introduced to another of Cara's sisters, Sara Hennell, who had heard all about what Mary Ann termed the 'Holy War' from the Brays, and was anxious to meet this daring apostate. Sara, whose love and knowledge of literature, art, and music immediately attracted Mary Ann, would remain one of her closest friends and most faithful and important correspondents, though they inevitably grew apart as the years progressed. In October she also met Elizabeth Brabant (known as Rufa, the pet name Coleridge had given her because of her red hair), who was in love with the consumptive Charles Hennell, though she was forbidden to marry him on the grounds of his poor health. She was the only daughter of Dr Robert Brabant, an eccentric surgeon from Devizes, who had learned German especially in order to read the new biblical criticism that was flourishing on the Continent, none of which was available in English translation. In May 1839 Brabant had visited Weimar and met David Friedrich Strauss, one of the foremost German biblical critics and author of *Das Leben Jesu* (*The Life of Jesus*), which Brabant had read. In 1841, Joseph Parkes, a radical politician and lawyer, promised to fund a translation of the *Leben Jesu* in England, if Hennell could arrange a suitable translator. He first asked Sara, who felt herself unequal to the task, and then Rufa Brabant, who set to work on the translation in 1842. When Dr Brabant finally agreed to allow Hennell to marry his daughter in November 1843, however, Rufa was still only a short way through the first volume, and Hennell asked Mary Ann to take over the job. Her knowledge of German was by this time extensive. She had been learning the language (along with Italian, French, and the classical languages) since 1840, and had read widely in German literature, including Goethe, Schiller, and Lessing. The Strauss translation would nevertheless prove daunting. It ran to nearly 1,500 pages in its German edition, and entered into a detailed mythical interpretation of each and every one of the biblical narratives of Jesus's life, arguing that the miracles should be understood not as events, whether natural or supernatural, but as sacred stories drawn from ancient sources. Strauss's dialectical method was intricate and exhaustive, and the work, which took her more than two years, was physically debilitating and morally dispiriting, as if she herself were being forced to account for each unconvincing article of faith one by one. Cara Bray reported to Sara Hennell, who was consulted regularly on matters of translation, that Mary Ann had become pale and sickly, and was suffering from dreadful headaches: 'She said she was Strauss-sick—it made her ill dissecting the beautiful story of the crucifixion' (*Letters*, i. 206). Mary Ann was paid £20 for her work, and the book was finally published, without its translator's name, on 15 June 1846. Because of this fluent, faithful translation (still the standard English version of the work), Strauss had 'an impact on English and American thought he never otherwise could have attained'.[12]

Trapped in a provincial town, Mary Ann was also worn down by boredom and loneliness. As far as we know she had only two tentative relationships during this whole period, both of them dismal failures. The first was with Dr Brabant himself, who invited Mary Ann to visit him in Devizes in 1843, just after the wedding of Rufa

CVCA Royal Library
4687 Wyoga Lake Road
Stow, OH 44224-1011

and Charles Hennell. Flattered by the attentions of an old man who appears to have been frankly lascivious, she became intimate with him, and was smartly banished from the house by Brabant's (blind) wife and sister-in-law. The second relationship was with a young painter (or picture-restorer) from Leamington who proposed to her in 1845 after knowing her only a few days. Mary Ann was taken by surprise, and clearly entertained the idea for a day or two before she quickly put an end to the affair.

Early in 1848 she also had an another flirtation, carried on entirely by letter, with Mary Sibree's brother, John. Her father's health was declining rapidly by now, and she was far from well herself, nervous and cramped by the drudgery of nursing and the pettiness of provincial society, while intellectual controversies to which she had contributed something herself in her translation of Strauss were as far out of her reach as the Europe that was exploding in revolutions. Sibree was studying for the ministry, reading Strauss, and finding his faith dangerously unsteady. Mary Ann, writing to Sara Hennell, mischievously confessed to an uncharacteristic 'fit of destructiveness . . . which might have been more easily gratified if I had lived in the days of iconoclasm' (*Letters*, i. 241). The letters she wrote Sibree are also quite uncharacteristic, meriting, as Rosemarie Bodenheimer observes, 'a bluntness of expression that is otherwise virtually absent in the George Eliot correspondence'.[13] They are long, excited, unguarded, even reckless, the letters of an intelligent woman desperate to be heard. But they are also the least sincere as well as the most playful of all George Eliot's letters, perhaps the only time she sets out to scandalize her correspondent.

By February 1849, Robert Evans was close to death and Mary Ann described her life as 'a perpetual nightmare—always haunted by something to be done which I have never the time or rather the energy to do' (*Letters*, i. 276). Since the Strauss translation, in fact, she had written a few reviews and other pieces (including the series 'Poetry and Prose from the Notebook of an Eccentric') for the Coventry *Herald*, which Bray had bought in June 1846. In March she also began a translation of Spinoza's *Tractatus-theologico-politicus* (from Latin), but soon gave up this task. She continued to read voraciously, however, including important contemporary writers and works such as *Jane Eyre* (1847), George Sand, and (apropos of John Sibree) J. A. Froude's *The Nemesis of Faith* (1849), considered the most dangerous novel of religious doubt of its time, which depicted its hero, preparing for ordination, torn by scepticism (Mary Ann reviewed it enthusiastically for the *Herald*). Froude, an Oxford don, was expelled from Oriel College and his book publicly burned; like others who were supposedly 'a little cracked', he turned up at Rosehill. *The Nemesis of Faith* was published by John Chapman, who described himself as a 'publisher of works notable for their intellectual freedom' (*Biography*, p. 82). Chapman had also published the translation of Strauss, and he was to play an important role in the next phase of Mary Ann Evans's life.

Robert Evans did not die until 31 May 1849, however, and the drawn-out final months of his life left Mary Ann on the verge of nervous illness. Immediately after the funeral, she jumped at the chance the Brays offered her to spend some time in Europe. Her father had left her £2,000 in trust, and with the modest income in interest yielded from this sum (around £90 per year), she would be able to live independently, if sparingly, for a while; certainly the money would go further in Europe. On 12 June they left for France, Italy, and Switzerland, and when the Brays returned home on 25 July, Mary Ann stayed on in Geneva, first at a *pension* in Plongeon, and then at the home of François D'Albert-Durade and his wife. D'Albert-Durade, a painter with a deformed spine, painted her portrait and accompanied her back to London when she returned, after seven months away, in March 1850.

On her return, Mary Ann—always known to her most intimate friends by her pet name from childhood, Polly, and to Cara and Sara as 'Pollian' (a play of Sara's on Apollyon)—changed her name again, to Marian. She did not begin to sign herself Marian Evans, however, until after January 1851. That was the month she published her first substantial piece of writing in one of the great nineteenth-century quarterly magazines, the *Westminster Review*. It was a review of Robert Mackay's *The Progress of the Intellect, as Exemplified in the Religious Development of the Greeks and Hebrews*, which John Chapman had just published. The previous October when she was at a loose end after the Geneva holiday, and staying at Griff with the Isaac Evanses (who apparently expected her to settle into maiden-aunthood there), Chapman and Mackay had visited Rosehill and commissioned the piece. The following month she delivered it to Chapman in person, spending a fortnight at his home at 142 Strand,

London. Built as a hotel, Chapman conducted his publishing and bookselling business from this house, lived there with his wife, Susanna, two of his three children, and his mistress Elisabeth Tilley, and took in 'literary' paying guests, many of them from America. Marian returned to Coventry on 2 December, but by 8 January, when the review was just published, she was back in London, living as one of Chapman's boarders at 142 Strand.

John Chapman, who had studied medicine in Paris, was a publisher and bookseller of considerable influence in London. Although he was, as Herbert Spencer later recalled, 'the only respectable publisher through whom could be issued books which were tacitly or avowedly rationalistic',[14] he was by no means a marginal figure in London literary culture.[15] But despite his ambitions for the business, and a taste for a *succès de scandale* (including *The Nemesis of Faith*), Chapman lost a lot of money in the book trade, and gave it up altogether in 1858 to practise as a physician and run the *Westminster Review*, which he bought in 1851 and controlled for thirty-five years. For the first two and a half years of his incumbency as proprietor he was only the nominal editor, however; in June 1851 he asked Marian to be the journal's 'secret' (and unpaid) editor.

Chapman's confidence in her was not founded solely on Marian's translation of Strauss, her review of Mackay's *Progress of the Intellect*, or her reputation amongst the Coventry set. In the six months since she had arrived in London he had developed an intimate relationship with her. In fact, on the evidence of Chapman's diary, it seems probable that it was already a sexual relationship less than three weeks after Marian moved into 142 Strand.[16] Needless to say, these goings-on were quickly brought to light by Chapman's jealous wife and mistress, who conspired together to have Marian removed. On 24 March she returned to Coventry. Chapman's diary records that she 'was very sad', and 'pressed' him for 'some intimation of the state of [his] feelings'. He told her that he 'felt great affection' for her, but that he loved his wife and mistress too, 'though each in a different way': 'At this avowal she burst into tears'.[17] Although the relationship ended there, and Marian was distraught at Chapman's ultimate rejection, the *Westminster* negotiations continued between Rosehill and London through the spring and summer, and Marian was invited to edit the journal. She had written the prospectus and began to solicit articles long before Chapman was able to persuade his wife and mistress that she should be allowed back to 142 Strand. She returned strictly under probation on 29 September, and set about preparing the first number in earnest.

A couple of days later, at one of Chapman's famous Friday night soirées, Marian met Herbert Spencer, who worked on *The Economist* just opposite Chapman's house in the Strand, and had already published his first book with Chapman, *Social Statics* (1850). With their shared intellectual interests (she introduced him to the work of the French positivist philosopher Auguste Comte) and cultural interests, Marian and Spencer quickly became close. As *The Economist*'s subeditor he had free tickets to the theatres and the Opera, which he and Marian attended frequently together over the early months of 1852. Spencer also recalled in his autobiography how during the late spring and summer they would spend hours walking up and down a balustraded terrace on the roof of the Somerset House basement beside the Thames (for which Chapman had a key), 'discussing many things'.[18] Spencer was attracted to 'the greatness of her intellect conjoined with her womanly qualities and manner',[19] and they became intimate, but like Chapman he was put off by Marian's plainness. As Gordon Haight notes, in her letters to the Brays 'there are never more references to her "ugliness" than during the months of her involvement with Spencer' (*Biography*, p. 115).

Marian spent July and August 1852 at Broadstairs in Kent, where Spencer was a frequent visitor, and her feelings for him intensified as the summer progressed. Sometime earlier they had agreed—he more readily than she—that they were not in love (*Letters*, ii. 22). But rumours were circulating that they were already engaged, and over that summer Marian did fall hopelessly in love with him. On 16 July, she wrote him a letter that provides perhaps the clearest evidence we have of her passion and dignity:

I know this letter will make you very angry with me, but wait a little, and don't say anything to me while you are angry. I promise not to sin any more in the same way.

My ill health is caused by the hopeless wretchedness which weighs upon me. I do not say this to pain you, but because it is the simple truth which you must know in order to understand why I am obliged to seek relief.

I want to know if you can assure me that you will not forsake me, that you will always be with me as much as you can and share your thoughts and feelings with me. If you become attached to some one else, then I must die, but until then I could gather courage to work and make life valuable, if only I had you near me. I do not ask you to sacrifice anything—I would be very good and cheerful and never annoy you. But I find it impossible to contemplate life under any other conditions. If I had your assurance, I could trust that and live upon it. I have struggled—indeed I have—to renounce everything and be entirely unselfish, but I find myself utterly unequal to it. Those who have known me best have always said, that if ever I loved any one thoroughly my whole life must turn upon that feeling, and I find they said truly. You curse the destiny which has made the feeling concentrate itself on you—but if you will only have patience with me you shall not curse it long. You will find that I can be satisfied with very little, if I am delivered from the dread of losing it.

I suppose no woman ever before wrote such a letter as this—but I am not ashamed of it, for I am conscious that in the light of reason and true refinement I am worthy of your respect and tenderness, whatever gross men or vulgar-minded women might think of me. (*Letters*, viii. 56–7)

But nothing came of the 'painful affair' (*Letters*, viii. 42 n. 5). Spencer, anxious that his part in it should not be misrepresented after Eliot's death, later recalled that it dragged on 'through the summer of 52, on through the autumn, and, I think, into the beginning of 53' until

At length it happened that being with Lewes one afternoon when I was on my way to see her, I invited him to go with me (they were already slightly known). He did so. This happened two or three times; and then, on the third or fourth time, when I rose to leave, he said he should stay. From that time he commenced to go alone and so the relation began—(his estrangement from his wife being then of long standing). When I saw the turn matters were taking it was, of course, an immense relief to me. (*Letters*, viii. 42 n. 5)

His friend was George Henry Lewes, whom Spencer described to his father thus in 1851:

Lewes is about 34 or 35, of middle height, with light brown long hair, deeply marked with small-pox, and rather worn-looking. He is very versatile. He is a successful novelist and dramatist, writes poems occasionally, is an actor, a good linguist, writes for the reviews, translates for the stage, is a musical critic, and is, as you may suppose, deeply read in philosophy. He is a very pleasant companion. He is married and has three children.[20]

Grandson of the comic actor Charles Lee Lewes, Lewes was

involved in Dickens's celebrated amateur troupe, and had performed professionally in the provinces in his own play. But his reputation was chiefly as a writer of articles and reviews on an astonishing range of literary, philosophical, and scientific topics. He was almost inexhaustible, producing material for all the leading journals (except the *Quarterly Review*), as well as plays, translations, fiction, and his *Biographical History of Philosophy* (1845-6). Although a professedly generalist work, this book introduced English readers to the (then still untranslated) positivist philosophy of Comte. Equally progressive in politics, in 1850 he and his best friend Thornton Hunt (whose father was the Romantic essayist Leigh Hunt) began a radical weekly, the *Leader*, to which Lewes contributed most of the 'Literature' section, and reviewed theatre under the dandyish nom de plume of 'Vivian'. (These reviews later influenced George Bernard Shaw.)

Lewes was a highly unusual-looking man, as Spencer hints, with an idiosyncratic personal manner. Considered the ugliest man in London, his appearance—he had a pale, pitted face, domed at the forehead and narrow at the chin, and a massive fleshy lower lip protruding from beneath a lank moustache that stretched across to unite spare long wisps of beard growing on the outermost regions of his chin—was often described as 'that of a monkey' (see p. 22).[21] Indeed the Carlyles, with whom he was on close terms, affectionately dubbed him the 'Ape'. But he also had fine eyes and great charm, was a highly entertaining raconteur, skilled at mimicry, and given to buffoonery and flippancy, which masked his underlying seriousness and, often, his unhappiness or illness. He was also an honest man, and generous in his dealings. As Jane Carlyle said of him, 'he is the most amusing little fellow in the whole world—if you only look over his unparalleled *impudence*, which is not impudence at all but man-of-genius *bonhomie*', one discovered 'no spleen or envy, or *bad* thing in him'.[22] He was difficult to get to know, however, and many people (especially including the Brays and Hennells) disliked the 'mercurial little showman',[23] being scornful of his dilettantism, suspicious of his politics, and appalled by rumours of his private life.

In 1841 Lewes had entered into an open marriage with Agnes Jervis, the intelligent and beautiful daughter of a Radical MP. Agnes made a significant contribution to her husband's growing reputation for productivity and versatility during the 1840s, anonymously

George Henry Lewes with Pug, 1859

Sketch of George Eliot by Samuel Lawrence, 1957.

collaborating with him in numerous French translations and other work. They had five children together, of whom only the three middle boys survived: Charles Lee, Thornton Arnott, and Herbert Arthur. In 1850, two weeks after their youngest son, 22-month-old St Vincent Arthy, died of measles, however, Agnes gave birth to another child, Edmund, the first of four she was to have with Thornton Hunt. Lewes, an avowed proponent of free love, duly registered the child in his own name, and continued to support Agnes and the children (Hunt's as well as his own) until his death. In 1852, however, after the birth of a second child, Lewes could no longer countenance the arrangement and he left Agnes to her relationship with Hunt. Unable to divorce her (by agreeing to register Edmund Lewes as his own he had tacitly condoned the adultery, and forfeited any grounds), he became disillusioned, embittered, and despairing. Later in his journal he recalled what a 'debt of gratitude' he owed Spencer for his friendship over these months: 'My acquaintance with him', he wrote, 'was the brightest ray in a very dreary *wasted* period of my life. I had given up all ambition whatever' (*Biography*, pp. 271–2).

In the same journal entry, Lewes continued: 'I owe Spencer another, and a deeper debt. It was through him that I learned to know Marian—to know her was to love her—and since then my life has been a new birth. To her I owe all my prosperity and all my happiness. God bless her!' (*Biography*, p. 272). In late summer 1852 they were both still too bruised to embark on another relationship, however, and they did not fall in love immediately. In fact it seems that Marian actually disliked Lewes's superficiality at first (and certainly, as an editor, she was not always complimentary about his journalism). By April 1853, however, she was writing to Cara Bray: 'Mr. Lewes especially is kind and attentive and has quite won my regard after having a good deal of my vituperation. Like a few other people in the world, he is much better than he seems—a man of heart and conscience wearing a mask of flippancy' (*Letters*, ii. 98). By the time she moved out of 142 Strand into lodgings at 21 Cambridge St., Hyde Park Square, six months later in October, it seems likely that Lewes had confessed his unhappiness to her, and that an intimacy was established.

At this time Marian resigned the editorship of the *Westminster Review* and agreed to undertake another translation for Chapman—

of Ludwig Feuerbach's *Das Wesen des Christenthums* (*The Essence of Christianity*)—while Lewes, anxious to prove himself a more substantial intellect, was writing up his *Leader* articles on Comte into a book, *Comte's Philosophy of the Sciences*, and preparing a new biography of Goethe. In April, overwork caught up with him (not for the first time), and he fell ill and was sent away to the country to recover. In his absence, his friends, and especially Marian, filled his columns for the *Leader*. In spite of this added pressure she managed to finish the Feuerbach translation by the end of May 1854, only five months after beginning work on it. It was a much easier job than the Strauss: shorter, and '*for a German*—concise, lucid and even epigrammatic now and then' (*Letters*, ii. 141). After the ruthless analytical naysaying of Strauss, too, Feuerbach presented the exhilarating, and to Marian highly congenial, argument that the idea of God was the expression of the essence of man. The human standpoint, Feuerbach argued, is the 'essential standpoint' of religion (as she translated the title of chapter 19). Divinity is really human perfection, God human love. Feuerbach's radical idea retrieved religion from the repressive orthodoxies of the Church and extricated it from its relationship with the established social order. For Marian, Feuerbach's cardinal antithesis of an inner truthful 'essence' and an imposed outer 'form' would become crucial. She was about to enter into a relationship that could never be formalized as a marriage, but was as sacred as any formal bond. She was also about to begin a career as a novelist in which she would show that the truthfulness of ordinary experience could never be contained in the half-truths of formulaic narrative structures. It was the only book of its author's in which the name Marian Evans appears on the title page. She received £30 for it.

With the Feuerbach out of the way, Marian considered moving in with Lewes, but finally decided against it. Instead they would declare their relationship from a distance, travelling together to Europe, where Lewes was to continue research on Goethe. On 20 July 1854, they left for Weimar and Berlin, where they were to stay for eight months, out of direct hearing of the storm which raged over the scandalous elopement in their different circles back in England. During this journey Marian found intense happiness and stability for the first time since her early childhood at Griff. She and Lewes were accepted in German society. They travelled widely, saw a great deal, and worked hard, quickly settling into the pattern of companionship and work that would mark their rich productive lives together. They took part fully in each other's projects, but not to the extent of hindering each other's progress. Every day they read aloud to each other, both from their own manuscripts, and from the books they were reading. It was the beginning of an intimate reciprocal intellectual relationship.

In March 1855, the couple returned to England, fully prepared to be spurned for their unconventional relationship. For a month Marian waited in Dover, reading Shakespeare intensively and continuing doggedly with a translation of Spinoza's *Ethics* begun in Berlin, while Lewes went to London to gain Agnes's promise that she would never try to bring about a reunion. With that promise secured, Marian joined her husband (as she henceforth referred to him) at 8 Victoria Grove Terrace, London. Two weeks later they moved to a house in East Sheen, near Richmond, where they stayed barely four months before shifting to lodgings nearby at 8 Park Shot, Richmond. This was to be their home for more than three years. In November, Lewes's *Life of Goethe* was published, and Marian finished the first in a series of major articles she was to write for the *Westminster Review* between then and the end of 1856 (having successfully made the transition from unpaid editor to paid writer whilst in Germany in 1854).

The Leweses did receive visitors on their return. In fact, two of Marian's first three visitors were women—Rufa Hennell, and Bessie Parkes, daughter of Joseph Parkes, the Radical MP who had originally funded the Strauss translation. When her father first heard about the elopement, he was outraged and forbade his daughter to communicate with Marian. Determined, however, to develop the friendship, Bessie made occasional clandestine visits, and received Marian's letters enclosed in those to mutual friends Barbara Leigh Smith and Chapman (themselves involved in a liaison at this time). Like other scandalized freethinkers, Parkes had been affronted not by the nature of this relationship—it was quite acceptable for men and women to conduct extramarital affairs—but by its openness, which must, after all, have seemed provocatively scornful of the values of respectable society. The plain contradictions in various accounts of the affair did not seem to matter. Lewes, a man with a reputation for unhealthy sexual appetites, had abandoned his Bayswater *ménage à trois* to live with a bluestocking and ruin her;

Marian—nicknamed the 'strong-minded woman' by the Carlyles—
was a marriage-wrecker. Chapman, drawing on his own experience
and his knowledge of the Spencer affair, put it about that Marian's
desperate sexual loneliness and need of being loved had drawn
Lewes to act recklessly. George Combe raised the question of sanity
in a letter to Charles Bray:

an educated woman who, in the face of the world, volunteers to live as a
wife, with a man who already has a living wife and children, appears to me
to pursue a course and to set an example calculated only to degrade
herself and her sex, if she be sane. If you receive her into your family
circle, while present appearances are unexplained, pray consider whether
you will do justice to your own female domestic circle, and how other
ladies may feel about going into a circle which makes no distinction
between those who act thus, and those who preserve their honour
unspotted? (*Letters*, viii. 130)

Even her old Coventry friends, who were quite willing to tolerate flex-
ible marital arrangements among themselves, were taken aback, and
their relationship with Marian never quite returned to its old footing.

Lewes, of course, could go about unrestricted, but Marian was
unable to visit anyone in society or receive visits from respectable
women, a situation only finally broken down by her fame in the
1870s, when she was sought out even by royalty. But she was deeply
happy and sure of the rightness of her conduct. As she had shown
during the 'Holy War' with her father, her confidence in her own
moral judgement made her capable of great determination and courage. Although she felt no need to defend the morality of her decision
to the world at large, however, she did feel the need to prove its
seriousness: its solemnity and essential respectability. This is not to
suggest that she craved the approval of 'respectable' society, as is
often assumed. She was horrified to think that her actions might be
misconstrued, but not because she cared for what the world, or the
world's wife, thought. She took it upon herself to live out, in the
defiant isolation of her exile, a new kind of respectability—an open
avowal of honesty and decency of conduct, in which her behaviour,
unconventional and bringing upon her the stigma of respectable
people, was elevated to a higher duty, authenticated by a supreme
'truth to feeling'. As she wrote to Sara Hennell in September 1855,
'if there is any one action or relation of my life which is and always
has been profoundly serious, it is my relation to Mr. Lewes', adding:

'Light and easily broken ties are what I neither desire theoretically nor could live for practically. Women who are satisfied with such ties do *not* act as I have done—they obtain what they desire and are still invited to dinner' (*Letters*, ii. 213–14). Not being invited to dinner had its undoubted advantages as well. Marian Evans Lewes, freed from 'petty worldly torments, commonly called pleasures' (*Letters*, iii. 367), was enormously productive.

In the spring of 1856 the translation of Spinoza was finished (though it was not published), and Marian was working as a higher journalist, testing her capacity to earn a living by producing regular articles and reviews for the *Leader*, *Westminster Review*, and other journals. At the same time she enthusiastically joined with Lewes in his new interest, natural science, and in May decided she could carry on her own work just as well away from London at the coast, where he wanted to collect specimens for his 'Sea-Side Studies'. Lewes, whose intellectual tendencies had been, in Henry James's words, 'of the drifting sort',[24] had been attacked by T. H. Huxley in the January 1854 issue of the *Westminster*, who accused him of being 'a mere book-scientist' (*Letters*, ii. 132 n. 8). Stung, Lewes set about equipping himself with practical scientific skills and vowed to undertake an ambitious study not just of marine life, but of animal physiology. Relations between physiology and psychology would occupy him off and on for the rest of his life.

The Leweses spent most of May and June at Ilfracombe on the north Devon coast, and all of July and the first week of August at Tenby on the south coast of Wales. Here, Marian recorded in her diary, she did 'no *visible* work', but 'absorbed many ideas and much bodily strength; indeed, I do not remember ever feeling so strong in mind and body as I feel at this moment' (*Journals*, p. 62). Here, too, lying in bed one morning,

my thoughts merged themselves into a dreamy doze, and I imagined myself writing a story of which the title was—'The Sad Fortunes of the Reverend Amos Barton'. I was soon wide awake again, and told G. He said, 'O what a capital title!' and from that time I had settled in my mind that this should be my first story. (*Journals*, p. 289)

Fiction 'had always been a vague dream' of hers, she confessed in this section of her journal (entitled 'How I Came to Write Fiction'), but she had always thought herself 'deficient in dramatic power, both of construction and dialogue' (*Journals*, p. 289), though capable in description. She did not get a chance to prove it one way or the other, however, until the couple returned to London, and she had cleared commitments with the *Westminster Review*. 'Amos Barton' was begun on 22 September 1856, and finished six weeks later on 6 November. Lewes was enthusiastic and, as they had agreed, he submitted the story to John Blackwood, who was publishing instalments of the 'Sea-Side Studies' in his *Blackwood's Edinburgh Magazine*. The story was accepted as the work of a friend of Lewes who wished to remain anonymous, and so began a famous publishing partnership, which produced the most detailed and revealing of any correspondence between a Victorian writer and her publisher.

On Christmas Day 1856, a week before 'Amos Barton' appeared in the January number of *Blackwood's*, Marian began her second 'scene' of clerical life, 'Mr Gilfil's Love-Story'. On 4 February 1857, in a letter to Blackwood over this follow-up story (and still unknown to him) she declared for the first time her intention of assuming the pen name George Eliot. It was chosen, she later told Cross, because 'George was Mr Lewes's Christian name, and Eliot was a good mouth-filling, easily-pronounced word' (*Life*, pp. 212–13). Stories in *Blackwood's* were still unsigned at that time, however, and the nom de plume would not be attached until the stories came out in volume form in January 1858. From that moment the mysterious identity of George Eliot became a topic of curiosity and fierce controversy across the country, intensifying further with the publication of the third story, 'Janet's Repentance', written in the Scilly Isles and Jersey and based on her memories of John Jones's Nuneaton curacy in the late 1820s.

Whilst in Jersey Marian also decided, after nearly three years' silence on the subject, to contact her brother Isaac and sister Fanny and announce her changed state:

You will be surprised, I dare say [she wrote to Isaac on 26 May 1857], but I hope not sorry, to learn that I have changed my name, and have someone to take care of me in the world. The event is not at all a sudden one, though it may appear sudden in its announcement to you. My husband has been known to me for several years, and I am well acquainted with his mind and character. He is occupied entirely with scientific and learned pursuits, is several years older than myself, and has three boys . . . We are not at all rich people, but we are both workers, and shall have enough for our wants. (*Letters*, ii. 331–2)

As she explained to Sara Hennell, she wrote simply to ensure that 'if any utterly false report reaches them in the first instance, their minds will be prepared not to accept it without reserve' (*Letters*, ii. 342). Isaac replied through the family solicitor, and demanded that the family cease all communication with their sister. Marian was devastated; but, true to his word, Isaac remained silent until 1880, when she married Cross and was safely respectable again.

Meanwhile Marian apparently thought of extending her *Blackwood's* series to include a story about a clerical tutor. After the mild sentimentality of 'Mr Gilfil's Love Story', however, Blackwood was uneasy with the dark, anti-Church tones and unsentimental realism of 'Janet's Repentance', and she decided to conclude the series and turn her attention to a full-length novel. It was to be constructed around the germ of a story told to her in 1839 by her Aunt Samuel Evans, the wife of her father's brother, who had been a Methodist preacher in the days before women were banned from the ministry, and had prayed all night with a young girl condemned to death for child murder, rousing her to confession and penitence. *Adam Bede*, the resulting novel, took her just over a year to finish, and was written at Richmond and during two trips to Germany in the spring and summer of 1858. It was published on 1 February 1859, just before the Leweses left Richmond for good, taking a house, Holly Lodge, at Wandsworth, which they had settled on after a long search for quiet suburban areas in which Marian could pursue her writing.

Adam Bede was not serialized in *Blackwood's* but published directly in three volumes, and was a runaway success. Within days of its release rumours of Marian's authorship were buzzing around in her circle. Lewes, unwilling to surrender the incognito, wrote a sharp letter to Chapman emphatically denying that Mrs Lewes was the author. Although there was apparently some disagreement between him and Marian about the strict necessity for a bare-faced lie, Lewes had no difficulty with his position, arguing with himself in his journal on that same day that 'the very existence and possibility of anonymity would be at an end if every impertinent fellow could force you either by confession or implication to admit the truth of his questions. Therefore I hold a man in no respect forfeits his truthfulness in denying questions put to him as to anonymous writing unless those questions be in themselves warrantable, and not simply curiosity' (*Letters*, iii. 12).

The whole matter of the incognito was complicated, however, by the unexpected emergence of a rival claimant to the identity of George Eliot. This was Joseph Liggins, who had been born at Attleborough, and had lived at one time on the Isle of Man, but who was again living in the Midlands when *Adam Bede* was published. Rumours of Liggins's authorship had in fact begun in connection with *Scenes of Clerical Life* as early as June 1857, when Marian's sister Fanny, recognizing 'some figures and traditions connected with our old neighbourhood', first reported his existence. The name 'George Eliot' was not known to the public at that time, of course, and Marian rather disingenuously replied that 'Blackwood informs Mr. Lewes that the author is a Mr. Eliot, a clergyman, I presume' (*Letters*, ii. 337). Liggins himself never publicly confirmed his claim to the authorship, but simply allowed the rumours to multiply unchecked. So effective was his strategy, aided by the ill-advised continuing silence of the Leweses, that by the summer of 1859, the Liggins myth had taken hold. It was vigorously defended in letters to *The Times* (where Lewes printed angry, but still anonymous, letters of denial), and by its high-profile supporters, including Florence Nightingale. Liggins was applauded for refusing to take payment for the work from Blackwood (always a subject of some delicacy for Marian), and was actually offered charity. In the end, as the Leweses became increasingly taken up with the business of discrediting Liggins, they decided they could no longer be bothered upholding an incognito that would soon surely be revealed anyway. In July Marian's authorship of *Scenes of Clerical Life* and *Adam Bede* was finally disclosed to the public, and the veil of anonymity was lifted— not without controversy, as it was charged in some quarters that the couple had actually invented Liggins to cause a stir and promote sales of *Adam Bede*. Significantly, the Liggins affair so distracted her during the spring of 1859 that she temporarily left off work on her new novel—what was to be *The Mill on the Floss*—and wrote a short Hawthornian romance about identity and secrecy, 'The Lifted Veil'.

There were other sadnesses, too. Marian's favourite sister, Chrissey, dogged with ill luck all her life (her improvident husband had died in 1852, and she lost two children to typhus), had contracted tuberculosis. At Isaac's command she had stopped writing to her sister in 1857, but in February 1859, a month before she died, she defied him and wrote a letter informing Marian of her illness and expressing her regret for the breach. 'It has ploughed up my heart', Marian wrote to Cara Bray (*Letters*, iii. 23). Lewes, fearful of the effect the news would have on her, noted in his journal, 'Polly . . . seems much affected, and I almost wish the silence had never been broken. She had got used to that' (*Letters*, iii. 24 n. 9). These personal difficulties could not but become deeply entangled with her work, however, for she was being drawn back by sorrow into memories of childhood happiness, and forced again to confront the pain of Isaac's silent rejection, just as she was beginning work on a new book which she intended to be 'a sort of companion picture of provincial life' to *Adam Bede* (*Letters*, iii. 41). This was her most autobiographical novel. Its title, *The Mill on the Floss*, was not finally decided upon until January 1860, but it is clear that she had already conceived the broad structure of the story of the Dodsons and Tullivers by January 1859, when she 'went into town . . . and looked in the Annual Register for cases of *inundation*' (*Journals*, p. 76). By 16 October, she had completed the first volume; volume ii was done three months later, on 16 January 1860, and volume iii only two months after that, on 21 March. For complex reasons negotiations with Blackwood for this novel were protracted and fraught with misunderstandings on both sides, and terms were not settled until the end of 1859. *The Mill on the Floss* was published on 4 April 1860, and did much better than Marian had hoped, consolidating her reputation and sales.

A week before *The Mill on the Floss* was published, the Leweses left for three months' holiday in Italy, returning home via Switzerland, where Lewes's three sons were at school. The eldest, Charles, was just finishing his education and that summer accompanied them home. Later that year, on Anthony Trollope's advice, he took the Civil Service examination and won a clerk's position at the General Post Office in London, prompting the Leweses to move at last from the outer London suburbs, where Marian had never been happy, to a more central position in town. In September they moved to 10 Harewood Square while they looked for a London address, and two months later moved to 16 Blandford Square, where they lived until the summer of 1863. Meanwhile, Lewes's other sons remained at school. In October 1863, the second eldest, Thornton (Thornie), who was not staid and reliable like his older brother (he failed the Civil Service exam), left for South Africa, where he established a farm. In 1869, he fell acutely ill with tuberculosis of the spine, returning to London in May, but only surviving until 19 October, when he died at home with his father and stepmother. Herbert (Bertie), Lewes's youngest son, joined his brother in Natal after learning the farming business in Scotland; he too died young, on 29 June 1875.

Soon after her return from Europe, Marian informed Blackwood of her intention to write an Italian novel (in Florence Lewes had suggested that the character of the charismatic fifteenth-century monk Savonarola might be the basis of a good story). Nothing came of these plans immediately, however. Instead, barely a month later, she had begun another English story, *Silas Marner*, in which she added to her characteristic provincial realism new elements of legendary romance and allegorical fable. This short novel, finished in six months and published on 2 April 1861, was an immediate critical and commercial success. A fortnight later the Leweses set out again for their spring holiday, returning to Italy with the express purpose of making notes for the 'great project' Marian had alluded to the previous summer (*Letters*, iii. 307). They stayed in Florence for a month, studying as well as sightseeing and visiting their friend Trollope's brother Thomas and his family. Back at home for the summer, progress on the new novel, *Romola*, was painfully slow. To make matters worse, Lewes was suffering from a mysterious wasting illness, which led them to try the water cure at Malvern, but without much improvement in the patient. At the same time, Marian's preparations still involved so much detailed research into Florentine history, customs, language, and costume, that she was buried in study for months on end, at home and at the British Museum ('She seems to be studying her subject as subject never was studied before', Blackwood remarked (*Letters*, iii. 474)). Always wracked with self-doubt and anxiety when a book needed writing, and burdened with headaches and vague illnesses that only dispersed when it was finished, Marian was almost paralysed by the enormity of this project, and though she had notes for many scenes she could not fairly make a start. Lewes, desperate for her to do so, asked Blackwood, who was coming to visit in December, to convince her that a historical romance was not 'the product of an Encyclopaedia' (*Letters*, iii. 474).

Marian resolved finally to begin in earnest with the new year. The writing was agony, however, and she did not finish the novel for eighteen months. To add to her difficulties she put herself under the additional pressure of bringing the novel out in serial form—her first to be published in this demanding way, where the story would have to begin appearing in the magazine long before she had finished writing it (*Scenes of Clerical Life*, although it was published serially, was not a continuous narrative). Marian had agreed to magazine publication against her better judgement, only because she had received an offer of £10,000 from one of Blackwood's chief rivals, George Smith of Smith, Elder and Co. After protracted negotiations, the final agreed sum was only £7,000: double what Blackwood could offer. Serialization began in July 1862, eleven months before Marian finished writing the novel; it was published in three volumes by Smith, Elder and Co. on 6 July 1863. As she later remarked to Cross, she could 'put her finger on [*Romola*] as marking a well-defined transition in her life. In her own words, "I began it a young woman—I finished it an old woman"' (*Life*, p. 361).

Romola also marks a significant transition in the kinds of novel Marian wrote. For the first time (in her full-length fiction at least) she did not depend upon her own memories for inspiration, and chose to set a novel outside the English Midlands of her childhood. Also for the first time, politics and public life entered her fiction. More particularly, in the character of Tito, she began to explore the relation of political life to the development of an individual nature (*Letters*, iv. 97). She would become increasingly preoccupied with this problem—that 'there is no private life which has not been determined by a wider public life' (*Felix Holt, the Radical*, chapter 3)—as she herself moved slowly towards a more public life as a celebrated author (*Romola*, commercially and critically unsuccessful as it was, made her the most eminent novelist in England after Dickens). She still refused invitations to dinner, and married women—even the wives of close friends, like Trollope—did not visit. But gradually more and more people began to call on the Leweses, and when they finally bought a large house in London in 1863—The Priory, just north of Regent's Park, paid for out of the *Romola* earnings—they instituted the Sunday afternoon gatherings that would bring the wider public world to their door.

Exhausted from the effort of *Romola*, Marian did not begin her next novel for nearly two years, instead trying her hand at a play for the actress Helen Faucit, a friend of hers and Lewes's. But she could not make headway with it (transformed into verse, it ultimately became *The Spanish Gypsy* in 1868). Meanwhile, against all advice Lewes had taken up the editorship of a new radical journal, the *Fortnightly Review*, and Marian, worried about his health, was anxious to support him. For the first time in eight years she wrote a magazine review, and, perhaps sensitive that *Romola* had not been all that successful and had not reversed the fortunes of the *Cornhill*, contributed two other pieces for George Smith's new evening *Pall Mall Gazette*. She also began taking a renewed interest in contemporary public affairs, especially the controversy over proposed parliamentary reforms, which included the extension of the franchise to working men in the towns. Then, on 29 March 1865, she noted in her diary that she had begun a new novel. *Felix Holt, the Radical*, George Eliot's latter-day 'Condition-of-England' novel, took up this topical theme of reform and the enfranchisement of the working classes, though it set its action back in 1832, the year of the First Reform Bill. By the following April, when Lewes finally approached Blackwood (returning, after the venture with Smith, to the old firm), the novel was more than half finished. By the end of May 1866, following the usual laborious task of writing, it was done. *Felix Holt* was not a commercial success, however, nor much of a critical success.

Over the following three years Marian worked almost exclusively on various poetic projects. *The Spanish Gypsy*, the plot of which anticipates many of the issues in *Daniel Deronda*, took up a great deal of her time, and was finally not rewarded with either critical praise or sales. At this time, too, she wrote the 'Brother and Sister' sonnets, perhaps her most successful poems, and a cluster of other verses.[25] Sometime in the late 1860s, however, a new novel was beginning to take shape, and an entry in Marian's journal for 1 January 1869 records among her plans for the coming year 'A novel called Middlemarch' (*Journals*, p. 134). On 2 August she was writing the story of Lydgate and the Featherstone and Vincy families; over a year later, in December 1870, she had begun another story altogether, entitled 'Miss Brooke'. Sometime soon after this, she made the momentous decision to combine the two stories into a single novel, *Middlemarch: A Study of Provincial Life*. Towards the end of 1871, Lewes, who had long cherished the idea of publishing a George Eliot novel in serial parts (not in magazines, that is, but in separately published instalments), saw his opportunity with *Middlemarch*. When it became clear that the novel would run to the equivalent of four not three full volumes, he proposed that Black-wood publish it in eight half-volume parts at two-monthly intervals. The first part was published on 1 December 1871. When the eighth and final part of the novel appeared a year later (the final two parts came out at monthly not two-monthly intervals) *Middlemarch* was an outstanding success, and George Eliot's apparent decline in popularity with *Felix Holt* was spectacularly arrested.[26]

By 1873 Marian no longer lived in social isolation but led an increasingly busy social life which, although the Leweses now kept their own carriage (an unmistakable sign of wealth and respect-ability), was still largely conducted at home at The Priory, and for a summer or two at The Heights, the country home they finally purchased in December 1876 in Witley, Surrey. She and Lewes made many new friends at this time.[27] It was also a period of crucial female friendships for Marian. Relationships with woman had always been an important part of her life: the Hennell sisters; Bessie Parkes; and especially Barbara Bodichon, the feminist campaigner and painter, whom she first met at Chapman's in 1852, and who remained an intimate, sympathetic, and intuitive friend all her life. This remarkable relationship contrasted dramatically with Marian's later intimate friendships with women. Perhaps only Georgiana Burne-Jones, who first visited The Priory with her husband the painter Edward Burne-Jones in February 1868, offered friendship on the same equable terms. They became frequent visitors, and introduced the Leweses to William Morris and Dante Gabriel Rossetti. In July 1870 Georgie visited Whitby, where Marian was staying, and they became intimate friends. But the two other prom-inent women in Marian's life after 1870, Elma Stuart and Edith Simcox, both came into her life as fervid admirers of 'George Eliot'. Elma Stuart, who had learned wood-carving, sent Marian the gift of a book-slide through Blackwood's. It was the beginning of a passion-ate mother–daughter relationship. Stuart is even buried beside

George Eliot in Highgate Cemetery, her tombstone reading: 'whom, for 8½ blessed years George Eliot called by the sweet name of "Daughter"' (*Biography*, p. 452). Simcox, on the other hand, was a brilliant intellectual, trade union activist, and social reformer. She wrote on a wide range of subjects for many journals including the *Academy* and the *Nineteenth Century*, and was the author of *Natural Law: An Essay in Ethics* (1877) and a study of women and property rights in ancient civilizations. As her extraordinary 'Autobiography of a Shirt Maker' attests, she was, like Eliot, both an intellectual and a woman of passionate affections. She was also a lesbian, and her passionate sexual adoration of Marian seems, in the 'Autobiography' at least, to be almost obsessional. When she dedicated *Natural Law* to George Eliot 'with idolatrous love', Marian became seriously discomfited by Simcox's sexuality, finally making it clear to her in 1880 that the 'mother–daughter relationship' they shared could not continue (see *Letters*, ix. 202–3).

Marian's next novel, *Daniel Deronda*, was conceived late in 1873, and worked on steadily through 1874 and 1875. In October 1875, she and Lewes decided to repeat the *Middlemarch* scheme of part publication, with the difference that *Daniel Deronda* would appear in eight monthly parts. Book 1 was published on 1 February 1876, and concluded in September 1876, just three months after Marian had finished writing it. It was to be her last novel. She was 56 years old, and had never been completely well. All her life she had suffered more or less constantly from bad headaches, toothache, and neuralgia, and various debilitating nervous illnesses and digestive problems, and after 1874 from periodic attacks of kidney stones. Lewes's ill-health, on the other hand, had long been much more serious—probably in part from overwork—and by the 1870s he looked prematurely old and unwell. In June 1878, a couple of months after his sixty-first birthday, it was confirmed that he had cancer. Although neither he nor Marian seem to have realized, or dared to believe, that this illness was terminal, he became acutely ill in mid-November, and died, after days of agony, on the evening of 30 November 1878.

Marian's grief overwhelmed her, and she mourned Lewes in absolute solitude, seeing no one but his surviving son Charles for nearly two months, as she went through his unfinished work and determined that she would complete *Problems of Life and Mind* from his notes. Volume iv, *The Study of Psychology*, was ready by May 1879, and volume v, the last volume, by the end of 1879. She also put aside £5,000 to endow a George Henry Lewes Studentship in Physiology at Cambridge, but was unable to access the money in Lewes's account until she had changed her name by deed poll, which she did in January 1879, signing herself 'Mary Ann Evans Lewes'. In the mean time her own writing had been suspended. Just a week or so before Lewes had died, he had sent off to Blackwood the manuscript of her *Impressions of Theophrastus Such*, a book of idiosyncratic essays and character sketches by the eponymous essayist, who is by turns ponderous and jaundiced in character. Its publication was put off until May 1879, and Marian asked Blackwood to insert a notice explaining that the work had been completed before Lewes's death and held in reserve until then. Blackwood himself died on 29 October.

In February 1879, Marian began to see other people, including John Walter Cross, whom the Leweses had known well since 1869. Cross was a banker who handled Marian's investments with great success, and visited frequently at The Priory and The Heights, becoming close to them both (they called him 'Nephew'). He was the first person Marian admitted after her period of solitary mourning was over, and he became a frequent visitor, taking control of financial matters, and gradually becoming more intimate. On 9 April 1880 they decided to marry, and did so less than a month later, on 6 May, at St George's, Hanover Square, honeymooning on the Continent. On 17 May, Isaac Evans wrote to his sister to congratulate her on her marriage—the first letter she had received from him in more than twenty years. Back in England the couple bought a house at 4 Cheyne Walk, Chelsea, to which they moved on 3 December 1880. Eighteen days later, she died.

She was buried in Highgate Cemetery—the unconsecrated section—not, as one might expect, in Poets' Corner in Westminster Abbey. Cross had in fact approached the Dean of Westminster with a petition, but Eliot's atheism and common-law marriage were against her. T. H. Huxley, the biologist and agnostic (he had coined the word himself), put the matter bluntly: 'George Eliot is known not only as a great writer, but as a person whose life and opinions were in notorious antagonism to Christian practice in regard to marriage, and Christian theory in regard to dogma. . . . One cannot eat one's cake and have it too.'[28] The obelisk in Highgate bears two names, 'George

Eliot' and 'Mary Ann Cross'. It is surely significant that she would choose at the last to return to that particular spelling of her name, the one she had preferred during the years of her most intellectually intensive and painful experiences, 1837–50: the years after the death of her mother; of meeting the Brays and the Hennells; and, especially, of the 'Holy War' and its aftermath. Eliot's biographers agree, in general, that the 'Holy War' was the most momentous of the formative events of Eliot's life. Rosemarie Bodenheimer, in particular, has argued that the 'pattern of behaviour and response' established during this terrible quarrel with her father over her loss of faith was 'to characterize George Eliot's conflict-filled moments of decision in later life, and to create the uneasy blend of radical social critique and conservatism that shapes her fiction'.[29] Present in that fateful decision was the rebellious woman—the incipient paramour—and the respectable woman—the future Mrs Lewes, as she would insist on being addressed; the independent intellectual of advanced views and the emotionally dependent daughter, sister, partner, whose 'need to be loved' was overpowering;[30] and the speculative modern, bold in the risks she took with her art, who nevertheless preached moderation, caution, and duty to the past.

But was that the meaning of the ill-fated episode in 1842? The 'Holy War' brought home, literally, the implications of Mary Ann's decision. The challenge to established religious views carried with it a challenge to the established social and political order, as her father recognized immediately and with alarm. Her new position, deeply considered and final, admitting no possibility of revocation, was met with dismay, anger, and misunderstanding from the man for whom she felt (although writing in 1849, before she had met Lewes) 'the one deep strong love I have ever known' (*Letters*, i. 284). But this episode was so critical in the development of George Eliot not primarily because Mary Ann Evans feared, above all, the consequences of her unconventional behaviour: rejection by family and community; loss of respectability. Rather, her confrontation with her father and brother, and partial capitulation to their demands that she not destroy the family's good name, made vividly, painfully actual to her that characteristic condition of modernity which she was to make peculiarly her own as a novelist: the real meaning, at the level of lived experience, of what Raymond Williams called 'the co-existence of persistence and change'.[31] She learned then that this was no benign coexistence but a clash of 'two principles, both having their validity, . . . at war with each other', as she later described it in an essay on Sophocles' *Antigone* (*Essays*, p. 244). That clash of principles—the drive to dismantle old certainties by rationalist analysis, and the impulse to preserve old certainties by conservative instincts—informs Eliot's whole creative work, which may be described as a set of variations on a theme: the confrontation between hard facts and powerful feelings.

The later scandalous liaison with Lewes—usually adduced as an accompanying outbreak of rebellion—brought its own degree of suffering, but it can scarcely be compared with the 'Holy War'. It was risked within a very different context. Marian Evans was an independent adult moving in metropolitan circles of free-thought and in the sophisticated cosmopolitan Europe of advanced culture, secure in the love of Lewes: *empowered*. Mary Ann Evans had been 21 years old and wholly dependent upon her father, a man who had worked his way to a position of respectability in a small provincial community. How hard must it have been for her to write those words: 'I could not without vile hypocrisy and a miserable truckling to the smile of the world . . . profess to join in worship which I wholly disapprove' (*Letters*, i. 129)? The fact that she *did* truckle to the smile of the world—did obediently go back to church for the sake of appearances—is sometimes overlooked. But what else that was in her power ought she rather to have done, as the narrator remarks of Dorothea at the end of *Middlemarch*?

And how, later, could she not have lived openly with Lewes? To have acted a deception, as she had in Coventry, was by then impossible to her. Unfortunately, being true to her feelings could look all too much like having your way and hanging the consequences. From this problem comes Eliot's great theme—what has been called the 'representative' question of her realism: not that of 'the shifting relation between passion and duty' (*The Mill on the Floss*, book 7, chapter 2), but the question 'where the duty of obedience ends, and the duty of resistance begins' (*Romola*, chapter 55).[32] Obedience and resistance do not carry quite the same connotations as respectability and rebellion, and the insinuation of that Eliotean keyword, duty, into both sides of the equation reminds us just how Victorian both Eliots were: how 'the *duty* of resistance' might not altogether satisfy our idea of a rebellious writer. 'George Eliot' was born out of a highly unconventional and, to later observers, decidedly un-Victorian act of defiance. Had Marian Evans not met and fallen in love with George Henry Lewes, and not resisted the extreme pressure on a middle-class woman to behave respectably, the novels of George Eliot might never have been written: *would* never have been written, she herself believed at the crucial turning-point of her career with the success of *Adam Bede*.[33] But it was not the act of a rebellious person—an insurgent. Nor should we, perhaps, be so quick to dismiss the sibylline Eliot as Eliza Lynn Linton did, and as later generations have done, almost as a reflex, with an instinctive distaste for the moralism, the *wisdom* of George Eliot. It is too easy to claim *our* insurgent and repudiate *their* sibyl (the Victorians', I mean). For to encounter Eliot's wisdom in the pages of her fiction is an extraordinary experience: electric, it can make us gasp in recognition and wonder, and leave us as entranced and puzzled as the young Henry James.

CHAPTER 2

THE FABRIC OF SOCIETY

England in 1819 and After

ON the face of it, no Victorian novelist is more Victorian than George Eliot. She was born in 1819, the same year as Queen Victoria, and her literary career, from 'Amos Barton' (1857) to *Impressions of Theophrastus Such* (1879), coincides with a period of unrivalled prosperity and social stability in England.[1] This is the period we now associate with the heyday of 'Victorianism', and later generations (taking their cue from the Edwardians, who were determined to shake off their heavy heritage) have sometimes found in Eliot the epitome of everything that was odiously self-satisfied about Victorian attitudes: the uninhibited and complacent confidence in one's own powers and in England's upward progress; the solemn and stifling moralism; the prudishness and philistinism. It is important to keep in mind, however, that the England in which Eliot grew up—and the years of her childhood and youth were by her own account the most significant of her life—was neither Victorian nor prosperous. The year 1819, after all, is not chiefly remembered as the year in which the future queen was born. It is remembered as the year in which a detachment of 600 hussars rode into a crowd of more than 50,000 working people attending a peaceful rally in support of moderate political reform in St Peter's Fields, Manchester, killing eleven civilians and wounding hundreds more with their sabres. This is the year memorialized in Shelley's famous sonnet, 'England in 1819'. King George III—'old, mad, blind, despised, and dying'—was in the last year of his long reign (1760–1820), although his dissolute and extravagant son had ruled in his place as prince regent since 1811. The Napoleonic Wars had ended in 1815, sending English manufacturing industry into crisis. Unemployment had risen sharply, a run of bad harvests had led to chronic food shortages, and widespread rioting broke out. A Tory ministry under the leadership of

Lord Liverpool responded to the growing discontent and increasing politicization and insurgency of the populace with a combination of repressive measures and clandestine intimidation. In January 1817, after a missile had shattered the window of the Prince Regent's coach on the way to the opening of Parliament, Habeas Corpus (the guarantee that no one could be imprisoned without trial) was summarily suspended. In the following months political meetings were outlawed, freedom of speech was curtailed, and spies and enforcers were planted everywhere, quashing (or in many cases wantonly inflaming) unrest and violently suppressing the spread of political radicalism. The ruling classes associated radicalism with Jacobinism, the ideology of the most extreme revolutionaries of the French Terror of the mid-1790s.[2] In this vein, Shelley ends his poem by prophesying a bloody revolution in England, a 'glorious Phantom' that may 'Burst, to illumine our tempestuous day'.

For reasons that remain the subject of debate among historians, this prediction of an uprising to rival the American and French Revolutions was never fulfilled. Nor was the 'Peterloo massacre' (named in ironical reference to the 1815 Battle of Waterloo) ever repeated, even when England was plunged into the terrible depressions and turbulent class struggles of the 1830s and 1840s. This is all the more remarkable considering how much worse things got before they got better. In 1839 and again in 1842 ('there was no gloomier year in the nineteenth century', according to Asa Briggs[3]) and 1848 Parliament turned away representatives of the working-class Chartist movement who had drawn up a People's Charter calling for universal male suffrage, the secret ballot, equal electoral districts, abolition of the property qualifications for MPs, payment of MPs, and annual general elections. The Chartists had massive popular support, and presented petitions carrying millions of signatures. Yet they failed, and no revolution came to pass. The economy gradually revived over the course of the 1840s, and by 1850 was beginning to expand, aided by the surge in railway development, which mobilized capital and streamlined transportation routes for raw materials and manufactured goods. The Great Exhibition held in London in 1851—the first exposition or world's fair—marked a turning point in the mood of the nation. By the mid-1850s things had improved dramatically, and the dangerous atmosphere of protest and revolt had almost completely dissipated. This was not because the majority of English men and women were better off: there were still terrible inequalities in the distribution of wealth. Yet as the century progressed, English social structures and institutions showed remarkable resilience—or rather the English people showed remarkable faith in those institutions. This optimistic culture of consensus insulated England from the liberal revolutions devastating Europe in 1848 and the nationalist movements and wars that broke out on the Continent in the decades following. There were periodic outbreaks of violent class protest in England over those decades (most notably on the eve of the Second Reform Act in 1867, when workers rioted in Hyde Park in London), but nothing to rival 1819 or the 1830s and 1840s. Even agricultural and industrial depression, which struck again in 1873, could not return the much larger, more robust economy to the condition it had been in during the hungry Forties (although it should be said that more than a quarter of the population still lived in poverty in 1873). It did, however, signal the onset of a general economic downturn that would outlast the nineteenth century and lead, eventually, to England's decline as a world power. When George Eliot died in 1880, therefore, the Victorians were once again facing economic uncertainty and intensified social distress. But by this time, liberal democracy was entrenched—although it would take half a century before the entire adult population would have the right to vote in parliamentary elections.

Eliot belonged, then, to the generation that came of age in the aftermath of the Revolutionary Wars in America and France and the Napoleonic Wars in Europe, and stood at the forefront of an unprecedented expansion in industrial production and an unprecedented extension of the sovereignty of ordinary people. Her generation was country-bred, but increasingly likely to live in towns or cities. It was a generation better fed and longer-living than any in the entire previous history of Europe: for this reason, and because of a huge influx of immigrants from Ireland, the population more than doubled over Eliot's lifetime, from 12 million in 1821 to nearly 26 million in 1881.[4] Despite the general drift of the population away from the countryside into the overcrowded cities, agriculture remained a significant employer of the English population throughout the century: roughly one in five men worked in the sector in 1841; roughly one in seven in 1881.[5] Fundamentally, though, the nature of the English economy had changed by 1819. The intensification of capital investment in industry after the Napoleonic Wars (the textile industries initially, and heavy industry after 1850) and highly efficient new technologies of industrial production and distribution brought about a massive reorganization of the economy, new kinds of work, new kinds of wealth and status, and new kinds of poverty. This was a period of intense social suffering, unrest, and violence, and a period of remarkable energy and optimism.

The three basic components of this revolution were coal, steam, and iron. James Watt developed the first efficient coal-driven steam engine in 1775, and by 1779 steam-powered textile mills were already in operation in Britain, although it was not until the 1810s that the textile industry began widely using Cartwright's power loom (first developed in 1787). The potential of steam for goods haulage and commuter travel was also quickly recognized. Already by the turn of the century coach travel in England was becoming more efficient, with turnpikes (toll gates) improving the quality and safety of road surfaces. But the first roads were not macadamized until 1819, and until then goods were transported throughout Britain along the canal systems, the first nationwide distribution network of the industrial revolution. Begun in Britain in 1757, the canals were not long finished before the railways superseded them. In 1801 Trevithick built a prototype steam-powered rail locomotive, but the first practical locomotive was not produced (by George Stephenson) until 1814. The Stockton–Darlington public railway began service in 1821; and in 1822 trains began to be used to haul raw materials, and steamships to transport manufactured goods around the world.

This was an astonishing period of technological advancement, transforming the city into the very image of modernity, with 'its smoke, its dirt, its bustle, its deformation of the face of nature, and the . . . rudeness of its millions'.[6] Modern life was new in an entirely new way, and the self-identity of Eliot's generation was intimately tied up with its acute consciousness of this newness. Part of her importance as a novelist rests with the fact that she was one of the great chroniclers of modern experience and the sensibility it produced. Hers was the first modern generation in the world, the first generation, that is, to be sensitive to their modernity, and look back to the immediate past—the past of their parents—as if across a chasm to the pre-modern age. More importantly, Eliot—unlike Dickens, say—does not look out from the modern city onto the pre-modern countryside. Those who remained in rural areas and occupations felt the shattering impact of all these changes too; indeed, for Eliot, and later for Hardy, the villages and towns of the English countryside became equally important sites of the modern. There, an entrenched social and economic order with its old patterns of life focused on the local community gave way just as suddenly to new orders of being, changing the very nature of everyday life in small local communities for ever. It was for this reason—the *concentration* of the effects of radical social and cultural change—that Eliot could legitimately represent the localized experiences of small communities in provincial backwaters as the generalized experience of modernity.

It is instructive in this regard to compare Eliot with Thackeray, whose novels also look back to this adjacent pre-modernity. Writing in 1860, Thackeray saw in that quintessentially Victorian technology, the railway, the ultimate symbol of the modern:

Your railroad starts the new era, and we of a certain age belong to the new time and the old one. . . . We elderly people have lived in that prae-railroad world, which has passed into limbo and vanished from under us. I tell you it was firm under our feet once, and not long ago. They have raised those railroad embankments up, and shut off the old world that was behind them. Climb up that bank on which the irons are laid, and look to other side—it is gone.[7]

Eliot was eight years younger than Thackeray, yet her experience of industrial modernity, and her representation of it, seems dramatically closer to that moment when everything changed. She grew up on an estate near provincial Coventry, not in metropolitan London. In the Midlands it was not the advent of the railway that symbolized the advent of the modern: in 1825, the railway had hardly got going, and there were barely thirty miles of track in the whole United Kingdom. Rather, it was the radical transformation of the countryside, the transformation of the physical and social landscape, that symbolized the modern. That landscape had begun to change long before the development of the steam engine, as rural populations increased in the eighteenth century and fell into grinding poverty, devastated by the loss of common lands, and subject to fluctuations in international trade. One of the most traumatic effects of this was also the least visible: the loss of localism. Industrial modernity tends to homogenize and universalize experience (factories and slums do not have a local character), so that local concerns are never *just* local, but are mediated by national or global conditions. During Eliot's lifetime global economic movements constantly affected the price of textiles and the price of bread (in 1856, for example, Eliot's Coventry friends the Brays were forced out of business by a depression in the ribbon industry caused by fluctuations in the supply of cotton from America). During this period, too, local time was replaced by standard time (to allow for safe train timetabling), and local dialects were gradually supplanted by standard English. In the villages, farms, and towns of Eliot's upbringing, new time and old time, new social formations and old, local and global concerns, all coexist, as the famous Introduction to *Felix Holt, the Radical* attests:

In these midland districts the traveller passed rapidly from one phase of English life to another: after looking down on a village dingy with coal-dust, noisy with the shaking of looms, he might skirt a parish all of fields, high hedges, and deep-rutted lanes; after the coach had rattled over the pavement of a manufacturing town, the scene of riots and trades-union meetings, it would take him in another ten minutes into a rural region, where the neighbourhood of the town was only felt in the advantages of a near market for corn, cheese, and hay, and where men with a considerable banking account were accustomed to say that 'they never meddled with politics themselves'. The busy scenes of the shuttle and the wheel, of the roaring furnace, of the shaft and the pulley, seemed to make but crowded nests in the midst of the large-spaced, slow-moving life of homesteads and far-away cottages and oak-sheltered parks. Looking at the dwellings scattered amongst the woody flats and the ploughed uplands, under the low grey sky which overhung them with an unchanging stillness as if Time itself were pausing, it was easy for the traveller to conceive that town and country had no pulse in common, except where the handlooms made a far-reaching straggling fringe about the great centres of manufacture.

Eliot grew up amidst 'the large-spaced, slow-moving life' of the Arbury estate, where her father worked as manager and land agent. Arbury was, as a social structure, still basically feudal in appearance: a large landed estate owned and passed down through the generations of a single family, the Newdigates. Much of the Arbury land was given over to farming, and all of its pastures would have been enclosed (by hedgerows) when Eliot was growing up. This practice had been going on in Britain for centuries, but the rate of enclosure accelerated spectacularly in the early nineteenth century. This was partly because it became necessary to supply food much more efficiently to the rapidly growing urban populations, and partly because during the Napoleonic Wars the importation of foreign corn had been stopped by enemy blockades, so that English agriculture was effectively protected, and enjoyed boom conditions. Whatever the reason, enclosure led to the dramatic reduction or abolition of common farming lands which under traditional social arrangements had allowed agricultural workers to grow their own food and supplement the income they received from the squire. Once enclosed, the landlord leased out his farms to tenant farmers, as Squire Donnithorne does to the Poysers, who in turn employed local agricultural workers—the descendants of cottagers and yeomen farmers—as wage earners on very low seasonal wages.

Arbury was not just an agricultural estate laid out around the big house, however. It also had a productive coal mine, and transported coal via the canal system to the great industrial cities where it was used to fire machinery in factories. In the Arbury villages, too, textiles were woven by handloom weavers who worked out of cottages owned by the squire, just as Silas Marner does. But unlike Silas, who produces cloth for the local population, the handloom weavers were really modern industrial operatives: part of 'far-reaching straggling fringe' of the industrial centres, as Eliot puts it in the *Felix Holt* Introduction. The majority of the cloth they wove was bought for export by clothiers (merchants who went from village to village). Although power looms were in use extensively in factories in the Midlands by 1811, handloom weavers still outnumbered factory-based power-loom workers in England by a factor of nearly two to one in 1819.[8] Yet by this time they were a doomed workforce. The output of a single factory worker on a power loom was much greater than that of a handloom weaver, and it was only a matter of time before the old ways disappeared. When the average wage of handloom weavers fell from 21s. a week in 1802 to less than 9s. in 1817, the threat to their livelihoods became so acute that they organized themselves and protested by damaging or destroying machinery (known collectively as Luddites, these groups were active between 1811 and 1816). The weavers struggled on, but by the middle of the 1840s prices were falling steeply and no increase in productivity could yield an increase in their incomes. They were finished, and their tragic situation became emblematic of the displacement of entire labour groups by machine production. Yet their persistence for half a century is also worth noting: for until the 1830s a significant proportion of the major British manufacturing industry of the nineteenth century, the textile industry, was still being carried out in what look like traditional social formations—in villages built centuries before out of local stone and thatch on land owned by the local aristocracy or gentry, or in one of the nearby market towns. As the Introduction to *Felix Holt* shows, distinctions between an old rural and a new industrial England were blurred in the Midlands of the early nineteenth century.

Eliot's generation also lived through the greatest period of economic and territorial expansion in the history of the world, and died just as Britain, in depression at home, was beginning to recognize, and take advantage of, the symbolic and ceremonial value of its vast empire. By the end of the nineteenth century, that empire covered one quarter of the globe and took in one quarter of the world's population. Yet, as J. R. Seeley wrote famously in *The Expansion of England* (1883)—a best-seller of the 1880s, and often credited with firing the imperial imagination of ordinary Britons—Britain 'conquered and peopled half the world in a fit of absence of mind'.[9] It is true that before the 1880s Britain thought of its empire more or less as India—in 1876 Parliament passed Disraeli's Royal Titles Act, making Queen Victoria empress of India—and only began to engage in 'constructive imperialism', the active promotion of a British Empire united in its constitutional, economic, military, and social policies, in the land-grabs of the last decades of the century. Yet Britain had substantial imperial holdings during George Eliot's lifetime, and the dominance of its free-trade economic policy after 1850 ensured the existence of a flourishing 'informal empire' driven by commercial and financial interests. Increases in foreign trade, particularly where the primary products of overseas countries were turned into manufactured goods in Britain, enticed the British into extensive capital investment and liberal credit provision abroad. Moreover, the Victorians were a nation of emigrants; and Britain, because it dominated international shipping and communications, was a powerful imperial presence, criss-crossing the globe with naval officers, missionaries, and traders.

Nevertheless Britain did also significantly expand its colonial possessions over the period of Eliot's life. In 1819, settled British territories were comparatively few and scattered: a string of provinces along the east coast of India and isolated shipping and trading outposts in the Far East (Singapore was acquired by Raffles the year Eliot was born); New South Wales and Van Diemen's Land in Australia; the Cape of Good Hope and three territories on the west coast of Africa; the Caribbean and what was left of British North America after Britain lost the American War of Independence. By 1880, India was under direct rule of Britain (after the disbanding of the East India Company in 1857 and the subsequent Indian Mutiny), and the Burmese peninsula was British territory. Britain had gained the all-important control of the Suez Canal (purchasing 44 per cent of the shares in 1875), which opened up the East to Europe. White settler colonies were prospering in Australia (where gold was discovered in 1851) and Canada (where Rex Gascoigne pledges to go after Gwendolen rejects him in *Daniel Deronda*), both of which, along with New Zealand, became self-ruled dominions in the 1850s. As the century progressed, Britain pushed further into Africa. Livingstone crossed the continent in 1853, and was found by Stanley in 1871. George Henry Lewes's sons Thornie and Bertie were farming in Natal (annexed by the British in 1843) in the 1860s. The British won victories against the Ashanti (1874) and Zulu (1879) and had just been defeated in the first Anglo-Boer War at Majuba Hill (1880) when Eliot died.

The Age of Reform

It was not until the late 1820s and early 1830s that the governing classes formally acknowledged what had been taking place in the British economy and British society over the previous half-century or more by recognizing the importance of the middle-class manufacturers, merchants, and capitalists, and giving them the vote. In the year Eliot was born, political power was still shared by those who had benefited from constitutional arrangements made in the late seventeenth century. Parliament in 1819 was not an institution for the representation of individuals, but the representation of property. It was dominated by two opposing parties: Whigs and Conservatives. The Whigs, whose origins can be traced back to the late seventeenth century, were the party of the wealthiest and most powerful landed interest: the aristocracy and old gentry. By the nineteenth century, however, the Whigs, who thought of themselves as 'friends of the people' and as socially progressive, were formative moderate Liberals (although the 'Liberal Party' was not formally labelled until 1868, when Gladstone became prime minister). They recognized that economic wealth was shifting away from the land and towards manufacturing (indeed, as we have seen from the example of Arbury, many of them had themselves entered industry), and were accordingly ready to remodel the political structure to accommodate the newly self-conscious middle classes: they became committed to parliamentary reform. On the other hand many Conservatives, whose number included bankers and industrial magnates, were opposed to reform: they supported the authority of the monarchy and the Established Church, and were committed to preserving traditional structures and institutions. Only after Sir Robert Peel's 'Tamworth Manifesto' of 1834 (put forward after the First Reform Act had been passed) did these Conservatives compromise, and accept to a small degree the inevitability of moderate reform.

The age of reform may be said to have begun in 1830—the year *Middlemarch* opens. That year, after fifty years of Tory rule in the House of Commons, a Whig, Earl Grey, became prime minister and prepared England for parliamentary reform by proposing to abolish a number of rotten boroughs (constituencies which had as few as a handful of voters, but still returned one or two Members of Parliament) and create new constituencies for the leading industrial towns in the north. Believing he did not have a sufficient majority to carry the bill, Grey was compelled to request the king, William IV, to dissolve Parliament in April 1831. With wide popular support for his reform agenda he won the election victory, and in September of that year succeeded in pushing the Reform Bill through the Commons. It was defeated in the Tory-dominated House of Lords, however (sparking an outbreak of reform riots in several British towns). In desperation, Grey approached William IV in May 1832, asking him to create a large number of Whig peers in order to get the Reform Bill through the Lords. The king refused, Grey's government resigned, and William IV invited the Conservative leader, the Duke of Wellington, to form a government. Wellington was unable to persuade key members of his own cabinet (most notably Peel, the Tory reformer who had carried through wide-ranging judicial reforms, and the Catholic Emancipation Act, in the late 1820s) to oppose reform openly against what was so manifestly the will of the people. Fearing revolt, the king was left with no choice but to invite Grey back into office. Threatened with the creation of a large number of new Whig peers, to which the king had agreed this time, the House of Lords passed the Reform Act.

Even after the successful passage of the Act, Parliament remained an institution devoted to the representation of property, not individuals. In the boroughs (the towns sending a Member to Parliament) men living in houses with an annual value of at least £10 were eligible to vote. As a measure to extend sovereignty, therefore, the Reform Act was extremely modest. It satisfied middle-class radicals, but disappointed the expectant working classes: only one in seven adult males was given the vote; and many rotten boroughs remained (it was not until the 1880s that the electorate was resolved into single-member constituencies of roughly equal population).

But the real significance of the 1832 Act lies not in the limited extent of the reforms it achieved itself but in the culture of reform it initiated in England. It opened the door to further parliamentary reforms, and in due course (though not without considerable resistance) the franchise was extended: to every male adult householder living in a borough constituency (and any male lodger paying £10 for rooms) in 1867 (giving the vote to about 1.5 million men); and to working men in the countryside in 1884. Progress was slow, however. Before the 1867 Act, according to the Radical MP John Bright, 'only sixteen out of every hundred men' were on the electoral rolls and half the House of Commons was 'elected by a number of electors not exceeding altogether three men out of every hundred in the United Kingdom'.[10] By 1911, still only sixty out of every hundred adult men, and no adult women, had the vote: universal adult suffrage was not in fact achieved in Britain until 1928, long after it was achieved in some other countries (such as Australia). But just as importantly, the 1832 Reform Act opened the door to other wide-ranging reforms which overhauled and modernized British institutions, dramatically improved the social conditions of the population, and entrenched Britain as the dominant world power. These reforms had begun in the 1820s, but only a reformed Parliament could be truly sympathetic, it was felt, to the demands for change in other specific areas, and the rate of reform accelerated significantly after 1832.[11]

The greatest achievements of the post-Reform Act period were in the areas of economic reform, institutional reform, reform of religious rights, and the reform of living and working conditions. Some, like the 1833 Abolition of Slavery Act (the culmination of forty years of legislative change instigated by Clarkson and Wilberforce in 1791), were tremendous monuments to human progress. Others, like the 1850 Public Libraries Act, which infinitesimally advanced the ideal of universal publicly funded education, were less spectacular; but they too were effective in contributing to long-term change.[12] Many reforms which were undertaken with the intention of renovating moribund, inefficient administrative entities had profound social side effects, both for good and ill. As an example of the good, the common-law prohibition on married women owning their own property (including the wages they earned after marriage) was eroded by a series of Acts (the 1857 Divorce Act, which gave deserted women the same property rights as single women, and the Married Women's Property Acts of 1870 and 1882) which were passed under pressure from a combination of sustained middle-class feminist campaigns (see the section 'The Woman Question' later in this chapter) and reform of the Law Courts. On the other hand, the notorious Poor Law Amendment Act of 1834—which compelled those unable to find work to seek relief in parish workhouses, where conditions were deliberately made harsh to discourage them from applying—was motivated equally by the need to reform corrupt and inefficient administrative systems (and reduce poor rates) and to revolutionize the ideology of government social support. As Dickens so graphically depicted it in *Oliver Twist* (written in 1836–7, virtually as soon as the effects of the Act became apparent), the new Poor Law was driven by an unfeeling and inhumane utilitarianism (which held that people were essentially self-interested, and innately motivated to do what was needed to better themselves), and it erred in allowing social theory to dictate social policy. Yet it has been argued that in 1839 only one-seventh of all those receiving public assistance in England were in workhouses: the overwhelming majority still received the dole at home.[13] Moreover the Poor Law, although it was scarcely immune from administrative corruption or inefficiency itself, was innovative in applying the principle that the state had a responsibility to provide uniform standards of support to the poor, laying the foundations, ironically, for the welfare systems of the twentieth century.

As the 1834 Poor Law Amendment Act shows, Victorian administrations, whilst they advocated laissez-faire economics in principle (that is, the minimization of government interference and the maximization of market forces in economic activity), were highly interventionist in the social sphere (and in fact, as we shall see, increasingly regulatory in economic matters). Many of the reform bills put forward to Parliament were the end-product of a long process of information-gathering that mobilized a vast apparatus of parliamentary committees of inquiry, Royal Commissions, Whitehall bureaucracies, pressure groups, and specialist (especially scientific) institutions. This was the age of blue books—the detailed reports of Standing and Select Committees of the Houses of Parliament and Royal Commissioners, so named because of their blue covers—which reported on virtually every aspect of Victorian national and imperial administration, trade and industry, finance, the military, social problems, work, education, emigration, and religion.

In particular, Victorian governments and bureaucratic agencies closely monitored the living and working conditions of the poor crowding into the cities from the countryside and from Ireland (whilst largely neglecting the equally appalling conditions of agricultural labourers and struggling tenant farmers left on unimproved estates like Mr Brooke's in *Middlemarch*). Social reform had a moral dimension for the reforming Victorian middle classes, who did not view the poor as victims of social inequality or crushing market forces but as either morally deficient (a delinquent class, associated with drunkenness, prostitution, crime) or incapable, in any case, of self-reform. Many of the most enduring achievements of the age of reform were responses to urban industrial living conditions that badly needed improvement: not responses to poverty itself, which had been caused in the first place by the very system that made the reforming classes rich and powerful. This was one of the great contradictions at the heart of Victorian society. Capitalism was enshrined as a force for moral regeneration. It encouraged enterprise, and rewarded thrift with the benefits of capital accumulation; it was expansive, and benefited everybody in the long run, and, in a genuinely free market, those benefits were available to anyone willing to work hard. The self-made man was the hero of the rising capitalist classes at the mid-century, commemorated in stirring biographical accounts in Samuel Smiles's best-selling *Self-Help* (1859), one of the period's sacred texts.

Social reforms, therefore, although they did genuinely seek to improve the living and working conditions of the lower orders, and were responsible for putting in place the infrastructures of the modern city (proper roads, sewerage systems, clean water), were also forms of external social control imposed by the ruling classes on an unrepresented majority of working men and women. This is manifestly the case in a measure like Peel's Metropolitan Police Act of 1829, for example, which, in the climate of lower-class social unrest leading up to the First Reform Act, established the prototype of the modern police force. Ten years later, once again in the face of organized working-class activism (Chartism this time), the Rural Constabularies Act established police forces to control outbreaks of violence in the counties. But perhaps the most visible sign of the intervention of reform in working-class living conditions was in the areas of public health and housing. In 1842, Edwin Chadwick, a disciple of Jeremy Bentham (the founder of utilitarianism, who held that actions are right in proportion as they tend to promote happiness, wrong as they tend to produce the reverse of happiness) and secretary of the Poor Law Board, published his *Report . . . on an Inquiry into the Sanitary Condition of the Labouring Population of Great Britain*. Among his findings, Chadwick reported that disease was always found in connection with poor living conditions: 'atmospheric impurities produced by decomposing animal and vegetable substances, by damp and filth, and close and overcrowded dwellings' that prevailed 'amongst the population in every part of the kingdom'. Significantly, Chadwick's report also acknowledged that the 'formation of all habits of cleanliness' among the poor was 'obstructed by defective supplies of water' and poor ventilation.[14] In the long run this represented a threat to economic production (disease was weakening the poor and their offspring, producing an inferior class of workers), and a threat to social control, because the poor were 'less susceptible of moral influences' than a healthy population.[15] The Public Health Act of 1848 and the 1866 Sanitary Act attempted to deal with these issues, compelling local authorities to improve sanitary conditions and provide sewers (connected to new houses) and running water, and appoint sanitary inspectors.

Not all Victorian reforms were interventionist in this way,

however. At the other extreme, the Corn Law Act of 1846—after the parliamentary reforms, the most significant Victorian reform—was designed to lessen government interference. The Corn Laws, instituted in 1815, ordered that no foreign corn (that is, food grains) could be imported into Britain until domestically grown corn reached an exorbitantly high price. As Eric Hobsbawm describes them,

The Corn Laws ... were not designed to save a tottering sector of the economy, but rather to preserve the abnormally high profits of the Napoleonic war-years, and to safeguard farmers from the consequences of their wartime euphoria, when farms had changed hands at the fanciest prices, and loans and mortgages had been accepted on impossible terms.[16]

For nearly thirty years the price of food was so high (proponents of Corn Law reform claimed it was kept artificially high) that working-class families in cities and towns suffered terribly. The general economy was deeply affected, too, with the domestic market for manufactured goods remaining permanently depressed because consumers were spending most of what they earned on staple foods.

The repeal of the Corn Laws is of enormous symbolic significance because it represented a long-fought-for victory won by the manufacturing and capitalist interests over the landed interest, and was a decisive moment in the shift of power away from the landowning classes, who were to maintain their dominance of Parliament for many decades after the 1832 Reform Act. More particularly, it was a victory of free trade over protectionism, won by the powerful Anti-Corn-Law League, founded in 1838 by a group of radical manufacturers from the northern industrial cities, led by Richard Cobden and John Bright. The League believed that free trade was the only way forward for the British economy, and they applied systematic pressure to successive governments (by electing Members to Parliament, for example) which culminated in the phased retraction of the Laws by Peel between 1846 and 1849 (under pressure from the Irish potato famine). The Leaguers' faith in the profound economic benefits of free trade was almost immediately justified, as Britain entered its long economic boom period (1850–73).

Free trade was an essential feature of laissez-faire ideology, reaching back to Adam Smith's *Wealth of Nations* (1776): the free market was an international market, and traded equally in domestic and

foreign commodities. It could be relied upon to operate most efficiently and fairly if left to its own devices. At home, however, the
free-traders' laissez-faire vision of economic progress came into constant conflict with ideals of social progress and the regulatory practices needed to ensure such progress. This conflict was most evident
in the 1840s, when the laissez-faire, anti-reform principles of the
Manchester School reached the height of their influence. Yet even
then governments allowed a free rein of the market only in matters
of pure capitalist enterprise, such as the railway mania which ruined
many investors. On the other hand the forties were also the era of the
Factory Acts, which little by little achieved more humane working
conditions for women, children, and young people, in the face of
free-trade mill owners driven exclusively by the profit motive. The
first of these Acts, in 1833, had restricted working hours for children
and youths (in the textile industries only). Eleven years later, in
1844, a superseding Act reduced children's hours of work further,
and stipulated that youths and (significantly) women in the textile
industries could not be required to work more than twelve hours per
day on weekdays and nine hours on Saturday. This was reduced
further in the 1847 Factory Act, which was still open to abuse by the
shift system, so that in 1850 the law was modified yet again to dictate
specific hours of work for women and young people.

Victorian reform was energetic and far-reaching. By the time Eliot
died in 1880, the legal system had been rationalized (seven courts
were united into the High Court of Justice in 1873), and political
process cleaned up (through such measures as secret ballot). The
army was in the middle of a long phase of restructuring, and the
foundations of the modern industrial relations system were being
laid: the activities of trade unions (such as picketing) had been legal-
ized, independent inspectors of factories were required, and
employers were made liable for the well-being of their employees in
the workplace (a forerunner of workers' compensation). Education
Acts were in place, introducing universal non-denominational education for children, and the right of enrolment at Oxford and
Cambridge was extended beyond practising members of the Established Church. The age of reform left no aspect of the daily lives of
the Victorians untouched.

Social Class and Social Life

It is already evident that British society during Eliot's lifetime was class-based, and that the age of reform was the age of the middle classes. But who exactly were the middle classes, and how were they set apart from those above and below them? To answer these questions, we need to examine briefly the origins of class-based society in Britain. As a way of describing society the idea of 'class' dates only from the late eighteenth century, so in 1819, when Eliot was born, it was a relatively new way of thinking about the differentiation of social groupings (the term 'working class' dates only from 1813, when it was first used by Robert Owen). Rich and poor had existed side by side, of course, since the very beginning of human society, and social inequality was especially pronounced in pre-industrial Britain. In the countryside the most distinctive pre-industrial formation was the landed estate, with its farms, villages, parish church, and common lands, which grew out of the integration of Norman and Saxon feudalism in the twelfth and thirteenth centuries, and continued to exist in more complex forms after Britain had become industrialized, and to interconnect in complex ways with the newer social formations growing out of industrial capitalism. Put simply, the earlier formation of landowners and dependent yeomen, artisans, and labourers, was a grouping based not on class but on *rank*, or social station. The relationship between Arthur Donnithorne and Adam Bede (in a novel set at the end of the eighteenth century) is a clear example of how rank differs from class. Arthur, the young squire-in-waiting, is the very embodiment of self-satisfied ease and moral indolence, who entertains paternalistic fantasies about his future as a benevolent and beloved landlord. These are also fantasies about the continuance of rank and its unearned privileges. He believes that, with 'a prosperous, contented tenantry', he will become 'the model of an English gentleman—mansion in first-rate order, all elegance and high taste—jolly housekeeping—finest stud in Loamshire—purse open to all public objects—in short, everything as different as possible from what was now associated with the name of Donnithorne' (*Adam Bede*, chapter 12). Arthur is in for a rude shock, but not in the form of an uprising of his tenants. The Donnithorne estate, mismanaged as it is by the family, preserves the idea of a harmonious system of social differences based on birth and property, and maintained by the benevolence of the powerful and the deference of the powerless: 'the bond of attachment', as Southey called it.[17] Thus, Arthur and Adam, although they come to blows over Hetty, retain a mutual respect for each other (which Eliot does not question: see Chapter 4, below). Adam retains respect for Arthur's *station*, which is worthy of respect no matter who occupies it, and in exchange Arthur respects Adam's *character*, which is an ideal reflection of the integrity of the entire system.

Neither of the two men, nor anyone else in Loamshire for that matter, conceives of himself as a member of a class to whom he also owes his identity and loyalty. They identify themselves solely by their place in a vertical hierarchy (along which they have a limited degree of mobility, as Adam does, rising up the social scale through his efforts)—or, more commonly, a pyramidal hierarchy, with the great mass of 'common people' at the base. Arthur may conceivably think of his tenants as an undifferentiated mob, but never as a *class*. By the time Eliot wrote *Adam Bede*, however, the class system was long entrenched (and indeed Adam's social mobility has all the hallmarks of middle-class social ideology: see below). Because class is not based on hereditary rights and responsibilities and the exclusive ownership of landed property but on the new economic divisions of land, capital, and labour, it differs in fundamental ways from rank. Under the class system an individual's identity is not determined by his or her place in a fixed hierarchy of caste but within a particular class: it therefore introduces a notion of class interest, and of a society actually *based* on inequality, not on some preordained order. Class is a complicated term, in which interest groups, occupational groups, and sectional religious groups may overlap. Unlike rank, it presupposes the existence of conflict and tension between classes, and it stratifies and sectionalizes society along lines that are openly recognized as unequal: working and housing conditions, food and leisure pursuits, types of illnesses and lengths of lifespans. If Arthur does not question the loyalty of his tenants, nor would it occur to him that they might organize themselves sufficiently to question their living conditions or make demands of their landlord. Such action is inconceivable in a small local community where everyone's livelihood depends on the big house, where few people can read or write, and where there is little communication with other districts. In other words, Arthur's farm labourers were not, on the whole, conscious of themselves as a class (although on some accounts working-class consciousness was forming in Britain at about the time *Adam Bede* is set). Factory workers or clerks or professionals, on the other hand—members of a social class—tended to live together in cities and interact among themselves, read the same newspapers, go to the same pubs, and so on. The relationship they had with other classes was not a personal relationship but a relationship based in economic transactions (in 1829, Thomas Carlyle had already observed that the 'sole nexus' between men in industrial societies, was the 'cash payment' nexus). Industrial operatives found it no less impossible, for lack of sufficient economic or cultural capital, to improve their conditions or make demands of their social superiors, but their identity was no longer determined by their preordained place in the social order.

This is not to say that British society, even in the early nineteenth century, comprised only an upper, a middle, and a lower class (or that class-based society completely supplanted ranked society). There were numerous subclasses, which multiplied and blurred as the economy and society became more multifaceted. Agriculture declined in relative importance, and industrial production techniques became more refined and factory work more specialized. Standards of living rose, greater numbers of women entered the workforce, and levels of formal education began rising. People were not just better educated but generally better off, with a greater range of lower-middle-class occupations available (a class of office clerks, for example, arose to service the growing international commercial empire in the last quarter of the nineteenth century). Even among the higher classes, there was increasing diversity. Before about 1750, these classes exclusively comprised those with titles, from the monarchy down to the baronetcy; and the gentry, the untitled landowners (gentlemen and gentlewomen, or esquires) who had held land in their families, often for many generations or centuries. Sir James Chettam (in *Middlemarch*) and Sir Hugo Mallinger (in *Daniel Deronda*) are Eliot's only aristocratic landowners, and they are lowly baronets. Sir Hugo's nephew, Grandcourt, is heir to the baronetcy (he is, Gwendolen decides, 'the most aristocratic-looking man she had ever seen' (*Daniel Deronda*, chapter 11)). But most of Eliot's landowners, like Squire Donnithorne, the Transomes, and Mr Brooke, are gentry. What both ranks have in common is the

hereditary right to landed property, which was often preserved by
the legal process known as entail, a measure taken to prevent any
future heirs to the estate from selling it in whole or part, or
bequeathing it to others. Usually, entailed estates passed down
through the male line, and were ceded to another branch of the
family if the male line died out. The Transomes in *Felix Holt*, for
example, came into land entailed on the male line (in 1727: only
about one hundred years before the events of the novel) which would
pass to the Bycliffes, the basis of Esther Lyon's claim on the property (she is actually a Bycliffe; Harold Transome, the supposed heir,
is actually a Jermyn). Likewise the Mallinger estate in *Daniel
Deronda* is entailed, and passes to Grandcourt because Sir Hugo has
only three daughters.

By 1800, the composition of the gentry had been changing gradually as greater numbers of wealthy merchants, industrialists, and
professionals used their money to retire into land and enjoy the
status it carried and the appearance of permanence and antiquity it
bestowed on their family name. Over the course of the nineteenth
century, more and more new money went into landed property (leading to something of a boom in country house building), and more
and more wealthy middle-class people moved into 'high society',
performing its rituals—the London summer 'season', the coming-
out balls, and so on—and sending their children to Rugby, and on to
Oxford or Cambridge. As the aristocracy set about reforming and
modernizing itself, it also embraced these upper-middle-class arriv-
istes, approving their new titles and welcoming them to country
society. For their part, the middle-class elite was not motivated solely
by acquisitiveness to emulate upper-class values and mores (though
they were certainly deferential to the upper classes). Their aim was
more actively to appropriate the power and status associated with
rank whilst projecting middle-class ideologies onto old values they
perceived to have become decadent and in need of revitalization.
Men of the upper classes were gentlemen by birth; men of the
middle classes began to style themselves as gentlemen. Making use
of national symbols, most obviously the medieval knight and the
code of chivalry (popularized in such novels as Charlotte Yonge's
The Heir of Redclyffe (1853) and Thackeray's *The Newcomes* (1853–
5), and perpetuated through the public-school system thanks to
novels like *Tom Brown's Schooldays* (1857)), the middle-class

gentleman was defined not by birth but by *conduct*. The concept of breeding accordingly became realigned with a form of moral refinement. What resulted was a social category that cut across, and confuted, class categorization. Being a gentleman was a form of class display—it was, like a house or clothes, a class indicator—but it was subtly different in that its function was to efface, not to display, the money at the heart of middle-class social power. Gentlemanliness was also something intangible, and apparently arbitrary: a disposition; a way of carrying oneself and one's authority effortlessly and inconspicuously; yet which excluded, by the mystique of its codes and rituals, the pretenders—those with *just* money.

In other words, it excluded most of the middle classes: women most obviously (who were constrained by more powerful and pervasive ideological codes and rituals of femininity, centred on domesticity, family, and the idea of womanliness: see the section on 'The Woman Question' later in this chapter); but also the majority of middle-class men. This was primarily because the term 'middle class'—denoting those who did not live off inherited wealth and did not have to earn a living by manual labour—comprised an increasingly wide range of occupations and incomes during the period of Eliot's life. Low-paid, low-status employees such as shop assistants, railway guards, and office clerks were middle class, even though they earned less (usually much less) than £100 per year; so were rich industrialists, merchants, bankers, and high-ranking soldiers and civil servants. Members of the skilled working classes like Caleb Garth in *Middlemarch*, who struggled to educate their children, nevertheless entered the middle classes when they took on, as Caleb does (and as Eliot's father did), estate management. At the other end of the scale, the younger sons of the landed classes joined ambitious middle-class young men in taking positions as beneficed clergymen (this is Fred's intended destiny in *Middlemarch*; and the Reverend Gascoigne in *Daniel Deronda* was plain Captain Gaskin before he took orders 'and a diphthong' (chapter 3)).

The complexity of middle-class relations may be seen in the town of Middlemarch. Eliot's novel is set just before the Reform Act of 1832, so she is writing back from a time (1871–2) of middle-class social and political dominance to the historical moment when that dominance may be said to have begun in earnest. One dimension of class relations in Middlemarch is the subtlety of social interactions between the landed classes and the town middle classes. Eliot captures these interactions through various mediating figures, most prominently Lydgate, whose doctoring takes him between the two realms, but also Bulstrode, for example, whose capital does the same, and Will Ladislaw, whose buried past does the same; through social events (Dorothea's wedding party, to which Brooke invites the local bourgeoisie; the funeral of Featherstone); and social attitudes (Rosamund's envy of Dorothea, the townspeople's contempt for Brooke). Eliot also, however, captures the delicate social dynamics within the middle classes, defined as they are 'with great nicety in practice, though hardly expressible theoretically' (*Middlemarch*, chapter 23). Even in the early 1830s, a family of 'old manufacturers' like the Vincys 'had kept a good house for three generations, in which there had naturally been much intermarrying with neighbours more or less decidedly genteel' (chapter 11). The intermarrying to which Eliot refers, however, is not between the manufacturing middle classes and the gentry: the notion of gentility, while it suggests the upper classes, refers rather to middle-class wealth and respectability. Vincy himself, for example, marries the sister of Nicholas Bulstrode, the pious banker 'who predominated so much in the town that some called him a Methodist, others a hypocrite, according to the resources of their vocabulary' (chapter 10). Vincy's daughter Rosamond is courted by Ned Plymdale, son of the crooked local silk-dyeing magnate, whose capital comes from Bulstrode. Peter Featherstone, who made his money out of manganese (used in the production of glass and steel), buys into land at Stone Court, but his brother-in-law is Caleb Garth, his nephew is Fred Vincy, and his illegitimate son uses the Featherstone inheritance to buy into a money-changing business at a seaport.

Eliot insists in *Middlemarch* that these are distinctions of rank, not class; and in any case the novel rarely dips below the level of the solid town bourgeoisie. Even the Larchers, the town carriers, do well enough to buy a fully stocked mansion. And although Mrs Garth was a schoolteacher before her marriage, she is not a member of that later urban lower-middle class that included teachers (like Hardy's Sue Bridehead) as well as the numerous classes of post office clerks and stenographers that may be found in novels after the 1870s (in Gissing, for example, and later in Forster's *Howards End*). Nor does *Middlemarch* concern itself directly with the rural labouring class

(Dagley, with whom Mr Brooke has a set-to over estate housing, is a tenant farmer), much less with Vincy's factory workers.

The wide range of Victorian middle-class occupations and incomes does not really tell us what the adjectival term 'Victorian middle-class' is referring to, however. This is because it is being used less often to describe a social group and more often as a set of relatively unified ideologies and values assumed to be shared by members of that group, and given as the dominant ideologies and values of the society. Considered as virtues, these values may be summed up as pious respectability, earnestness, ambition, energy, optimism, and national pride; viewed in a less flattering light (as they often were by the Victorians themselves), they may be summed up as hypocrisy, anti-intellectualism and philistinism, and jingoism. These values actually came out of the world-view of a small number of industrial and commercial elites of evangelical background, for whom utilitarianism and the general political outlook known as liberalism were most congenial (on evangelicalism and liberalism, see the section 'Religion and Society', below). But they were enormously influential in the Victorians' self-definition. They were popularized by political leaders such as Gladstone and by numerous conduct manuals and magazines. They were disseminated (and criticized) by influential social critics such as Carlyle, Ruskin, and Arnold, and by cultural producers: middle-class novelists (Dickens in particular) and poets (Tennyson in particular), but also painters (whose work was widely circulated in the form of engravings), popular dramatists, and powerful commercial interests in the culture industries (Mudie of the circulating library: see Chapter 3, below).

Because of the dominance of these ideas and values, it is difficult to see the Victorian lower classes independently of the relationship they bore to the middle classes, who perceived those below them either as anarchic and criminal—the drunken, unruly mob indifferent to English institutions and traditions (as in the *Felix Holt* riots); as a fantasy of a rational and deferential proto-bourgeoisie (Felix himself); or as inhabitants of an exotic and mysterious underworld—'darkest England'—living 'an inner, secret life which perpetuated traditional values and patterns of behaviour, essentially of rural origin, into the new urban industrial society'.[18] The lower classes, or 'lower orders' as they were sometimes called, referring back to the language of rank, were as socially stratified as the middle classes.

The censuses of the mid-century list well over a hundred different working-class occupations from agricultural labourers (which included farm servants as well as outdoor farm workers) and domestic servants (these two categories were by far the largest) to textile workers, coal miners, dressmakers, washerwomen, coach-makers, and railway engine stokers. But within each of these categories—especially the different categories of industrial work—there were wide variances between skilled and unskilled workers. In addition to these, a vast urban underclass, living in extreme poverty, carried on innumerable other occupations: costermongers (street fruit and vegetable sellers), water-carriers, cigar-end finders, old wood gatherers, ballast-getters, and street photographers. These occupations were first described in detail in Henry Mayhew's extra-ordinary *London Labour and the London Poor* (1851; initially pub-lished as a series of reports in the *Morning Chronicle* newspaper). Mayhew's reports were based on interviews, and are a good example of the way serious social investigation served both the philanthropic interests and sensation-seeking tastes of the Victorian middle classes. Dickens, too, exploited the exoticism of the urban underclass, writ-ing and publishing in his magazine *Household Words* numerous 'trav-ellers' tales' of his and his contributors' 'descents' into the unmapped slums (usually accompanied by a policeman). Likewise, his fiction, and in particular *Our Mutual Friend* (1864–5), is some-thing of a catalogue of the occupations of the London poor, includ-ing dustmen (refuse recyclers), lamplighters, bell-ringers, Thames watermen, crossing-sweepers, and old clothes dealers.

At the other end of the social scale were the skilled wage earners, effectively a working-class elite, or working-class aristocracy. This leading subclass (those enfranchised by the 1867 Reform Act) emerged out of the pre-industrial category of skilled artisans (like Adam Bede), with their craft guilds and societies, and out of the traditions of popular radicalism, with their division of 'the "industrious" or "productive classes" on the one hand, and the "idle" or "unproductive" on the other'.[19] They were the best-paid and best-educated working men, who enjoyed high status amongst their peers (significantly the working classes themselves discrimin-ated between the deserving and undeserving poor). Merging at points into the lower middle class—and certainly middle class in their values and aspirations—the artisan class (the name stuck) ranged from foremen and shop-floor managers to skilled tradesmen (cabinetmakers, boilermakers, master printers, and so on). This was the most politically active and politically powerful sector of the working classes. William Lovett, for example, whose London Working Men's Association was a focal point for the growth of Chartism in the mid-1830s, was a cabinetmaker and president of the Cabinet Makers' Society.

Lovett's moderate Chartism may have failed (he was challenged by more radical leaders as the movement grew), but the artisan classes remained enormously influential both in the advancement of working-class activism (the trade union movement, the co-operative movements, and later Marxian socialism) and in the consolidation of working-class cultural identity in Britain. Also important to the latter was the creation of distinct working-class leisure and cultural pursuits, aided by the steady growth of literacy and increases in available leisure time. Industrial work was characterized by regularity and uniform intensity: unlike agricultural work it was not seasonal but controlled by machines that could generate maximum capital returns for investors by running all day and all night. This new work culture produced new kinds of leisure, and produced too a struggle for control of working-class recreation by the paternalistic middle class. This may be described as a struggle between what the middle classes saw as 'rational' and 'irrational' forms of recreation. In early industrial England, the most irrational of all free-time activities, drinking, was more or less completely dominant. In part this was fuelled by the evangelical insistence on restricting public entertainments on Sundays, the only day working people were not required to clock on (Dickens, a leading agitator for Sunday entertainments, memorably describes the oppressive noise of church bells in London on Sundays in *Little Dorrit* (1855-7)). As the Victorian period progressed and these rules relaxed, however, organized recreational activities (rambling and hiking, organized tourism) and recreational spaces (parklands, the seaside) became an essential part of respectable middle-class life, and the ideals of open-air activity and athleticism were accordingly passed down to workers, in the establishment of football clubs, for example, which promoted discipline, teamwork, and national identity. Likewise middle-class cultural pursuits were imposed from above on working-class communities. Enlightened manufacturers like Titus Salt (whose Saltaire was one of the leading 'planned' working-class communities in England) hired special trains to transport all his factory workers to the 1857 Manchester Art Treasures Exhibition.

Education was also seen as an important form of rational recreation for workers. The utilitarians founded the Society for the Diffusion of Useful Knowledge (SDUK) in 1825, which laid the foundations for the emergence of popular scientific and technical education in Britain during the period. At about the same time mechanics institutes were set up in Scotland and London, with the aim of offering a more general range of educational opportunities to workmen. Neither succeeded, however. Mechanics institutes failed because the annual subscription fee of one guinea was too steep for all but the highest ranks of skilled workers, because few workers were motivated to attend lectures after a twelve-hour day, and because the institutes wrongly assumed that their subscribers had some elementary educational background. They were also too bluntly paternalistic and conservative to succeed widely with the working classes (women were excluded until the mid-century, and the slightest hint of radicalism was quashed). The SDUK, too, although it produced pamphlets and tracts promoting scientific and technical knowledge, could not succeed without the intervention of the state.

It was not until 1870, however, that the state began to intervene even in elementary education. That was the year in which W. E. Forster's Elementary Education Act finally instituted a national system of government-supported education, after decades of wrangling between the various religious interests which had controlled education through charitable subscription: the evangelical ragged schools, which provided a rudimentary education of tens of thousands of poor infants and children between 1840 and 1870; the craft-based dame schools and Sunday schools; and the public and grammar schools run for middle- and upper-class children and supported by the Established Church. The legislation, which had been mooted by utilitarians like James Kay-Shuttleworth forty years earlier, constantly foundered on the question of funding. Who was to pay? Forster's bill got around the sectarian objections by setting up local boards of control for elementary schools paid for by local rates; and where there was an objection to local control, schools could remain voluntary and receive central funding. It was not until 1880, however, that school was made compulsory until the age of 10.

Religion and Society

The story of George Eliot's passage from the easygoing Anglicanism of her family in the 1820s to the severe Calvinistic evangelicalism of her youth in the 1830s and her crisis of faith and search for a secular alternative to Christianity in the 1840s is in many ways the story of religious experience in nineteenth-century England. This was a period of intense and turbulent disputation and upheaval in religion, a period in which matters of private belief had a critical impact on wider public social institutions and practices—both religious institutions and practices and beyond. The cultural authority of religion was under siege. Successive scientific discoveries, culminating in the sensational publication of Charles Darwin's *On the Origin of Species* in 1859, refuted the biblical narrative of creation, and challenged religion as the dominant mode of human explanation. Added to this there was a notable decline in church attendance as British society became more materially prosperous after the 1840s (42 per cent of the population did not attend a church of any kind according to the 1851 census), and the heat went out of the Evangelical Revival which had done so much to regenerate religious life in England in the late eighteenth and early nineteenth centuries.

Yet religion permeated every level of Victorian society, even as it grew more secular. The head of state, Queen Victoria, was also the head of the Church of England (or Anglican Church): the 'Established Church'. Under the system of inherited privilege the wealthy landed establishment also effectively controlled the Church. Clergy advanced their careers only through the patronage of the aristocracy and gentry, in the form of the endowment of 'livings' (which gave them property and income for life). This arrangement effectively replicated the social inequalities of the system as a whole, with a small number of wealthy gentry clergy dominating church government through their social connections while neglecting their parishes or leaving them to be run by poor curates (like Amos Barton). This system also actively discouraged religious fervour, associating it with the superstitious excesses of Roman Catholicism. In doing so the Church of England neglected the spiritual needs of many of its parishioners, especially those of the poor for whom life without belief was insupportable under the strain of poverty and sickness. In the second half of the eighteenth century, as the pace of industrial change intensified and conditions worsened for the lower classes, large numbers of those people began to practise a new, grass-roots religiosity inside the Established Church. An Evangelical Revival, led by John Wesley, swept across the country. Evangelical Protestantism was revolutionary in that it challenged the authority of dominant religious institutions and dogmas: individuals were alone with their God, and made a solemn personal commitment to their faith. At the heart of Wesleyanism, or Methodism, was the experience of conversion: that life-changing moment when we recognize our sinfulness and can be reborn in Christ. The radical tendencies of early Methodism may be seen in the inclusive character of its constitution and worship: it had no church hierarchy; permitted anyone (including women) to preach (as Dinah does in *Adam Bede*); and conducted services outdoors. The revival quickly spread to older Nonconformist churches, such as the Baptist and Congregationalist churches ('Nonconformist' because they did not conform to the disciplines or rites of the Anglican Church as outlined in the Thirty-Nine Articles; they were also known as 'Dissenters'). After Wesley's death, Methodism split into numerous smaller denominations, in many cases reinstating the hierarchical structures of old and abandoning the most radical aspects of Wesleyan Methodism (as when Dinah is forbidden to preach at the end of *Adam Bede*).

It was not until the 1830s that the Anglican Church responded officially to the Evangelical Revival by pledging to reform itself. By that time, however, evangelicalism had already penetrated deeply into the Established Church, creating a powerful 'Low Church', which, along with the popular Nonconformist sects in the northern cities, succeeded in carrying evangelical ideas and attitudes to the middle classes, where they shaped the Victorian age in the most profound way, by *moralizing* it, so that even when the revival lost its impetus (by about 1850) and became the object of considerable revilement, its job had effectively been done. This is obvious in Eliot's atheistic humanism (see Chapter 6, below), but also in novelists like Dickens and Wilkie Collins, who lambasted 'Exeter Hall' (the derisory name for the whole evangelical institution, named after the London annual meeting place of evangelical missionary and bible societies) in novel after novel—think of Mrs Jellyby in *Bleak House*, Mrs Clennam in *Little Dorrit*, or Miss Clack in *The Moonstone*—but whose whole world-view was shaped by the quintessentially evangelical, and Victorian, qualities of earnestness and moral conduct.

If the term 'evangelical Protestantism' describes a wide range of doctrines, beliefs, and ecclesiastical practices shared by Low Church Anglicans and Nonconformist sects, it also tends to obscure the firm distinctions in class and status between evangelical Anglicans and Nonconformists, to say nothing of the fine distinctions between the Nonconformist denominations which multiplied during the nineteenth century.[20] Thus, George Eliot later described herself as having been 'a strong Calvinist' (*Letters*, iii. 175) under the influence of Maria Lewis, and the sympathy she showed in her fiction towards Chapel (particularly in 'Janet's Repentance'), led to the common assumption that she had grown up a Nonconformist. In fact, despite her antagonism towards the Church of England '*as a system of thought*' and her conviction that it was 'the least morally dignified of all forms of Christianity', she insisted that it made up such a 'portion of my earliest associations and most poetic memories, it would be more likely to tempt me into partiality than any form of dissent' (*Letters*, iv. 214). Maria Lewis had in fact been trenchantly anti-Nonconformist, refusing even to take a position as governess in a Nonconformist family; and Robert Evans, like Theophrastus Such's father, was 'a Tory who had not exactly a dislike to innovators and Dissenters, but a slight opinion of them as persons of ill-founded self-confidence' (*Impression of Theophrastus Such*, 'Looking Backward').

At the other extreme from the evangelical Low Church was an equally controversial Anglican wing: the Anglo-Catholic High Church. In the 1830s conservative High Church theologians at Oxford dedicated themselves to renewing the latitudinarian (or doctrinally indifferent) Church of England not by taking it in the anti-intellectual and anti-hierarchical directions of the Wesleyans, but by appropriating Catholicism, arguing in effect that the Church of England was the one true apostolic church, and that the Thirty-Nine Articles were not in fact incompatible with the teachings of the Roman Catholic Church. These inflammatory arguments were laid out in a series of *Tracts for the Times* (1833–41) by the leading proponents of what came to be called the 'Oxford Movement' or 'Tractarianism': John Henry Newman, John Keble, and Edward Pusey. Newman, rebuffed, converted to Catholicism in 1845; but his was not the only way. The Anglo-Catholic or Ritualist movement subsequently gained significant ground inside the Church of England.

As the middle classes gained political power in the early decades of the nineteenth century, the Anglican Church's dominance of public office came under challenge, and religious pluralism progressively weakened the power of the Established Church—although disestablishment, the formal severing of Anglicanism from its role as the church of the nation, was never successful (even though the English Church was disestablished in Ireland). Nevertheless there was a gradual extension of religious rights through the period. In 1828 the Test and Corporation Acts of 1661 and 1673 were repealed, allowing Dissenters to hold government office and participate in local government, and changing the Anglican constitution into a Protestant constitution. An important series of legislative reforms (some of them precipitated by the Irish question) also removed the disabilities on Catholics in Victorian Britain. In 1829 the controversial and divisive Catholic Emancipation Act was passed by the Duke of Wellington's Tory government. This Act allowed Catholics to sit in Parliament for the first time since the Elizabethan period. And in 1858 the Jewish Disabilities Act was finally passed (after several attempts) enabling Jews to sit in both Houses of Parliament.

The Woman Question

With the possible exception of Queen Victoria herself, no figure better exemplifies the complexity of Victorian attitudes to femininity than Florence Nightingale. In 1852, just two years before she demonstrated her enterprise and administrative genius by leading a contingent of nurses to the battlefields of the Crimea, Nightingale was so desperate about her future as a woman living at home with her well-to-do parents that she contemplated suicide. Instead, she wrote *Cassandra*, an impassioned and bitter polemic on women's oppression, in which she asked: 'Why have women passion, intellect, moral activity—these three—and a place in society where no one of the three can be exercised?'[21] *Cassandra* was not published until 1928, by which time Nightingale had long been immortalized not as a brilliant Victorian administrator but as an icon of Victorian femininity: the lady with the lamp, whose mission to sick and wounded soldiers was an extension and glorification of woman's innate domestic gifts, as natural and instinctive as raising children, supporting husbands, or looking after ageing parents. Nightingale's historical fate testifies to the enduring power of certain reactionary Victorian ideas about the nature of woman and her proper role in the world. *Cassandra* should not be thought of as an aberration, however, a lone secret jeremiad against an oppressive patriarchal system by a woman whose frustrated intellect, passion, and moral sensibility would soon find a suitably wide field for their exercise. On the contrary, it is one of a huge number of texts, public and private, in which ideas about women's nature and role in society were energetically put forward and contested. In hundreds of newspaper and magazine articles, letters to the editor, lectures and scientific studies, parliamentary debates and legal cases, conduct books, private letters by men and women of all classes (from Queen Victoria down), novels, poems and plays, satirical cartoons, and Royal Academy pictures, the Victorian middle classes talked about and argued about what they called 'The Woman Question'. At stake, it was widely believed, was nothing less than the social stability and moral well-being of the entire nation. For the ruling class the conservative ideal of 'womanliness'—the term describing those women for whom marriage and maternity were the highest vocation—was essential to that stability and well-being.

The 'womanly woman' of the popular conduct books and public debates—and her opposite, the feared and persecuted unwomanly or 'fallen' woman (the terms used to describe prostitutes)—was not so much a social fact as an ideological fiction, however. The vast majority of women actually did work outside the home, in factories and sweatshops, or as servants, governesses, teachers, or nurses; in doing so they did not risk becoming unwomanly. Nor was womanliness simply an ideal to which women of all classes could aspire. It is perhaps better understood as a representation which functioned to naturalize women's inequality, so that 'the legal subordination of one sex to the other'[22] was a cause for celebration, not complaint:

Man for the field and woman for the hearth:
Man for the sword and for the needle she:
Man with the head and woman with the heart:
Man to command and woman to obey.

Tennyson, *The Princess* (1847)

As these lines show, the Victorians understood femininity primarily in relation to its (first-named) opposite, masculinity. The new authority of the biological sciences reinforced the idea that women and men were fundamentally different, physiologically and psychologically, and made for different roles. On the other hand, to a liberal philosopher like John Stuart Mill, such arguments were specious. In *The Subjection of Women* (1869), he and his wife Harriet Taylor argued that 'what is now called the nature of woman is eminently an artificial thing—the result of forced repression in some directions, unnatural stimulation in others'.[23] Taylor and Mill were prominent figures among the small number of middle-class women and their male supporters who organized sustained campaigns against women's legal disabilities and social disadvantages throughout the Victorian period and into the first decades of the twentieth century. The most vital of these was the campaign for female suffrage. But when the first petition to extend the vote to women was presented to Parliament in 1851 it became clear that several other reforms would need to be achieved first. Married women could not be given the vote, for example, if they did not first legally exist: which, according to English law, was the case. Women became *femes coverts* or covered women, and were absorbed into their husband's legal identity upon marriage. Under the same law they could not sue their husbands either, since they were not legally separate from them—and a man could hardly sue himself! For that reason women could not obtain a divorce until the 1857 Matrimonial Causes Act established divorce courts and gave women (very limited) access to divorce (it was fewer than twenty years earlier, in 1839, that the Infant Custody Act gave separated mothers the right of custody of their children).

These laws were the legal expression of the ideology of femininity by which middle-class women were constrained in industrial England: they were not expected to work; they were not required to be educated beyond a certain level; and had no reason to participate in public life. As a substitute for political power women were held to possess the power of 'moral influence' over husbands and children, an extraordinarily potent idea in Victorian society, with its hint of sexual power beneath the moral rectitude of the domestic angel. Women's influence, radiating outwards from the sanctuary of the home, counterbalanced the vicious competitiveness of the capitalist marketplace, the horrors of war, the violence and unbridled sexuality of the streets, and the unthinkable un-Englishness of the rest of the world. To advocate higher education for women, allow them entry into full-time paid work in the professions or in business, permit them financial freedom and property of their own or the power to take legal action or enter Parliament, represented a threat to the entire social system. Numerous conduct books written for middle-class women disseminated this doctrine of woman's influence,[24] and warned of the dangers of public life and the terrible risks to women who, like George Eliot, deviated from the feminine ideal and lived outside middle-class codes of morality.

CHAPTER 3

LITERARY AND CULTURAL CONTEXTS

Literature and the Arts in an Unpoetical Age

GEORGE ELIOT's journal records the following events in spring 1864:

[March] 8. Received cheque of £150 from Blackwood.

11. Went to hear Judas Maccabaeus with Mr. Burton.

27. Mrs. Bray spent the day with us and in the evening G. and I set out on a journey to Glasgow . . .

[April] 4. Had a delightful letter from Thornie dated Jan. 28 from Pietermaritzburg, Natal. Then G. and I went to see Mr. Leighton's pictures in his Studio.

6. Wednesday. Mr. Spencer called for the first time after a long correspondence on the subject of his relation to Comte.

9. Went with Mr. Owen Jones to the Kensington Museum to see Mulready's pictures and the Indian Courts.

10. Grandmamma dined with us.

18. We went to the Crystal Palace to see Garibaldi.

19. George went into Herefordshire.

May 4. We started for Italy with Mr. Burton.

(Journals, pp. 119–20)

These terse entries are typical of Eliot's journals. They tell us something about family events, social engagements, and everyday domestic and financial dealings. They hint at momentous public occasions—Garibaldi's triumphant presentation in Sir Joseph Paxton's quintessentially mid-Victorian building, the prefabricated glass and steel Crystal Palace (originally built for the Great Exhibition in 1851)—but offer few opinions about those occasions. They are neither especially demonstrative nor reflective. They are a matter-of-fact record of events, personages, and achievements, and seem to belong in a Puritan tradition of self-examination which took the long view of daily life. Important and unimportant matters alike mount up steadily over time into something substantial and worthwhile; and each entry is a receipt of knowledge (or money) accumulated, of distinction and social acceptance won at the cost of struggle, self-doubt, and ill health, all duly recorded.

Eliot's journals also tell us a great deal about the everyday cultural lives of well-off, educated Victorians, the vital centres of Victorian high culture, the social networks in which it was produced, and the close relationship between cultural production and Victorian society. Eliot attends a performance of a Handel oratorio with a stalwart of the artistic establishment (Frederic Burton's portrait of Eliot was exhibited at the Royal Academy in 1867). She views neoclassical paintings by Frederic Leighton (who had illustrated *Romola*) in a studio in Kensington fitted out to resemble a Turkish palace. She accompanies the architect Owen Jones (who designed the interior of the Crystal Palace for the Great Exhibition, and the interior of the Leweses' new house, The Priory) to a show of archetypal English daily-life scenes by an Irish-born painter, William Mulready, showing in a museum founded by Prince Albert (whose idea the Great Exhibition was) and devoted to the celebration of Victorian industrial and cultural progress. While there they also visit the India Courts, interior spaces that, like Leighton's studio, replicate the architectural forms of Greater Britain (Jones, whose *Grammar of Ornament* (1856) incorporated design motifs from around the world, was the leading orientalist and functionalist among Victorian theorists of architecture and design). And like others of their class, they entertain, and they travel. She and Lewes take a short trip to Scotland—travelling first class on the train, no doubt—and Lewes retires into the countryside for a week or so before they regroup to spend the remainder of spring in Italy, where it was cheap, and where so many culturally acquisitive Victorians made their version of the Grand Tour, the cultural journey through Europe taken by generations of the wealthy English.

There ought to be an air of leisureliness about these journal entries, the leisureliness of the privileged classes pursuing culture. Yet, cursory as they are, and even in holiday mood (Eliot was between books: exhausted by *Romola*, she had not yet started on *The Spanish Gypsy* or *Felix Holt, the Radical*), they bristle with the purposeful energy of the mid-Victorians. In the background, out of sight, we sense the constant writing and the constant business of *being* a writer. There are the long correspondences, with Spencer and many others, the dealings with publishers and exchanges with other writers, and the unrelenting intellectual intensity of Eliot's everyday life: the hundreds of books she read on subjects related to virtually every department of intellectual inquiry, and each devoured in a day or two as soon as it came out. The extent and density of Eliot's reading is felt in the commanding range of literary and intellectual reference in her fiction, most obviously in chapter epigraphs and direct allusions, but also in the texture of the language itself. No less important, though, was this broader cultural life—music and theatre, the visual arts and architecture, travel and leisure—which Eliot participated in with the same passion and seriousness, which is vividly represented in her fiction, and which is the context out of which that fiction was written.

When she attends that performance of Handel's *Judas Mac-cabaeus*, for example, held at Exeter Hall in London, the strong-hold of English evangelicalism, Eliot is engaging in one of the most Victorian of cultural activities: listening to sacred music written by a great composer, an honorary Englishman whose *Messiah* was probably the most performed piece of classical music during the period, and came to be emblematic of British imperial progress. Eliot was a regular concert- and opera-goer (one of Queen Victoria's daughters, Princess Louise, sketched her at a concert in 1877), and an accomplished amateur pianist. Her tastes (like those of many music-lovers still) tended to the mainstream Viennese and German classical and Romantic repertoire: Haydn and Mozart, Beethoven and Schubert. She largely ignored the contemporary composers of her own country (who had to struggle against widespread indifference), and was lukewarm about the most progressive Europeans. Wagner's music, like Herr Klesmer's in *Daniel Deronda*, she found 'an extensive commentary on some melodic ideas not too grossly evident' (chapter 5), although she deeply admired Liszt, whom she had met with Lewes in Weimar in 1854. In Eliot's fiction, the great music of Western Europe is a touchstone of the protagonists' moral development: the noblest expression of the human spirit, it was emotionally complex yet powerfully immediate, a 'pregnant, passionate language' (*The Mill on the Floss*, book 6, chapter 6) intuitively grasped, a glorious affirmation of the inner meaningfulness of existence in a post-religious age. Musical metaphors and allusions to musicians and compositions abound, as do scenes of middle-class music-making. Eliot had little interest in the musical culture of the rural lower classes. *Adam Bede* and *Silas Marner*, the most obviously rustic novels, are both conspicuously unmusical (despite the 'great dance' scenes in chapters 25 and 26 of *Adam Bede*). There is no folk singing or dancing, and no local bands or church choirs that were the cultural heart of small communities, although the latter are distantly alluded to in the Rainbow in *Silas Marner* (chapter 6). Nor does Eliot pay any attention to urban working-class music or the commercial music hall, both central aspects of Victorian culture. What interests her is the music of the middle-class drawing room, where high culture is popularized and vulgarized. Before the gramophone (not widely available until after Victoria's death), popular music circulated in the form of sheet music, one of the largest and most profitable sectors of the publishing industry in Victorian England. The rapid expansion of this sector after 1850 was in part due to its ability to sell into the same market both lowbrow forms (popular ballads and hymn tunes) and 'serious' music repackaged for the drawing-room piano and voice (most notably popular arias and the popular Romantic piano repertoire led by Chopin). When Klesmer points out to Gwendolen that the Bellini aria she has just performed is the product of a 'puerile state of culture', he is not being critical of Italian opera but the 'passion and thought of people without any breadth of horizon' (*Daniel Deronda*, chapter 5). These are the people Matthew Arnold dubbed the 'Philistines' in *Culture and Anarchy* (1867): the industrial bourgeoisie, who effectively controlled cultural production in Victorian Britain.

This was a 'deeply *unpoetical*' age, Arnold had complained in a letter in 1848: 'Not unprofound, not ungrand, not unmoving:—but *unpoetical*.'[1] What was there in modern city life from which to make authentic poetry—authentic art of any kind? Must poets, painters, architects, and composers look to the past, as Arnold did, to its universal stories and elevated styles, for the moral grandeur with which to represent 'an era of progress, an age commissioned to carry out the great ideas of industrial development and social amelioration'?[2] Or were the 'best and most original ideas' to be derived from the poet's own time?[3] These were burning questions for mid-Victorian artists and writers, whose creative achievements and failures were alike born of a struggle to produce the best and most original work in a climate of pervasive and seductive industrial and material progress, and one of increasing social cohesion. There was no true avant-garde in mid-Victorian Britain and little space outside mainstream or 'official' culture. Musical originality was stifled by the absence of a vigorous musical culture for composers to work in, literary originality by the famously puritanical book trade, architectural originality by the various competitions for major public projects, and artistic originality by the Royal Academy. But cultural practices were not in fact heavily policed by centralized institutions; the problem was, many of those institutions were populist—or, more bluntly, commercial. This was particularly true of the Royal Academy. Although it trained artists in its schools to produce 'Academic' art (art characterized by strict hierarchies and conventions of representation and rewarded for its command of draughtsmanship and technique), its huge annual public exhibitions encouraged painters to produce images for wide popular consumption. The progressive improvement of engraving techniques led to a boom in reproductions of the most successful pictures from each summer's RA show, and even to the advent of one-painting blockbuster shows which turned large profits from ticket sales and the sale of engravings.

William Powell Frith's urban panorama *The Railway Station* (1862; p. 79) was the most famous solo-exhibition-cum-cultural-extravaganza of the period. It shows a crowded platform in Isambard Kingdom Brunel's lofty Paddington Station, with jostling porters and engineers, soldiers and families, criminals and detectives, aristocrats and newly-weds, foreigners and cabmen, and shabby genteels—representative figures of the age. Organized by an impresario, Louis Flatow, the show was so popular that barriers had to be erected around the picture and a policeman stationed permanently beside it. Viewers of all classes paid at the door to marvel at the photographic realism with which Frith depicted the scene. This was a crowd assembled to view its ideal self—well-behaved, admiring, docile before culture. What they saw, and what they bought and took home as engravings, was the spectacle of Victorian England in all its energy, industry, and underlying order, raised to the status of high art.

Frith claimed that his paintings met with critical disapproval because they were unpictorial and challenged prevailing definitions of high art.[4] Such was the physical scale of *The Railway Station* that reviewers and cultural critics were alarmed by the conjunction of its

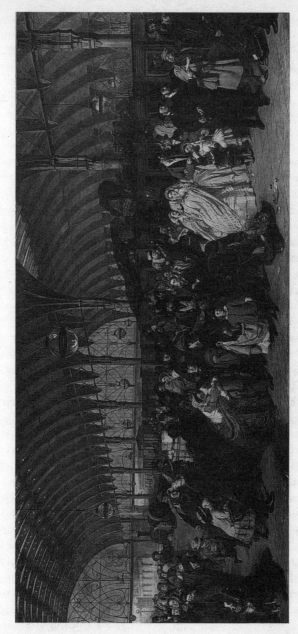

William Powell Frith, *The Railway Station*, 1862

benign journalistic modernity and its pretensions to history painting (the highest form of academic painting, representing historic, legendary, or literary episodes on a large scale and in a grand and noble manner). Modern life was repellent to those who believed that only mythical, allegorical, or historical subjects were worthy of being called art. Yet *The Railway Station* is hardly a radical painting—compare it with Manet's roughly contemporaneous *Dejeuner sur l'herbe* (1863), for example—because it leaves academic assumptions about art largely undisturbed (technical bravura is still its measure of greatness, and its composition is traditional) and because it mistakes universality for that mild bourgeois substitute, the common touch. Here in epitome are the leading concerns of Victorian art and literature, and the chief reasons for the unevenness of Victorian cultural production. *The Railway Station* makes claims for the historical significance of contemporary culture but cannot represent the keynotes of that culture—its ordinariness, its ugliness, its progressiveness—without reference to artistic conventions that only serve to reduce its vision of modern life to the level of anecdote and sentimentality.

A more uncompromising realism was being pursued at the same time, both in Britain and across the Channel in Europe. Of course, literature and the visual arts had privileged the realistic representation of individuals and social environments since at least the Renaissance, and forms of realism had progressed steadily since that time, aided by the rise to dominance of oil paint in the arts, with its remarkable facility for rendering the density and detail of objects, and industrial print technologies in literature, which made printed objects cheaper and more widely available, and so broadened literary subject matter and treatment to include the material interests of the middle classes. Among the most notable examples of bourgeois realism before the middle of the nineteenth century were seventeenth-century Dutch painting, with its calm domestic interiors and prosperous burghers, and the eighteenth-century English novel, exemplified by Samuel Richardson, which achieved a richly detailed psychological realism in its thick descriptions of the lives and intrigues of the gentry and bourgeoisie. Yet it was not until about 1850 that writers and artists, in France and Britain predominantly, responded to dramatic political and social change and rapid advances in science and industrial processes by turning towards a newly self-conscious realism. Their aim 'was to give a truthful, objective and impartial representation of the real world, based on meticulous observation of contemporary life'.[5] They did so with a new confidence in their 'capacity to master the physical world'[6] through technological progress (especially in new 'realist' technologies such as photography) and the techniques of empirical science. Eliot's fiction (although it has undeniable affinities with the English anecdotal tradition, especially *Adam Bede* and *Silas Marner*) is self-consciously and polemically realist. In this respect it occupies a central position in the history of realism as a radical aesthetic practice in mid-nineteenth-century Europe—alongside the novelists Balzac, Flaubert, the Goncourts, and Tolstoy, and the painters Courbet and Manet.

Eliot's best-known formulation of her own realism occurs in chapter 17 of *Adam Bede*, 'In which the Story Pauses a Little'. Her aim, she writes is

to give a faithful account of men and things as they have mirrored themselves in my mind. The mirror is doubtless defective; the outlines will sometimes be disturbed; the reflection faint or confused; but I feel as much bound to tell you, as precisely as I can, what that reflection is, as if I were in the witness-box narrating my experience on oath.

Eliot's is not an unselfconsciously reflectionist realism, therefore (as Frith's was, for example). Because 'it is a very hard thing to say the exact truth' (chapter 17), the realist's only recourse is to good faith, the sworn duty, as of a legal witness, to tell the truth, the whole truth, and nothing but the truth. The central problem for Eliot's realism, therefore—that it calls upon the authority of objective physical evidence, but cannot do so from any truly objective standpoint—is solved in essentially moral terms: truthfulness, once we accept that it cannot be fully achieved, is an even more urgent ethical responsibility. This is why Eliot's claim that art is 'the nearest thing to life' is framed as it is: 'a mode of amplifying experience and extending our contact with our fellow-men beyond the bounds of our personal lot' (*Essays*, p. 271).

In part this comes from John Ruskin. Eliot reviewed the third volume of Ruskin's *Modern Painters* in the *Westminster Review* in April 1856, remarking: 'The truth of infinite value that he teaches is *realism*—the doctrine that all truth and beauty are to be attained by a humble and faithful study of nature, and not by substituting vague forms, bred by imagination on the mists of feeling, in place of definite, substantial reality. The thorough acceptance of this doctrine would remould our life; and he who teaches its application . . . is a prophet for his generation'.[7] Eliot's realism made large claims for the representation of ordinary life—what she called in several essays 'the working-day business of the world' (*Essays*, p. 302)—in high art. Like Frith, she held that the unexceptional lives of unexceptional people were worthy of serious treatment, not the comic, grotesque, or picturesque treatment they were usually accorded in traditional hierarchies of art. There was always a risk, however, of realism slipping into sentimentality, cliché, or contrivance. This is what happened to mainstream Victorian pictures of contemporary life after the mid-1850s (with some exceptions): they are now largely consigned to the decorative tradition of 'Victoriana'. Frith had altogether loftier aims, but his confused aspirations to high art and popular acceptance left him—and almost all the best Victorian painters—stranded between progressive realism, academic history painting, and genre painting.

As many subsequent critics of the period have observed, Victorian art is bad art precisely because the Victorian bourgeoisie were so obsessed with these ideas of 'high art': in Arnold Hauser's words, 'the bad taste which dominates its architecture, painting, arts and crafts is partly the result of its self-deception—of the ambitions and pretensions which muffle the spontaneous expression of its nature'.[8] At its worst, Victorian culture was kitsch culture, a triumph of middle-class intellectual mediocrity. But even at its best it was—at least from the standpoint of the cosmopolitan modernism which succeeded it, and which valued formalist experimentation and art for art's sake—something less than art. At its most exploratory and inventive, at its most self-critical and restless, it was a bourgeois art. That is why the most modern society in the world failed to produce the most modern art in the world. Paradoxically, it was too powerful: the moral and intellectual leadership of world-dominating British capitalism was unchallenged in the arts because there was no position to challenge it *from*. Even when Victorian art and literature is penetrating and caustic in its criticism of the society which produced it (in Dickens, most famously, but also in Eliot herself) it is criticism directed from one middle-class Victorian to others of like mind in the public sphere, and conceives of art as a social and moral instrument. When we think of Victorian art and literature, therefore, we still marvel at its descriptive power, which in a fundamental way celebrates the bourgeois values of moral seriousness and thoroughness. Victorian artists and writers were pre-eminently 'artist-thinkers',[9] for whom art was not primarily about aesthetics but ethics and social criticism. The Victorians demanded that art have a moral function; even at its most formally experimental, therefore—and Eliot is one of its great experimenters—theirs was a culture with a purpose.

In a sense the novelists had greater scope for innovation because they were not burdened with the responsibility of reinvigorating the high-art tradition, but rather had the opposite problem of raising the cultural status of a high-profit low-mimetic form. The poets, however, struggled to accommodate modern-life narratives, settings, and themes to decidedly unmodern verse forms inherited from the past. Some, like Arnold, gave it up in despair: his best-known poem about modern life, 'Dover Beach', sits uneasily with his most ambitious poem about the mid-Victorian experience, the classically set 'Empedocles on Etna'. Others, such as Clough, Patmore, Tennyson, and the Brownings, experimented boldly with the domestic narrative that dominated the Victorian novel. Tennyson, in particular, struggled against the self-consciousness that crippled the Victorians, and the populism that encouraged them to be so skilfully and blandly fluent and expressive—in poems like *The Princess* (a sort of modern-dress history painting in verse); *Locksley Hall* and *Maud* (ultramodern in their explorations of psychic disturbance); and most especially *In Memoriam, A.H.H.*, a long elegy on the sudden death of his friend Arthur Hallam which modulates into a profound expression of mid-Victorian anguish and affirmation.

Yet if there was no thoroughgoing counter-culture in Victorian Britain, there were significant moments of dissent and significant forms of resistance practised by artists and writers who remained within the cultural mainstream because there was nowhere else to go. One such moment was the extraordinary phenomenon of the Pre-Raphaelite Brotherhood, a group of young artists (and, more marginally, writers) who joined together in 1848 with the aim of rejecting the artifices and conventions of academic art. Their name signified their approach. Academic art had its origin in, and took its authority from, the great Renaissance master, Raphael. Therefore the PRB (as they signed their first paintings) took its inspiration from the more vigorous art of 'Pre-Raphaelite' quattrocento Italy. The first Pre-Raphaelite subjects, exhibited in a storm of controversy in 1849 by J. E. Millais, William Holman Hunt, and Dante Gabriel Rossetti, took academic conventions and stood them on their heads.[10] At first they chose literary and religious subjects—the staple of history painting—but gave them an immediacy and sensuality that scandalized the art public. They flouted academic conventions of composition, and applied unmixed colours to a wet white ground in order to achieve high saturation, uniform intensity, and sharp detail. Their religious pictures—most notoriously Millais's *Christ in the House of his Father* (1849)—drew public accusations (from Dickens no less) that the PRB were Roman Catholic propagandists, whose realistic, humanized figures were blasphemous. They also exhibited literary pictures, but provocatively chose scenes from the sensual work of the (not yet canonical) Romantic poet John Keats and the lush medievalism of their contemporary, Tennyson. Just as controversial was their decision in the early 1850s to paint modern-life subjects (as Frith was beginning to do quite independently).

The Pre-Raphaelites' commitment to 'things of to-day'—urged by Ruskin, who was an influential supporter—may be seen too as an extension of their critique of the anecdotal tradition of the English School: they had radicalized historical painting; now they would reinvigorate the genre tradition. They did so in spectacular fashion, choosing for their first modern-life subject-pictures to paint prostitutes: Hunt's *The Awakening Conscience* (1854); Rossetti's unfinished *Found* (1854–5); the striking series of drawings Millais did in the early 1850s on related themes; and Brown's powerful and mysterious *Take Your Son, Sir!* (begun as early as 1851, and also unfinished). The prostitute was already established in religious and social discourse, fiction, and poetry, as the magdalen figure or 'outcast' (an adulteress or a seduced and abandoned woman). But the Pre-Raphaelites were the first to paint this figure in modern dress, and not disguised as a mythological, historical, or literary figure. These images scandalized bourgeois morality (Holman Hunt, for example, intended *The Awakening Conscience* to be a religious picture), but not for long. Modern-life art emerged from, and was ideologically bound up with, the supremacy of the British industrial bourgeoisie.[11] The Pre-Raphaelites, like their more conservative contemporaries, believed implicitly in the moral function of art—in its purposiveness.

The tradition of moral modern-life art they initiated quickly went the way of Frith's insipid panoramas, offering, instead of a vision of sunny civil orderliness, a vision of dark evangelical rectitude.

One of the extraordinary exceptions to this is Ford Madox Brown's *Work* (page 86). Begun in 1852 but not finished until 1865, it is one of the most ambitious and fascinating of all Victorian paintings, and it tells us a great deal about the cultural contexts of Eliot's intellectual fiction. An epic of modern life—the narrative pretext for its homage to that most Victorian of virtues is, after all, a traffic jam—*Work* is a spectacular example of the Victorians' efforts to reconcile history painting and genre painting. Unashamedly high art and unashamedly social realism, the painting shines with moral seriousness. This is a celebration of urban labour—it depicts navvies laying the sewage system in Hampstead (where Brown lived: he based the figures on the actual navvies that did the work). The size of the picture, its arched shape, and the heroic manner in which Brown disposes the figures all allude to the tradition of history painting, and especially to Raphael's *School of Athens* (1509–10), which depicts what Thomas Carlyle, the towering Victorian prophet of history, called the great 'brain-workers' of the ancient world—Socrates, Plato, Aristotle, Heraclitus, and the rest. Carlyle, in fact, is himself depicted in *Work*, along with F. D. Maurice, leader of the Christian Socialist movement and advocate of 'muscular Christianity', both of whom Brown admired for their invigorating philosophies of work.

Brown is not co-opting the cultural status of Raphael's great masterpiece because he wants to elicit a comparison between two great civilizations—a hubristic gesture if ever there was one—but because he and his contemporaries could only really make sense of what was happening to them by reference to the past. History was a vital explanatory enterprise for the Victorians. If modernity made them hyper-conscious of the present, it also made them conscious of the past in a new way. In short, Victorian consciousness *was* historical consciousness. This was a culture steeped in historical modes of thought, which raised history-writing to the highest level of intellectual discourse. Everything existed in time, and developed through time, and the present was a moment freighted with a significant past and tending towards a significant future. And how could the Victorians be unconscious of time? This period witnessed astonishing

Ford Madox Brown, *Work*, 1852–65

'Capital and Labour'. Cartoon in *Punch*, 1843

transformations in the fundamental nature of human temporal existence. Scientific investigation revealed that life on earth was much older than had previously been thought, and demolished the biblical time-frame of human history in the process. Simultaneously, industrial technologies were accelerating material change almost beyond comprehension, and reducing time to the small measurable units of factory time and railway time. In response, the Victorians constantly referred their modernity and its seemingly insoluble problems—what Carlyle called 'the Condition of England' in *Past and Present* (1843)—back to the authority of the cultural past, seeking explanations for what was going on around them in the continuities and contrasts between the bewildering present and the safely explicable past. They found them in the prehistory of the fossil records being uncovered for the first time by geologists. They found them in the classical cultures with which they frequently compared themselves. They found them by idealizing the art and culture of the Middle Ages (the architect and social critic Augustus Pugin's book *Contrasts* (1836), which compared the architecture of medieval and present-day England and called for a revival of Gothic styles, deeply influenced Carlyle and Ruskin). They found them in the art and culture of the expansionist commercial city-states of Renaissance Italy—especially Florence and Venice. They found them in England's own constitutional past, enshrined in the revolutions of the seventeenth century; and they found them in England's cultural past, enshrined in the literary histories that flourished in the century of the nation-state, and especially in that crowning achievement of English culture, the work of William Shakespeare.

At the other end of the cultural hierarchy, novelists began to have ideas above their station, and, in an inversion of the modern-life movement in the visual arts, sought to elevate what they already did—represent ordinary life—and endow it with something of the breadth and ambition of the higher arts, putting themselves on a more equal footing with poets and painters.[12] From the beginning of her career Eliot believed the novel could attain the grandeur of history and epic poetry, and her fiction explores the relationship between the 'grand historic life of humanity' and the 'ugly, grovelling existence' (*The Mill on the Floss*, book 4, chapter 1) of 'the faithful who were not famous' (*Felix Holt, the Radical*, chapter 16).

It is important to recognize that this realist imperative of Eliot's, although it was part of the Europe-wide shift towards objectivity in literature and the visual arts, paradoxically had its roots in European Romanticism. The Romantic period is usually thought of as 1780–1848 (taking in, for instance, *Wuthering Heights* (1847)), but its British heyday was over when Sir Walter Scott died in 1832. The Romantic tradition, however—its style and temper, its post-Enlightenment sensibility—remained dominant throughout the Victorian period, as we can see in Dickens and Tennyson, for example, or Rossetti. In this sense, Romanticism was not an influence so much as a set of assumptions about art and society deeply embedded by the 1850s, part of the texture of the culture in which Eliot lived and wrote: it 'penetrated the times with its leaven and entered into everybody's food', as she writes in *Middlemarch* (chapter 19). The influence of Romanticism is evident everywhere in her work: in the idea that intellect and imagination are not separate faculties; that the highest knowledge is felt knowledge; and that the feelings are the fountainhead of morality. Eliot is concerned with that which gives 'the most abstract things the quality of a pleasure or a pain' (*Middlemarch*, chapter 20); and with those moments when 'argument takes the quality of passionate vision' (*Daniel Deronda*, chapter 17). She reveres the creative imagination, and believes implicitly in its autonomy, as well as in the artist's special role in society. She privileges sincerity over style, and the particular case over the general rule. She strives to speak authentically, across social and cultural divides, appealing to all classes and not just the educated classes. Her language can be lyrical, her drama sensational, her characters impassioned. In all these features she is a Romantic.

In fact, Eliot's thought absorbs so many elements from so many key Romantic writers in Britain, France, and Germany that some critics have found it more helpful to think of her as a late Romantic rather than a Victorian.[13] There are certain problems with this. Eliot asserts the value of analytic rationalism and scientific empiricism, most obviously, those keystones of Enlightenment thought which the Romantics had rejected out of hand. She is also suspicious of the emotional extremities of Romanticism, as well as of the egotism that runs through it in the relentless self-projections of its poet-speakers. But it is undeniable that, in her post-Christian 'working-out of higher possibilities' (*Letters*, iii. 366), Eliot was consciously and complexly engaged with Romantic thought. She was deeply read in the German Romantics: the poet Friedrich Schiller ('our divine Schiller' (*Letters*, viii. 13)) when she was younger; and Goethe, whose work she came to know intimately through Lewes. She was also influenced by the French philosopher and novelist Jean-Jacques Rousseau, whose *Confessions* she read in 1849 (the experience 'sent that electric thrill through my intellectual and moral frame which has awakened me to new perceptions, which has made man and nature a fresh world of thought and feeling to me' (*Letters*, i. 277)). Rousseau introduced Eliot to that paramount Romantic value, *feeling*, as a corrective to the dehumanizing effects of any systematic rational thought (significantly, she read him after finishing the exhausting Strauss translation). Rousseau taught Eliot that reflection can be, as she puts it, electric. This insight informs the aspirations to ardent knowledge of her heroines: Maggie, Romola, Dorothea. It remained, however, for Eliot to find a way of integrating feeling and knowledge with moral action. She found one way in William Wordsworth.

Without Wordsworth's *Lyrical Ballads*, and his celebrated 1802 Preface to them, Eliot's realism could hardly have been imagined.[14] The defence of realism in *Adam Bede* (chapter 17) recalls Wordsworth's declaration of a poetry of 'ordinary things' in the Preface to the *Lyrical Ballads* when it appeals to 'the faithful representing of commonplace things'. Eliot's fiction is nowhere more Wordsworthian than in its solicitation to the reader to 'turn your steps' 'from the public way', towards objects and people 'which you might pass by, | Might see and notice not' (*Michael*); and towards the 'dreary intercourse of daily life', which is 'full of blessings' (*Tintern Abbey*). Even Eliot's instinctive repugnance to 'the men of maxims' has Wordsworthian overtones, cautioning us that 'to lace ourselves up in formulas . . . is to repress all the divine promptings and inspirations that spring from growing insight and sympathy' (*The Mill on the Floss*, book 7, chapter 2). Eliot's conception of the essential goodness of human nature, embodied in the affections, is a Wordsworthian conception; her idealization of the child as the centre of imaginative being, and her consecration of the pre-industrial past and the associations of the past, although put to quite different ends, have their roots in Wordsworth. She follows him in linking the high moral vocation of the artist to the fellow feeling engendered by the imagination: 'the only effect I ardently long to produce by my writings, is that those who read them should be better able to *imagine* and to *feel* the pains and the joys of those who differ from themselves in everything but the broad fact of being struggling erring human creatures' (*Letters*, iii. 111).

Eliot's characteristic narrative situations involve the clash of hard facts and powerful feelings, as I have said, and lead inevitably to compromise—and what is usually a melancholy destiny for her characters. Something of this comes out of her reading of Goethe: not the young Goethe of the *Sturm und Drang* (Storm and Stress) movement of the 1770s, but the titanic cultural authority of the 1820s, with his magisterially 'calm independence' of mind.[15] Goethe's rejection of *Sturm und Drang* Romanticism, and his embracing of observation and objectivity, were hugely important to Eliot. Her exemplar is not Werther, the suicidal artist-hero of Goethe's early *Die Leiden des jungen Werthers* (*The Sorrows of Young Werther* (1774)), but Wilhelm Meister, whose trajectory is from Romantic individualism to social accommodation.[16]

From Goethe, and from Rousseau, George Sand, and others, Eliot came to know the power of fiction as a vehicle for serious thought. Eliot's fiction should not be seen as a medium for the dramatic presentation of ideas, however, as Herbert Spencer believed when he exempted it from his ban on all fiction in the London Library, as if it were a series of solemn treatises in novel form. Fiction was for Eliot a *form of thought* itself, offering something that none of the dominant forms of Victorian thought—philosophy, theology, anthropology, sociology, political economy, history—could offer: ideas that were 'thoroughly incarnate, as if they had revealed themselves . . . first in the flesh and not in the spirit' (*Letters*, iv. 300). Recalling Carlyle, who taught that the 'End of Man is an Action, and not a Thought, though it were the noblest',[17] Eliot sought in fiction a new form of intellectual discourse, an integration of philosophical and aesthetic methods aimed at effecting moral and social action. Eliot chose to invest her formidable learning in a form of writing that still carried relatively little intellectual weight or cultural status. Her aim was to mould an English novel of ideas—a novel dealing, by and large, with commonplace people whose lives welcomed no abstract thought: unpoetic people. The range of cultural influences she drew upon for this enterprise was vast because her reading and learning was vast: from Greek drama (especially Sophocles), Shakespeare, and Dante, to Jane Austen and George Sand, and dozens, hundreds of others. But like her contemporaries, the most important cultural influence was the culture of modern life itself: the question, how to produce an art equal to the great achievements of the greatest nation on earth—and produce it in a deeply unpoetic age? More significant than the influence of Shakespeare's plays on particular novels, in this sense, was the profound and debilitating influence on Eliot and all the Victorians of what V. S. Pritchett memorably called 'Shakespearean longings',[18] their longings for a great national culture as vigorous and original as culture of the Elizabethans: a Renaissance for the industrial age.

Eliot and the Victorian Novel

There were good practical reasons, too, why Eliot chose fiction at the age of 37, just when she might have been expected to embark on some original philosophical writing (and indeed a book intriguingly entitled *The Idea of the Future Life* was advertised as forthcoming in 1853). Partly it was a question of money. Eliot had been writing and publishing, mostly anonymously, for more than a decade and had produced a handful of translations of obscure scholarly works and a steady number of essays and reviews. She was not a journalist in the sense Dickens was, or Thackeray, although, like them, her apprenticeship in an editorial office would prove decisive in the development of her ideas and narrative style—the distinctive compound of intellectual authority, clarity, and engagement that is the hallmark of her fiction. For five years between June 1851 and 1856 she was a leading figure in what the Victorians called the 'higher journalism', writing articles for the distinguished monthly and quarterly periodicals which introduced and debated the foremost ideas in philosophy, science, social criticism, and culture. Eliot was a paid writer only for the last eighteen months or so of that period, however. For most of it, from 1851 until 1854, she worked in the unpaid position of editor of one of the three major quarterlies in Britain, the *Westminster Review*.[19] Founded in 1824, the *Westminster* was a radical journal: stridently pro-reform and rationalist in religious matters, it was considered in some circles to be dangerously anti-establishment, but was nevertheless highly respected and aimed at a small educated upper- and upper-middle-class liberal readership. By the 1850s it had fallen on hard times, however, and Eliot's 'secret . . . Editorship' (*Letters*, viii. 23) was important in recalling it to pre-eminence.[20]

The anomalousness of this situation—being the unpaid, publicly unacknowledged editor of one of the most important periodicals of the day—became even clearer to Eliot when she surrendered the editorship with the intention of working as a higher journalist for a living. In doing so she entered a field where it was possible to earn the equivalent of a modest middle-class income (around £300 per annum), but extremely difficult. Lewes managed it, but was constantly unwell from the overwork endemic to a journalist's life. It soon became clear to Eliot that if ill health forced Lewes to back off (he wanted to pursue scientific interests in any case), the burden of their income must fall on her. The market for fiction in magazines was more lucrative than the market for non-fiction: she decided to pursue her intellectual interests as a novelist, not an essayist.[21]

The timing was right. At the beginning of 1855, Eliot was a virtual unknown. Five years later, with only three stories and two novels to her credit, she was being compared to Jane Austen and Charlotte Brontë (*CH*, p. 114), and had already earned more than £6,000 from the two novels, *Adam Bede* and *The Mill on the Floss*. This was a lot of money: the annual income of a doctor or lawyer at this time was in the range of £300–£800. It was also a lot of money for a novelist: about four times what Anthony Trollope, her popular near contemporary, made during the same five years out of five novels, including *Barchester Towers*. To some extent Eliot was lucky because she took up fiction just when the market for novelists was rising steeply. Charlotte Brontë, whose overnight success with *Jane Eyre* in 1847 was even more spectacular than Eliot's with *Adam Bede* in 1859, earned a fraction of Eliot's £1,700 under the much tighter publishing conditions of the late 1840s. Likewise, one of the most eminent and popular novelists of that period, Thackeray, took fully twenty years to make £6,000 out of his great novels *Vanity Fair* (1847–8) and *Pendennis* (1848–50). By the buoyant late 1850s, when Thackeray's enormous popularity was waning, he could still earn much more for *The Virginians* (1857–8) than he had at the height of his fame ten years earlier.[22] Trollope, too, in spite of his inauspicious start, went on to take spectacular advantage of the conditions, earning an average of £4,500 per year over twelve years in the 1860s and 1870s.[23]

By contrast, the great majority of Victorian novelists earned relatively little. This was because Victorian mainstream publishing and distribution practices were in the main conservative and restrictive, even oppressive, for novelists. Yet as Sutherland and others have shown, the Victorian period was the great age of the novel precisely *because of* these conservative and restrictive practices. Always severely under-capitalized, Victorian publishing stayed relatively stable during a period of volatile capital expansion by preserving an arrangement between itself and the main distribution agency for fiction, the circulating library (or commercial lending library), which cushioned it from risk. That arrangement, for all its tyrannical iron-handedness, permitted an unprecedented amount of fiction to be produced. At the same time, the industry was not altogether averse to higher-risk, higher-profit ventures, and entertained a small degree of entrepreneurial innovation. Publishers and authors—of the latter, most famously Charles Dickens, but also George Eliot—therefore had some freedom to experiment with new formats for their novels. At the heart of this arrangement, the commercial circulating library—the most pre-eminent of which was the massive Mudie's Select Library of New Oxford Street—was a book distribution system unique to Britain and its colonies.[24] Every Victorian novel, with the exception of those written for the lower-class markets, was shaped to a significant degree by Mudie's, which dominated (but did not monopolize) the market; and every important innovation in Victorian publishing was a response to this autocratic dominance. The most prominent of these innovations were the 'railway novels', cheap uniform volumes sold directly to commuters from W. H. Smith and Son's outlets on station platforms, and the period's three distinct forms of fiction serialization: publication in separate parts (the free-standing monthly serial, or part issue, popularized by Dickens); publication in magazines (becoming more dominant in the 1860s); and publication in cheap collective reissues.[25]

The dominant form of fiction, however, was the three-volume novel—the 'triple-decker'—which originated during the Napoleonic Wars, when paper was in short supply and new books were hugely expensive. A number of subsequent factors conspired to keep the price of new novels at this artificial level. In 1821 Sir Walter Scott's *Kenilworth* was published in three volumes and priced extortionately at 31*s*. 6*d*. for the library market. It turned out to be a prodigious commercial success, proving that novels priced for borrowers rather than buyers could also, on occasion, sell phenomenally well. *Kenilworth* established overnight the standard length and price for new fiction for the next seventy years. Until the 1890s the first editions of novels were routinely produced in costly bindings with wide margins and clear types, and kept well beyond the range of most readers (an affordable 6*s*. reprint in one volume usually followed, though usually not for at least a year). In the majority of cases, the triple-deckers had very small initial print-runs (generally 1,000 copies, and often less than half that number). Under modern conditions, even with much cheaper production costs, such a small run would give publishers almost no chance of making a return on their investment, and would be unlikely to be risked in the first place. In Victorian Britain, however, the retail price of a first edition was kept artificially high in order to discourage readers from purchasing it. Of the initial printing, more than half were sold (at generous discounts of up to 60 per cent) to Mudie's, where, for one guinea per year, subscribers could borrow one volume at a time to be exchanged as often as they wished (so that one novel, physically split into three volumes, could be loaned to three readers at a time).[26]

This unusual practice was upheld principally by the timorousness and conservatism of the publishing industry, and the enterprise of Mudie's proprietor, the strict Nonconformist Charles Edward Mudie, who exploited the cosy non-competitive publishing culture and succeeded in taking effective control of book publishing in Britain for forty years. The reasons for his success were simple. He introduced the idea of the 'select' library, which filtered out books deemed unsuitable for family reading, and was therefore able to tap into the substantial market of the newly respectable middle classes.[27] He also revolutionized book distribution. He built a palatial centralized emporium in London, established a vast branch and agency system throughout the country, and used the railway and postal service to ensure the rapid delivery of books that publishers were under pressure to supply immediately on publication and in quantity.

Mudie's may be said to have shaped Victorian fiction in two major ways: by producing books of mostly uniform size; and books that stayed within a fairly narrow range of values. Their practice of sustaining turnover by lending a volume at a time meant that they demanded standard three-volume novels, and this is one reason, though not the only reason, why Victorian novels are so long. They did accept shorter novels (such as the two-volume *Scenes of Clerical Life*) and longer ones (such as the four-volume *Middlemarch*), but these generally had less chance of success. Mudie's also exercised control over the content of fiction by refusing to buy books they considered to be morally objectionable, or if they did buy them, only keeping token supplies and excluding them from their advertised lists. This policy was to some degree responsible for the notorious prudery of Victorian fiction (though this has been overstated). So powerful was Mudie that authors and publishers alike fell into line, producing the kind of novel the library market demanded, in the form Mudie preferred. In spite of the mutual benefits of this system, publishers deeply resented the deference they were forced to pay him, and the discounts they were forced to give him.[28]

It might have been expected that the confrontational subject matter in *Adam Bede*—scenes of seduction, pregnancy, and infanticide—would have jeopardized its chances with the strait-laced Mudie; and that the irregular union between Eliot and Lewes, once it became public knowledge in 1859, might have made it impossible for her to get her books into circulation. Although there is some evidence to suggest that Mudie had threatened to boycott *The Mill on the Floss* on moral grounds because of Eliot and Lewes's irregular relationship (*Letters*, iii. 209), its success actually prompted him to invite 'Mr and Mrs Lewes' to a party at the opening of his new premises (*Letters*, iii. 360 n. 6a), which seems to indicate that, on some occasions at least, his notorious moral rigidity was used as an instrument to gain the upper hand in bargaining with publishers. Eliot's Edinburgh publisher, John Blackwood of William Blackwood and Sons, was well aware of this, and therefore open to any scheme that might circumvent Mudie's. In 1871, for example, he agreed to Lewes's plan to publish Eliot's next novel, *Middlemarch*, in eight two-monthly parts—resulting in the unusual four-volume length so essential to the 'stealthy convergence of human lots' (chapter 11) in that novel.

Blackwood's was not ideologically opposed to the principles on which Mudie selected or rejected books, of course. The overwhelming issue for the firm was profit margin, which was constantly being narrowed by intensive discounting.[29] Blackwood's was particularly combative in its dealings with Mudie's because, unlike other publishers, it was not aggressively entrepreneurial in pursuing new ways of controverting the library system. It had its roots in the eighteenth-century author–publisher coteries, and built its business strategies around these traditions. Blackwood assembled a strong, loyal list by reading manuscripts himself, developing personal relationships with his authors, and being fair and open with terms. The extensive surviving correspondence between Blackwood's and Eliot and Lewes attests to this company culture. It shows Blackwood carefully nurturing his author, reserving any discouraging criticism, reassuring her about sales and advertising, being generous and punctual with payments and copyrights, carrying out negotiations cordially and openhandedly, and even sending her a pug as a gift. On no account should this relationship, which stayed on terms of real friendship for most of Eliot's twenty-two-year career as a novelist, be viewed cynically. But it was the product of an established house strategy of Blackwood's, and the correspondence with Eliot certainly reveals, besides the mutual friendliness of the parties, an underlying current of mutual wariness between them as they each pursued their own best commercial interests.

Increasingly after 1850 publishers and novelists experimented with modes of publishing fiction other than the three-volume library edition followed by the 6s. one-volume reprint. Clearly this was not primarily to compete with Mudie's but to supplement the generally solid profits made out of sales of the short-run library volume. Dickens had established in the 1830s that serialized fiction could make money without jeopardizing subsequent volume sales, and experiments in serial fiction after 1860—most notably Smith, Elder and Co.'s *Cornhill Magazine*—were successful in attracting novel readers to magazines, and through them to publishers' fiction lists.[30] The staid and conservative Blackwood's had a decided advantage in this new market, because it owned one of the longest-running magazines to include stories and serial novels, the monthly *Blackwood's Edinburgh Magazine* (known by the nickname 'Maga'), which had begun in 1817. Its circulation was never higher than 10,000,[31] and it was more than twice the price of the *Cornhill*, but it was run soundly by Blackwood on the same principles as the book publishing division, and fostered a loyal group of contributors willing to accept less for their work than others might offer.

When George Eliot began writing fiction in 1856 Lewes was in close contact with Blackwood over his 'Sea-Side Studies', then appearing in *Blackwood's Edinburgh Magazine* in instalments. It made sense to try out 'Amos Barton' there. Blackwood, taking his cue from Lewes, who warned him to treat the morbidly sensitive Eliot with exceptional delicacy, quickly developed the habit of showing confidence in the work, offering encouragement, and keeping his reservations to himself. This resulted in Eliot being given an unusually liberal hand. For example, she insisted, incredibly for a new author, that she was unable to 'alter anything in relation to the delineation or development of character, as my stories always grow out of my psychological conception of the dramatis personae' (*Letters*, ii. 299). And Blackwood, well recognizing that he did not 'fall in with George Eliots every day' (*Letters*, ii. 352), reassured her:

In continuing to write for the Magazine I beg of all things that you will not consider yourself hampered in any way. Of course I will say when I think you are failing to produce the effect you intend or otherwise missing the mark, but unless you write entirely from the bent of your own genius or knowledge or observation it would not be worth my while to make any comments at all. (*Letters*, ii. 352–3)

Eliot recognized very quickly, however, that fiction written for family magazines like *Blackwood's* was much more subject to censorship than fiction written for volume publication. Mudie's may have been moral arbiters, but their subscribers were also *Blackwood's* readers, and magazines were intended to be read by (or to) members of the family who might not be permitted access to library novels. Blackwood's had its own vested interest in producing fiction suitable for 'family reading', and Eliot was extremely cautious about magazine serialization. Nor was she comfortable with the idea of a novel beginning its serial run, and being read and reviewed, before she had finished writing it, or comfortable with the high-pressure world of writing to deadlines. For those reasons she turned down the opportunity of publishing *Adam Bede* in *Blackwood's* and, following its success, resisted the temptation of earning a great deal more for

The Mill on the Floss by selling it to Dickens (who wanted it for *All the Year Round*), or his competitors, Bradbury and Evans, who offered £4,500 for it for their new magazine, *Once a Week*. It was inevitable, though, that in the rising market for major novelists after 1860 Eliot would eventually be enticed into the serial market, and away from Blackwood's. It happened with *Romola*, which George Smith wanted to stem the declining circulation of the *Cornhill*. He initially offered her £10,000, which would turn out to be the highest sum offered for a novel for the entire century. Eliot was finding the novel extremely difficult to write, however, and finally settled for £7,000 for twelve monthly parts, with the copyright reverting to her after six years. *Romola* failed, and Eliot returned to Blackwood's for *Felix Holt, the Radical*, which was also, by comparison with the early novels, unsuccessful.

In 1867, Blackwood decided to embark on a cheap illustrated edition of George Eliot's works (with the exception of *Romola*, held by Smith) to be sold initially in thirty sixpenny numbers, then bound into four volumes selling at 3s. 6d. each, to appeal to a new readership. Increases in literacy levels, in leisure time for reading, and (most importantly) in disposable income to spend on reading matter, were beginning to have an impact on the book trade, and publishers were keen to reissue titles by established novelists on their lists in cheap collective forms for sale in railway bookstalls and elsewhere.[32] Perhaps because the Eliot reissue was overpriced for the railway market, because of the 'superheated conditions' of the publishing world in the 1860s,[33] or because of Eliot's mid-career slump in popularity, the venture was a dismal commercial failure. For the same reasons, the Leweses' more daring and idiosyncratic experiment for *Middlemarch*—to publish in eight two-monthly parts, each the length of half a standard volume—ought not to have succeeded at all. Part issue, revived in 1836 with spectacular success by Dickens and Chapman and Hall for the shilling monthly *Pickwick Papers*, and still being used profitably by Dickens in the mid-1860s, was elsewhere well in decline by then.[34] Blackwood must have thought hard about the unusual format, but his determination to sidestep Mudie's won him over. Each part sold for 5s., and when the novel was published in four volumes it sold for 42s., and Eliot and Lewes offered Blackwood a choice of terms: purchase the English rights for four years for £6,000; or pay out royalties of 40 per cent on all sales of parts, first edition, and cheaper editions. His acceptance of the royalty offer was ultimately to Eliot's advantage, because *Middlemarch* sold much better than expected.[35] Eliot and Lewes had always negotiated terms astutely, protecting Eliot's copyrights and gradually favouring royalty agreements over fixed-sum fixed-term copyright sales. They also began to exploit the burgeoning market for syndicated fiction in the colonies, selling *Middlemarch* into the Australian market, and *Daniel Deronda* (which also earned a 40 per cent royalty from Blackwood's) into the difficult United States market (where international copyrights were not recognized, and British fiction was routinely pirated).

What is remarkable about Eliot's career—again compared to Trollope's career—is that she managed to succeed commercially and artistically despite writing relatively little. Most other Victorian novelists sold their copyrights to publishers for £200 or (usually) much less, and never earned another penny from them. As a consequence, they had to write more, and more quickly, often to a ready formula. Eliot's contemporary Margaret Oliphant, for example, wrote more than a hundred novels, several volumes of stories, biographies, and literary histories, as well as over two hundred articles for magazines. No one was more keenly aware of the sacrifices demanded by the Victorian literary system. In her autobiography (1899), she wrote of Eliot, half wistfully and half bitterly: 'Should I have done better if I had been kept, like her, in a mental greenhouse and taken care of?'[36] Eliot was also relatively unhampered by the puritanical gate-keeping of Mudie's, by and large avoided family magazines, and kept herself comparatively free from interference from her publishers, so that she could develop at her own pace and take her own directions. She could experiment with potentially unpopular themes and forms (having succeeded with feel-good pastoral of *Adam Bede*, she immediately abandoned it for the darker tones and stifling realism of *The Mill on the Floss*), and tackle commercially dangerous subjects (the Jewish question in *Daniel Deronda*). She was popular, yet she resolved not to give her readers what they wanted: 'Unhappily,' she warned Blackwood in 1857, 'I am as impressionable as I am obstinate, and as much in need of sympathy from my readers as I am incapable of bending myself to their tastes' (*Letters*, ii. 400). She was popular, but not *that* popular—by no means a writer of best-sellers in the modern sense. (In fact, the word 'best-seller' does not enter the language until much later in the century, with the advent of the mass market, and the increasing distinction between the large-scale production of commercial fiction and the small-scale production of literary fiction.) In its first year of publication some 15,000 copies of *Adam Bede* were sold; compare this with the staggering one million copies of Harriet Beecher Stowe's *Uncle Tom's Cabin* sold in Britain between 1852 and 1856.[37] Likewise, aggregate sales of Ellen Wood's sensational romance of adultery and crime, *East Lynne* (1861), reached 430,000 by the end of the century, more than all of Eliot's novels put together.[38] Yet Eliot earned a great deal more than either of these top-selling novelists. How are we to account for that? In part, Lewes's astute brokerage helped. Yet Eliot's novels were expected to circulate in the thousands, not tens or hundreds of thousands.

To answer this, we need to understand the extraordinary phenomenon that was Charles Dickens. By 1882, twelve years after his death, sales of Dickens's work had reached more than 4.2 million volumes. In 1836 his first novel, *Pickwick Papers*, had average sales of 40,000 per month at a shilling per monthly part (which only middle-class readers could afford); in 1870 the first instalment of his last novel, *Edwin Drood*, sold better—50,000 copies. As these figures show, he was easily the most popular and highest earning novelist in Britain. He was also the nation's greatest literary artist, and as such established a strong demand for literary fiction in the popular market. Only Eliot among the Victorians approached Dickens in this regard, and this was the key to her success. By comparison with him, her circulation was slight, of course, but because she demonstrated with her first novel that she could achieve both substantial popularity *and* literary prestige as a writer of rare genius, she became the hottest literary property in thirty years.

Uniquely, though, Eliot did so writing fiction that was intellectually demanding. It could be argued that she accomplished this only because she also introduced into the English novel a powerful new pastoral element: 'the family life of the English farmer, and the class to which he belongs' (*CH*, p. 115). To her contemporary readers, this was her greatest achievement, and *Adam Bede* and *Silas Marner* her greatest novels. But the idyllic cast of her early fiction was not the only reason for the enormous prestige and popularity she enjoyed then, and has continued to enjoy. She also introduced the novel of ideas into Victorian England, and fused it with an uncompromising fiction of ethics, producing what we might call, quoting the *Saturday Review* on *The Mill on the Floss*, the novel of 'fierce mental struggles' (*CH*, p. 119). She brought together the urbane discursive language of the metropolitan intellectual and the vigorous speech and common sense of the rural Midlands to mould a resolutely serious and highbrow fiction out of compelling and engaging stories. They were also unusually frank in their dealings with sex, as John Sutherland has observed, and so appealed simultaneously to a readership that was high-minded and one with a taste for 'adultery, elopement, . . . and nemesis in their novels'.[39] For Eliot, there was no contradiction in this. She wrote for adults, and was committed to realism: she simply told the truth about the lives of ordinary, fallible people. These people were also her readers, and Eliot's fiction conferred status on them—and on its publishers, which is why it was so highly valued.

What is even more remarkable about Eliot's career is that she managed all this *as a woman*. Not that practising women novelists were by any means uncommon in Victorian Britain—far from it. In fact, until about 1840, women dominated the fiction market, both as writers and readers. And although they were not altogether 'edged out', an important change took place after 1840.[40] The novel began its gradual transformation into a higher-status art form, coinciding with a reversal in the proportion of men to women novelists, a concomitant shift away from fiction addressed to a predominantly female readership, and a shift away from fantasy and romance towards realism.[41] A number of explanations have been put forward by critics for this last shift, which began in the mid-1840s and was more or less accomplished by the mid-1850s, when Eliot entered the market. Dickens's *Dombey and Son*, which seems to mark a significant turning towards the subject matter of everyday bourgeois existence (and which was a significant influence on the 'modern life' painters of the early 1850s), started its serial run in 1846 up against a field dominated by established romancers, most of whom are now unread (and many of whom were women), including G. P. R. James, the Countess of Blessington, Catherine Gore, Bulwer-Lytton, Captain Marryat, Catherine Sinclair, and Frances Trollope. By 1856, the field of English fiction looked very different: the old names still wrote and published their romances of high-society life, criminal life, exotic life, medieval life, life at sea, and so on. But there was a new emphasis on seriousness and topical relevance, and a new expansiveness and reach—a sense that the novel was an important representational form, not just escapist entertainment. Dickens's fiction had grown more artistically ambitious and darker in mood (though he continued to intersperse his major novels with Christmas romances and the like), and the experiment he had begun in *Dombey and Son* with large-scale formal structures for the narrative of modern urban life was taken successively further with each new project. The Brontës, unknown in 1846, were all already dead, leaving behind a collection of remarkable novels, including the epochal *Jane Eyre* (1847) and *Wuthering Heights* (1847), *The Tenant of Wildfell Hall* (1848), and *Villette* (1853), which had a profound effect on Eliot.[42] Elizabeth Gaskell, whose first novel, *Mary Barton*, appeared in 1848, had by then written a succession of important social-problem novels, including the controversial *Ruth* (1853), about a fallen woman; and indeed, as the hungry Forties came to a close the middle-class social-problem novel returned to vogue, taken up by the Christian Socialist Charles Kingsley and by Charles Reade, who brought a new strain of theatrical melodrama to the novel-with-a-purpose in his runaway best-seller *It is Never Too Late to Mend* (1856). Thackeray, known chiefly for his *Punch* burlesques in the 1840s, began serializing the highly influential *Vanity Fair* in 1847, which set him up as a powerful rival of Dickens (his semi-autobiographical *Pendennis* (1848–50) ran in parallel with Dickens's semi-autobiographical *David Copperfield* (1849–50)). In 1856, too, George Meredith published the first novel of a career that would continue into the twentieth century.

Even this rudimentary list shows how prominent women were among the foremost novelists of that decade; and if we add the names of Margaret Oliphant, Dinah Mulock Craik, Charlotte Yonge, and Geraldine Jewsbury—all of them significant figures in the history of the mid-Victorian novel—it can be seen that women were not eclipsed in the sphere of serious fiction. Moreover, all these women published under their own names, suggesting that when Marian Evans adopted the pseudonym 'George Eliot' in 1857, it was not, as is sometimes supposed, a common practice for Victorian women novelists to disguise their gender in order to succeed in the literary marketplace. It is true that in the same year Smith, Elder and Co. published the *Life of Charlotte Brontë*, the first biography of one of the most acclaimed woman novelists of her time, who had famously published under the (intentionally ungendered) pseudonym 'Currer Bell'. On the other hand, that biography was written by Elizabeth Gaskell, who published under her own married name. Like Gaskell, most Victorian women writers did not use pseudonyms; indeed, it has been proposed that 'men apparently were more likely than women to use a cross-gendered pseudonym'.[43]

Why, then, did Eliot adopt the pseudonym, why did she decide to keep it after her identity became known, and why insist on it through the rest of her career?[44] The answer to the first question lies with Lewes; the answer to the other questions with the nature of Eliot's fiction and its relationship to questions of gender and discourse. Marian Evans was at first a very reluctant novelist. Constitutionally self-doubting, hypersensitive to the slightest insinuation that she was incapable of meeting her own high standards, and ready to give up at any moment, she was persuaded to try her hand only because she knew she could do so in periodicals (where contributions were conventionally unsigned) in complete anonymity. As a journalist Eliot had learned how powerful anonymity was: it enabled her to write authoritatively and trenchantly across a wide range of social and intellectual issues on which women were not generally invited to give their opinions.[45] But the higher journalism required the cultivation of a particular voice, and few women were successful in breaking into the field despite the cover of anonymity. Eliot's most eminent intellectual forebear, Harriet Martineau, openly admitted that she trained herself to write like a man to succeed as a higher journalist (*Biography*, p. 268), and Eliot likewise honed her skills in the authoritative house style of the quarterlies and monthlies when she was editor of the *Westminster Review*.

Her final contribution to that journal was a significant one: a caustic review, completed only a week or so before she began work on 'The Sad Fortunes of the Reverend Amos Barton', and bearing the blunt title 'Silly Novels by Lady Novelists'. The essay was not, however, an unseemly swipe at Eliot's soon-to-be sister novelists from the safe cover of anonymity, as its title may suggest, despite the undoubted irony of the situation: an important defence of women's fiction staged as a conventional attack by an intellectual man on the inanities of the female popular romance. It begins wittily and aggressively:

Silly novels by lady novelists are a genus with many species, determined by the particular quality of silliness that predominates in them—the frothy, the prosy, the pious, or the pedantic. But it is a mixture of all these—a composite order of feminine fatuity, that produces the largest class of such novels, which we shall distinguish as the *mind-and-millinery* species. (*Essays*, p. 301)

This species of romance is described in detail by Eliot: the consummate heroine—beautiful, devout, and well read—who must pass through 'many *mauvais moments*', but comes out of them all 'with a complexion more blooming . . . than ever' (*Essays*, p. 303). This is not Eliot's principal target, however, for she is rather more interested in two subspecies of the silly novel—the '*white neck-cloth*' species, in which 'the Orlando of Evangelical literature is the young curate, looked at from the point of view of the middle class' (*Essays*, p. 318); and 'the most mischievous form of feminine silliness', the 'literary form' (*Essays*, p. 316). With her own scenes of evangelical clerical life in the front of her mind, Eliot's objection to the 'white neck-cloth' species is their falseness. Developing arguments she had made in other essays of this period (such as 'The Natural History of German Life': see Chapter 4, below), she contends: 'The real drama of Evangelicalism . . . lies among the middle and lower classes' (*Essays*, p. 318). And with a growing sense of commitment to a novel of ideas, Eliot attacks the so-called 'literary' romance, the ridiculous 'intellectuality' of which 'tends to confirm the popular prejudice against the more solid education of women' (*Essays*, p. 316).

Throughout her fictional career Eliot continued to explore these stereotypes, taking up aspects of the mind-and-millinery romance in Rosamond Vincy and Gwendolen Harleth, the white neck-cloth romance in Amos Barton, Edgar Tryan ('Janet's Repentance'), and Camden Farebrother (*Middlemarch*), and the oracular romance ('intended to expound the writer's religious, philosophical, or moral theories' (*Essays*, 310)) in everything she wrote. But this essay is significant for another reason. Eliot concludes on a rather different note, reminding her readers that women have produced 'among the very finest' novels: 'novels . . . that have a precious speciality, lying quite apart from masculine aptitudes and experience' (*Essays*, p. 324). There are clear echoes of Lewes in this. In an earlier piece of his, 'The Lady Novelists', he had looked forward to 'the advent of female literature', a literature that 'promises woman's view of life, woman's experience: in other words, a new element'.[46] 'We are in no need of more male writers,' he suggested provocatively; 'we are in need of genuine female experience. The prejudices, notions, passions and conventionalisms of men are amply illustrated; let us have the same fulness with respect to women.'[47]

It is worth noting, therefore, that Eliot chose anonymity and a male pseudonym at the outset of her fictional career not because she wanted to write like a man: she must have been sure that what she had to offer lay 'quite apart from masculine aptitudes and experience'. Indeed, quite a number of her first readers, including Dickens, the essayist Anne Mozley, and Eliot's feminist friend Barbara Bodichon, immediately recognized the author of *Adam Bede* as a woman. Nor did she fear the kind of criticism she herself had levelled at silly lady novelists. Rather, it was praise she feared. Emily Davies, founder of Girton College, put it best in 1868: that two of 'the greatest of female novelists should have taken the precaution to assume a masculine *nom de plume* for the express purpose of securing their work against being measured by a class standard', she wrote, 'is significant of the feeling entertained by women' (*Letters*, viii. 429 n. 9). Lewes himself expressed the same feelings at the height of the Liggins affair in June 1859, when, unknown to Eliot, he added a revealing postscript to a letter of hers to Barbara Bodichon:

It makes me angry to think that people should say that the secret [of George Eliot's identity] has been kept because there was any *fear* of the effect of the author's name. You may tell it openly to all who care to hear it that the object of anonymity was to get the book judged on its own merits, and not prejudged as the work of a woman, or of a particular woman. It is quite clear that people would have sniffed at it if they had known the writer to be a woman but they can't now unsay their admiration. (*Letters*, iii. 106)[48]

Lewes raises two quite distinct issues here, which hint there may have been *some* fear of the effect of Eliot's identity being revealed: the fact that novels would not get a fair hearing if they were known to be written by a woman; and if they were known to be written by a *particular* woman—a woman of possibly doubtful character, in other words, living openly in sin with a married man. The latter concern was certainly uppermost in their minds when the public disclosure of Eliot's identity coincided with their troubled negotiations with Blackwood over *The Mill on the Floss*. Because Blackwood had suggested Eliot publish the novel first in *Blackwood's Edinburgh Magazine*, where it would appear unsigned, she came to the conclusion that he had some concerns about the effect of the dropped incognito on the profits and reputation of his conservative, respectable firm, and that he may even have been reluctant to continue as her publisher once her identity was exposed. Blackwood denied all this, but behind the scenes there was in fact considerable disagreement among the partners and staff about whether the revelations would directly 'affect the circulation in families of any future work' (*Letters*, iii. 221). When *The Mill on the Floss* came out, he did worry that 'knowledge of the secret' had made reviewers and readers more critical of the novel, but increased sales vindicated his decision to publish, as she had requested, in three volumes, with the name George Eliot on the title page as before (*Letters*, iii. 290).

But Lewes was right in the Bodichon postscript: women *were* severely disadvantaged in the literary marketplace. No one knew better than he did how difficult it was for a talented lady novelist to get her work 'judged on its own merits, and not prejudged as the work of a woman'. In late 1849 and early 1850 he had betrayed Charlotte Brontë, with whom he had established a friendship by letter, in an insensitive, hurtful review of her second novel, *Shirley*. In November 1849, before *Shirley* appeared, Brontë had written to Lewes:

I wish you did not think me a woman: I wish all reviewers believed 'Currer Bell' to be a man—they would be more just to him. You will—I know— keep measuring me by some standard of what you deem becoming to my sex—where I am not what you consider graceful—you will condemn me . . . Come what will—I cannot when I write think always of myself—and of what is elegant and charming in femininity—it is not on those terms or with such ideas I ever took pen in hand; and if it is only on such terms my writing will be tolerated—I shall pass away from the public and trouble it no more.[49]

Very shortly afterwards, Lewes discovered Currer Bell's identity by chance, and could not resist making capital out of it in the *Edinburgh Review*. The review—which began ominously, declaring that the 'grand function of woman . . . is, and ever must be, Maternity'[50]— not only trumpeted that 'the authoress is the daughter of a clergyman!' who must 'learn to sacrifice a little of her Yorkshire roughness to the demands of good taste', but demanded that Brontë stop 'saturating her writings with such rudeness and offensive harshness, nor suffering her style to wander into such vulgarities as would be inexcusable—even in a man'.[51] Brontë was deeply hurt: she had assumed Lewes was a friend, and yet, she wrote to him, 'after I had said earnestly that I wished critics would judge me as an *author* not as a woman, you so roughly—I even thought—so cruelly handled the question of sex'.[52] In early 1857, when Marian Evans was assuming the pseudonym George Eliot, Lewes had not forgotten his discreditable conduct in this affair; for at about the same time he generously sent on to Elizabeth Gaskell the angry letters Charlotte Brontë had written him seven years earlier (one of them a single line: 'I can be on my guard against my enemies, but God deliver me from my friends!'[53]). There can be no doubt that Brontë's experience was at the front of Eliot's mind when she decided to assume the pseudonym. It forms an important part of Lewes's arguments to Blackwood in favour of anonymity: '*mystery* as to authorship will have a great effect in determining critical opinion', he wrote, adding, 'When Jane Eyre was finally known to be a woman's book the tone noticeably changed' (*Letters*, ii. 506).

In 1859, as the Liggins affair grew out of control and threatened the incognito, Eliot was faced with that same problem: would the tone of readers and reviewers noticeably change if *Adam Bede* and (imminently) *The Mill on the Floss* were known to be a woman's books? Eliot resolved to let the secret be known, against the better judgement of her publisher, who nevertheless believed that 'the truly good, honest, religious, and moral tone of all you have written or will write is such that I think you will overcome any possible detriment' (*Letters*, iii. 217). Whatever may have motivated that decision, it proved decisive in the subsequent development of Eliot's art. Her successful fabrication of a male author had established and verified the authority of the male narrative voice with which she had been experimenting (with uneven results) in *Scenes of Clerical Life* and *Adam Bede*. Being identified as a woman who, even so, chooses to retain the name 'George Eliot' and all that goes with that name, allowed her to declare openly her entitlement to that 'precious speciality, lying quite apart from masculine aptitudes and experience' (*Essays*, p. 324) *and* her right to go on pursuing the open fiction of the male storyteller. There were many advantages in this for a writer so deeply engaged with the masculine discourses of mid-Victorian society—politics, political economy, theology, law, and science. 'Writing of men with the same sympathetic completeness as of women', Gillian Beer has argued, Eliot's writing becomes 'an effortless representation of women's scope and authority'.[54] There were also advantages for a writer who was determined to insinuate women's experience into those discourses, and assert the centrality of women's experience in social and cultural advancement.

CHAPTER 4

ELIOT AND SOCIAL AND POLITICAL ISSUES

Society, Politics, and the Social Novel

IN an election speech reported in the *Daily Telegraph* on 8 July 1868, the political philosopher and Liberal candidate John Stuart Mill answered a question from a working man in the crowd who asked what advantages he (the man, that is) now enjoyed from having the vote (the 1867 Reform Act had just enfranchised working men in the towns, virtually doubling the size of the electorate—which still comprised, however, barely a third of the adult population). In reply, Mill declared that the man was now 'a citizen', with 'an equal right to be heard—to have a share in influencing the affairs of the country—to be consulted, to be spoken to, and to have agreements and considerations turning upon politics addressed to one'.[1] The effect of citizenship, Mill claimed, was to

elevate and educate the self-respect of the man, and to strengthen his feelings of regard for his fellow men. (*Cheers.*) These made all the difference between a selfish man and a patriot. (*Hear, hear.*) To give people an interest in politics and in the management of their own affairs was the grand cultivator of mankind. (*Cheers.*)[2]

Some seven months earlier, another man had addressed the newly enfranchised town workers on the same subject, and framed his argument in exactly the same way—setting 'selfishness' against 'cultivation'. Unlike Mill, however, he had pronounced that no amount of political participation could strengthen a selfish man's regard for his fellows. Indeed, the desire to participate was motivated precisely by selfishness, which only cultivation could overcome—eventually. Citizenship, at least in Mill's sense of the word, was not, of itself, a 'grand cultivator' at all, and democracy was a false god. This other political speech-maker was Felix Holt, whose 'speech' appeared in the pages of *Blackwood's Edinburgh Magazine*, a journal no working man was ever likely to read and no Liberal to read with any conviction. George Eliot's novel *Felix Holt, the Radical* had appeared before the Reform Bill was passed (15 August 1867) and was a calculated intervention into the debates over the benefits and dangers of giving working men the vote. Eliot's 'Address to Working Men, by Felix Holt', on the other hand, was written in late 1867, after the Act had passed into law. It was done at John Blackwood's explicit request, as a riposte to a speech of Disraeli's given on 29 October, in which the Prime Minister had declared, in language that must have seemed heretical to an old Tory like Blackwood: 'In a progressive country change is constant, change is inevitable.' These sentiments reveal just how entrenched liberal social ideas were by the 1860s. The principle of universal manhood suffrage was by then almost unanimously accepted (in principle at least—and of course 'manhood' disqualified women). Even the Conservative Party under Disraeli had stolen the Liberals' thunder and passed the Second Reform Act themselves. This was in part a response to growing economic prosperity in Britain: it was felt on both sides of politics that social progress could best be achieved through the extension of political rights to those classes that had made a significant contribution to economic progress.

The energy, indeed the vehemence, with which Eliot has Felix defend his unfashionable point of view may strike us now as surprising: is this the novelist who is supposed to exemplify mid-Victorian liberal humanism? Here is someone to whom individuals clearly matter—for whom all social inquiry must be 'checked and enlightened by a perpetual reference to the special circumstances that mark the individual lot' (*The Mill on the Floss*, book 7, chapter 2). Eliot's fiction showcases the central liberal values of tolerance and responsibility; and her plots characteristically turn on choice and the consequences of choosing. Her realism, moreover, is a distinctively liberal aesthetic form in that it 'involves the tactful unravelling of interlaced processes, the equable distribution of authorial sympathies, the holding of competing values in precarious equipoise'.[3] Yet, if Felix's intransigent rhetoric represents Eliot's political views in any degree, hers was obviously a somewhat different conception of the individual from that which, in liberal democracies at any rate, we now tend to take for granted: an abstract rational being whose freedom is essential to the systematic improvement of human life.

Victorian liberalism asserted the primacy of individual interests over the interests of an oppressive entrenched hierarchical social order, and conceived society as a set of rational institutions created by individuals to serve those interests. In liberal democracies, a 'good society' is self-evidently one committed to 'social justice, equity, freedom and progress'.[4] But for Eliot the ideal of a good society entailed a series of other questions which were only inadequately addressed in the liberal idea of individual freedom tempered by responsibility. What are social relationships? Are they relationships of power—that is, political relationships (a question at the centre of her fiction after *Romola*)? Are they economic relationships— relationships between capital and labour, producers and consumers, haves and have-nots (a question she pursues in *Silas Marner*)? If politics is predicated on domination, and economics on self-interest, can social relationships ever be moral? Is morality even relevant in the social sphere (a question running through *Daniel Deronda*)? Is there any necessary connection between social existence and moral sensibilities: or, to put it another way, are questions about the individual good and the social good really questions about goodness at all, or only about material advancement—from which all other forms of social progress and happiness stem? In Eliot's view, all political and economic questions are indeed at base moral questions, and social progress entails the growth of moral sentiment in individuals. When we speak of the moral *intensity* of Eliot's fiction, therefore, we do not just mean the concentration of its ethical force, but its insistence on the interconnectedness of human existence and the grounding of the moral life in the mutual acknowledgement of that interconnectedness.

The deep contradictions in Eliot's own social background and position resonate in that word 'interconnectedness'. She was a metropolitan rationalist and a member of the mid-Victorian industrial bourgeoisie who had, however, assimilated the organicist values of the hierarchical rural society of her childhood and youth. Society, for Eliot, was a body of institutions and relationships formed over a very long period of time. And *body* here is apt: an organic outgrowth of customs and traditions rooted in the past and still vitally meaningful in the present, in the enduring affective ties of family and community. Society, in Eliot's view, existed not primarily as a compact made between members of an economic state, nor as a system or structure explicable through social or statistical analysis, but as the totality of felt relationships that individuals shared with those around them. The affective nature of those ties was critical: where the intellect urged progress, the feelings urged caution and the preservation of continuity with the past. Society, Eliot wrote in 'The Natural History of German Life', a famous early essay on the social philosophy of a German contemporary, Wilhelm Riehl, was '*incarnate history*'. Any attempt 'to disengage it from its historical elements must ... be simply destructive of social vitality. What has grown up historically can only die out historically, by the gradual operation of necessary laws' (*Essays*, p. 287). Those social laws are effectively laws of nature (see Chapter 7, below). The long evolution of society is as inexorable and unalterable as the biological evolution of species. The responsibility for improvement lies with the moral evolution of individuals in their day-to-day relations, not with the wholesale and piecemeal reform of social institutions. That process of evolution, however, must and will take generations. To be distracted from the task by the prospect of immediate social gains is to risk all. Society, for Eliot, was (in Raymond Williams's words) 'a complicated inheritance',[5] and every individual action had complicated, unforeseen consequences: for just as '[we] who are living now are sufferers by the wrong-doing of those who lived before us; we are sufferers by each other's wrong doing; and the children who come after us are and will be sufferers from the same causes' ('Address to Working Men, by Felix Holt', in *Essays*, p. 419).

This vision of society as a complicated inheritance permeates Eliot's fiction. Just as all our emotions, thoughts, and actions bear 'subtle relations to our own past' (*Adam Bede*, chapter 18), so the emotions, thoughts, and actions of an entire society bear subtle relations to its own social past. The idea of 'incarnate history' suggests that we all of us physically embody, and carry forward through the generations, the nature of our collective being—our racial memory—in our customary acts, emotional responses, and social relationships. Social consciousness, in this sense, is something like a 'vision of consequences' (*Adam Bede*, chapter 31). It is arrived at only after an arduous and inevitably painful process of transformation—a self-awakening that is not possible until we have learned to 'lessen the evil consequences of the past, which is unchangeable' (*Adam Bede*, chapter 48) and acknowledge the incalculable effects of our actions on unborn generations. What is at stake for Eliot is the relationship between the legitimate claims of individualism and the imperative need for a 'coherent social faith and order' (*Middlemarch*, Prelude)—that is a struggle being played out everywhere in Eliot's fiction between liberal ideals, rooted in a Romantic concern for 'the untrammelled evolution of the "free spirit" ',[6] and conservative ideals. Like the great conservative thinker Edmund Burke, Eliot believed England was (in the words of the Victorian historian John Richard Green, describing Burke) 'a great living society, so complex in its relations, . . . whose institutions were so interwoven with glorious events in the past, that to touch it rudely was a sacrilege. Its constitution was no artificial scheme of government, but an exquisite balance of social forces which was itself a natural outcome of its history and development'.[7]

In spite of her conservative instincts, Eliot was too acutely conscious of the oppressiveness of the past—her own past weighed heavily down on her in the unbroken silence of her disapproving family—and too much of a realist to reverence altogether the great living society inherited from it. Rather, as the Liberal man-of-letters John Morley later noted (and regretted), Eliot was bound by a 'sense of the iron limitations that are set to improvement in present and future by inexorable forces of the past'.[8] Her complex and seemingly contradictory attitudes towards 'tradition' and 'progress', and towards 'society' and 'the individual', reflect the heaviness of this sense of limitations. Consider, for example, this important passage of narratorial commentary from *The Mill on the Floss*:

There is no sense of ease like the ease we felt in those scenes where we were born, where objects became dear to us before we had known the labour of choice, and where the outer world seemed only an extension of our own personality: we accepted and loved it as we accepted our own sense of existence and our limbs. Very commonplace, even ugly, that furniture of our early home might look if it were put up to auction: an improved taste in upholstery scorns it; and is not the striving after something better and better in our surroundings, the grand characteristic that distinguishes man from the brute—or, to satisfy a scrupulous accuracy of definition, that distinguishes the British man from the foreign brute? But heaven knows where that striving might lead us, if our affections had not a trick of twining round those old inferior things—if the loves and sanctities of our life had no deep immovable roots in memory. (book 2, chapter 1)

The narrator is at once critical of material progress here (that 'grand characteristic' of British manhood) and committed, as the novel is, to 'striving after something better and better in our surroundings': this striving, after all, drives the Dodson sisters' imperious codes of household management, and Mr Tulliver's ill-fated designs on Tom's 'eddication', but it also drives Maggie's struggle to escape the oppressive, reactionary community that is smothering her. This passage begins as though it were presenting a Romantic vision of childhood and the past sharply at odds with the 'oppressive narrowness' shared between narrator and reader in the rest of the novel: very commonplace, even ugly, those 'emmet-like Dodsons and Tullivers' are (book 4, chapter 1). Yet the inconsistency is only apparent, for the novel, while it forbids an uncritical nostalgia, demands that we hold true to the felt values and traditions of our past even as we must rise above 'the mental level of the generation before [us]' (book 4, chapter 1). We are, in any case, locked into the Darwinian struggles of our species, and, as Maggie declares to Stephen Guest in despair: ' "If the past is not to bind us, where can duty lie? We should have no law but the inclination of the moment" ' (book 6, chapter 14). The 'great temptation' (as book 6 is called) is the temptation to abandon the binding past in professing to progress towards something better. Betterment will duly come, but only through the same 'gradual operation of necessary laws' (*Essays*, p. 287). Eliot's faith in progress is faith in 'the onward tendency of human things' but the 'historical advance of mankind' can only come about, she argues, through the suffering of obscure people in suffocating places remote from history. Eliot in effect pushes beyond Burkean conservatism: where Burke values established social institutions because they are interwoven with glorious events in the past, Eliot values them because they are interwoven with the hardships of ordinary folk. In avowing that 'we need not shrink from [the] comparison of small things with great' (*The Mill on the Floss*, book 4, chapter 1), Eliot is responding, as a conservative, to a liberal impulse: the common people are given a share in the historical life of the nation.

As her fiction developed, Eliot grew more preoccupied with what it meant to reject one's inheritance, as Maggie tries and fails to do. Eppie in *Silas Marner*, and Felix and Esther in *Felix Holt, the Radical* all refuse the inheritances they are offered in favour of new bonds of love and obligation. To reject one's inheritance is to challenge the status quo; but that rejection entails another kind of conservatism: the homeliness of traditional lifeways in *Silas Marner*, or a stake in Felix's anti-modern artisanal values, with their veneration of an honest day's work and scorn for easy democracy.[9] Conversely, in *The Spanish Gypsy* and *Daniel Deronda*, Eliot came to insist, as Bernard Semmel argues, 'on the national inheritance, its distinctive ethos and network of traditions, as an heirloom that could not be forsaken by a person of principle'.[10]

This question of inheritance was a crucial one for the Victorians, for whom industrial modernity was both a liberation and an estrangement from the pre-modern past. The simultaneous autonomy and vulnerability of the modern subject is constantly rehearsed in the Victorian social novel. Orphans, most famously, appear in Victorian novels in proportions far in excess of their actual demographic incidence because they represented to the Victorians something of their own freedoms and fears—to create themselves out of nothing, unencumbered by a family identity that would tie them to the past, but ever anxious to find and reclaim their rightful place in a broken genealogy. But in other social narratives, too, the Victorians tried to imagine meaningful courses of action to deal with the traumatic newness of modern industrial existence. This was all the more urgent because many of the old sources of authority and cohesion—an established hierarchical social order, religious belief and its institutions, settled forms of work—fell by the way. In their place, new totalizing systems were tried: most notably, political economy, 'which sought to explain the whole movement of society in terms of the economic behaviour of its members' and utilitarianism, 'which sought to measure all human actions not by any absolute standard, in the manner of religion, but by the simple test of whether they contributed more or less good to the sum of human happiness'.[11]

The Victorian social novel was an important form of instrumental social discourse, taking its place beside (and offering trenchant critiques of) political economy, utilitarian statistical analyses, and parliamentary committees of inquiry. Originating in the turn-of-the-century political fiction of the radical William Godwin, social novels made use of a heightened mimetic realism to shock their (middle-class) readers into consciousness of acute social problems, and thereby promote or induce social change. The first generation of Victorian social novels—Frances Trollope's *Michael Armstrong, The*

Factory Boy (1839–40), for example, or Dickens's *Oliver Twist* (1837)—tackled specific social inequalities and problems such as child labour or the links between poverty and crime. But their successors, dubbed 'Condition-of-England' novels (in reference to what Carlyle called 'the Condition of England' question[12]), were more ambitious still, approaching the regeneration of the whole national life from the perspective of particular political or religious ideologies.[13] Eliot's fiction is an extension of that impulse to take a synoptic view of society, but it refuses to be didactic—to lapse from the picture to the diagram (*Letters*, iv. 300), as the social-problem novelists did, or as Eliot implied they did in her essay on Riehl. Her fiction also refuses to countenance the sentimental solutions offered by a social novelist such as Dickens, who—but for his bracing humour—encouraged

the miserable fallacy that high morality and refined sentiment can grow out of harsh social relations, ignorance, and want; or that the working-classes are in a condition to enter at once into a millennial state of *altruism*, wherein everyone is caring for everyone else, and no one for himself. (*Essays*, p. 272)

Eliot believed something ought to be done about social problems: Felix Holt, in the one novel of hers squarely in the tradition of social-problem fiction, is a close relative of Dickens's 'virtuous . . . artisans' (*Essays*, pp. 271–2) when he looks life 'fairly in the face to see what was to be done with it' (*Felix Holt, the Radical*, chapter 5). But as we have seen, Eliot eschewed the interventionist legislative solutions called for by social-problem fiction, and deplored their violations of aesthetic integrity—an integrity essential to both moral advancement and social amelioration. Populism in either politics or art was doomed. A book's real 'power over the social mind', she wrote to Harriet Beecher Stowe (rather pointedly, given the social influence of Stowe's enormously popular *Uncle Tom's Cabin*), is 'due to its reception by a few appreciative natures, and is the slow result of radiation from that narrow circle . . . but no exquisite book tells properly and directly on a multitude however largely it may be spread by type and paper' (*Letters*, v. 30–1).

By the time Eliot wrote the Riehl essay (in 1856), and was beginning to think about her own fiction, the social-problem novel had lost its impetus. Growing economic prosperity through the 1850s had considerably mitigated the appalling social conditions of the hungry Forties, and Chartism, the working-class political movement (against which the social novel was partly a middle-class reaction), had long collapsed. Without the benefit of the Riehl essay (which appeared unsigned in the *Westminster Review*), Eliot's first readers could be forgiven for not recognizing the ambitious aims she had for a new kind of social fiction in her modest, anonymous fictional debut—three scenes of provincial clerical life and the pastoral idyll *Adam Bede*. On the face of it, these stories have nothing in common with earlier narratives of urban industrialism and its evils, which focused on cities (Dickens's London, Gaskell's Manchester) or the mills and manufacturing towns springing up along rivers in Lancashire, Yorkshire, and the Midlands (Disraeli's *Sybil*, Charlotte Brontë's *Shirley*). They are, rather, self-consciously provincial—countrified, that is to say, and narrowly particular in their locale—and make a point of the backwardness of their people and places. They are also, by any measure, sedate affairs, set in a much less prosperous but somehow much more settled and secure past. And for all the social struggles they represent, one essential component of both social fiction and modern experience is missing—class conflict.

When Eliot proclaims, in the middle of the nineteenth century, that the task of the artist is all the more sacred 'when he undertakes to paint the life of the People' (*Essays*, p. 271), she is using the capitalized term 'People' in a way that harks back to the eighteenth-century language of social relations, to describe anyone whose rank is lower than that of 'gentleman'. But by the time Eliot was writing, the word also belonged to the vocabulary of political radicalism (which likewise originated in the eighteenth century) and assumed very particular meanings in the intense class struggles of the 1840s—for example in the title of the Chartists' list of demands, 'The People's Charter'. Eliot's use of the word has no explicitly radical overtones of that sort: she does not claim to paint the life of working-class or middle-class people, not only because that is likely to suggest an urban proletariat or bourgeoisie, but also because it presumes the predominance of horizontal social affiliations—across members of the same class right across the country—rather than the traditional vertical 'bond of attachment' (in the poet Southey's words[14]) up and down the hierarchical social orders or ranks. Eliot grew up on a farm on the edge of a landed estate in the Midlands in the first decades of

the nineteenth century, where, despite the entrenchment of industrial capitalism in the economic life of the region, social life was still
ordered (and kept orderly) by the binding 'chain of connection'
between the upper and lower ranks. Like most other English people
in the mid-nineteenth century, Eliot left the countryside and lived
the rest of her life in or around cities and large towns: in the suburbs
of Coventry, and later London. Yet, with the notable exception of
The Mill on the Floss, all her English novels are set in a neighbourhood dominated either by a great park and manor-house (the Donnithorne estate in *Adam Bede*, Transome Court in *Felix Holt*, Tipton
and Freshitt in *Middlemarch*, Monk's Topping and Diplow in *Daniel
Deronda*) or, in *Silas Marner*, by a large farm which stands in for the
manor-house among the local community. Even when her heroes and
heroines are not members of the privileged landed classes, they mix
to a greater or lesser degree in those circles: Adam Bede is a lowly
carpenter who knows his place, but his boyhood friend is the young
squire; even Silas Marner, like the poor misshapen surrogate father
of an enchanted princess in a fairy tale, comes into close contact with
the wealthy small gentry.[15] It is tempting to think that Eliot is replay-
ing in these settings the historical transition from a hierarchical
social order presided over by a closed system of power vested in the
land and wealth of the aristocracy and gentry, a system described in
the language of rank, to a social order defined by economic relations
between capital and labour and described in the language of class.
But as we have seen, she was deeply attached to the old traditions
and institutions, and her intellectual commitment to the notion of a
society based around mutual dependency and duty is simultaneously
a commitment to anachronistic social forms based on privilege, and
maintained by rites of deference and obligation. Eliot's ethics, in
other words, are bound up in her social conservatism, and not just in
her evangelicalism: 'that recognition of something to be lived for
beyond the mere satisfaction of self' ('Janet's Repentance', chapter
10) involved also a recognition of, and resignation to, social
inequality.

When in her first story Eliot stakes out the social terrain of her
fiction as 'the debatable ground between aristocracy and common-
alty' ('Amos Barton', chapter 4), her adoption of the language of
rank to describe social relations in Milby in the 1820s is unsurpris-
ing. When in her last novel, she writes that her heroine's family

occupied 'that border-territory of rank where annexation is a burning topic' (*Daniel Deronda*, chapter 3), things no longer seem so simple. It is true that the Davilows move, as Jane Austen's genteel families do, in gentry circles. But *Daniel Deronda*, written in the mid-1870s and set in the mid-1860s, explores the bizarre social formations engendered by rampant capitalism. It begins with countesses and tradesmen together at the gaming tables, in 'a striking admission of human equality' (chapter 1), and follows the restless lives of those newly formed, still-to-be-defined social groupings—what Hardy was later to call the 'metamorphic classes of society'.[16] That is quite a different 'border-territory', one which suggests that Eliot's use of the word 'rank' in a novel with such a consciously contemporary setting is deliberate. Eliot is wary of class: wary that the struggles of competing economic groups should underpin all social description, and wary of the language of social description itself, which is a calculated intervention in society.[17] Once social experience is 'wrought back to the directness of sense like the solidity of objects' (*Middlemarch*, chapter 21), in the everyday face-to-face dealings of one person with another, class is revealed in all its artificiality—its constructedness. This is why Eliot chooses provincial social life as paradigmatic of 'our old society' (*Essays*, p. 421), the society which has 'grown up historically' and pre-dates class-based society by centuries. Provincial settings offer Eliot a local particularity which is, to begin with, resistant to sociological generalization: she wants to tell the truth about *these* people, about *this* society. In so narrowly focusing her milieux, however—Loamshire is not Stonyshire, even if they are next door; Treby Magna is not Middlemarch—she is also trying to contest the assumption, in place by 1860, that these societies were, a generation earlier, already part of that larger overarching structure, class-based society.[18] So when Eliot writes about the 'subtle movement' of social groups in 'old provincial society', she is reluctant to relinquish the language of rank to describe

those less marked vicissitudes which are constantly shifting the boundaries of social intercourse, and begetting new consciousness of interdependence. Some slipped a little downward, some got higher footing: people denied aspirates, gained wealth, and fastidious gentlemen stood for boroughs; some were caught in political currents, some in ecclesiastical, and perhaps found themselves surprisingly grouped in consequence; while a few personages or families that stood with rocky firmness amid all this fluctuation, were slowly presenting new aspects in spite of solidity, and altering with the double change of self and beholder. (*Middlemarch*, chapter 11)

Setting her fiction in small (or smallish) rural communities offered Eliot a model of social relations that was thoroughly modern in economic terms, but kept the vocabulary of class at one remove. Mayor Vincy's unsteady wealth and status derive from his ownership of a ribbon factory which hires local wage labour: he is not a Middlemarcher in that sense but a capitalist who might have invested his capital anywhere. Provincial life being what it was, however, and technologies of communication and transportation being much less advanced during the 1820s, local social relations were in practice very much *local* relations. As Lydgate discovers, it is impossible to escape the 'particular web' of interdependence in a small town, or the 'hampering threadlike pressure of small social conditions, and their frustrating complexity' (*Middlemarch*, chapter 18).

The two main intersecting axes of provincial life in Eliot's English fiction are county society and town society. County society comprises (as well as landowners) tenant farmers (who may be well off, as the Poysers are on the Donnithorne estate in *Adam Bede*, or poorly off, as the Dagleys are on Brooke's estate in *Middlemarch*), rural artisans (skilled workmen, like Adam Bede or Caleb Garth), and agricultural labourers. Town society, represented in most detail in *Middlemarch*, is essentially the commercial society of rural England in the early industrial period. Some of Eliot's townspeople are manufacturers, as we have seen with Vincy, but her towns are essentially the hubs of agricultural commerce. St Ogg's in *The Mill on the Floss* is exemplary in this regard. What makes it modern is not the presence of local capitalists, but the presence of urban capital flowing in to producers (to take up the novel's dominant metaphor) and out again as local goods (and prices) bound, via transport and communication routes, for other towns and ports across the country. Tulliver is therefore the victim not of a local power struggle with Pivart upstream but a struggle between two rival producers in a modernizing agricultural industry. Lawyer Wakem is one of the many town professionals and businessmen in Eliot's fiction (lawyers, most notably, but also bankers, such as Bulstrode in *Middlemarch*, as well as auctioneers and land agents) who act as the point of articulation between local interests and the interests of capital. There is no better example of these intersections of agricultural and commercial production than the extended families of the Tullivers in *The Mill on the Floss*. Tulliver is a (mortgaged) small businessman: a mill owner, whose flour-making business turns local agricultural produce (grown by poor tenant farmers like his brother-in-law, Moss) into goods destined, via the river and canal systems, for national food markets. (The importance of the local import–export markets is underlined in the figure of Bob Jakin, who flourishes as a prosperous small trader.) The husbands of the Dodson sisters also reflect this intimate relationship between agriculture and commerce: Mr Deane works in a local firm (which employs Tom); Mr Glegg is a retired woolstapler; and Mr Pullet a gentleman farmer.

From her discussion of the peasantry in 'The Natural History of German Life' it might be expected that Eliot would explore the lives of agricultural labourers in her histories of 'unfashionable families' (*The Mill on the Floss*, book 4, chapter 3); and there are certainly moments when the lowest of the lower orders are on her mind. In *The Mill on the Floss*, for instance, the narrator pauses to defend the novel's 'tone of emphasis', by which Eliot means the vulgar stridency of its social critique. This 'wide national life', the narrator argues passionately, is based entirely on 'the emphasis of want':

good society, floated on gossamer wings of light irony, is of very expensive production; requiring nothing less than a wide and arduous national life condensed in unfragrant deafening factories, cramping itself in mines, sweating at furnaces, grinding, hammering, weaving under more or less oppression of carbonic acid—or else, spread over sheepwalks, and scattered in lonely houses and huts on the clayey or chalky cornlands, where the rainy days look dreary. (book 4, chapter 3)

The image is a familiar one from earlier decades (see the 1843 *Punch* cartoon, p. 86). But Eliot means, of course, the emphasis of Maggie's wants: the daughter of a petty bourgeois mill owner. There are no factory workers in Eliot's fiction, and the vast population of agricultural labourers is virtually invisible—the unworthy poor are not, she implies, the stuff of fiction: they ' "are not easily roused" ', as the Reverend Irwine says to Dinah in *Adam Bede* (chapter 8), and ' "take life as slowly as the sheep and cows" '. He redirects Dinah's attention to the ' "intelligent workmen" ' about the district, the Bedes.

The representative Eliotean 'peasant' is therefore the skilled artisan, the high-status craftsman labourer whose skills, passed down
from master to apprentice, link him back to medieval times (hence
the significance of the originary naming of 'Adam Bede'). What
characterized the skilled artisan was his independence, his control
over his own labour. By the end of the eighteenth century, as a
vast new class of unskilled factory labourers emerged, class-
consciousness was forged (according to E. P. Thompson's landmark
account of the 'making' of the English working class) by identifying
the rising proletariat with the proud tradition of independent
artisans.[19] But Eliot, as we have seen, was suspicious of this articulation of traditional social forms and class identity. As a result, she
ignores the real poor, effectively sanitizing the working class in order
to deal with them. For her, the artisan embodied the ideal of a
responsible, progressive worker, whose independence safeguarded
him from the corruptions of class, that corporate form of self-
interest which blinded its members to their responsibilities and capacities to pursue social relations independently and clear-sightedly,
and encouraged moral laziness and the tendency to 'convenience,
that admirable branch system from the main line of self-interest'
('Janet's Repentance', chapter 10), in which individuals lived 'from
hand to mouth . . . with a small family of immediate desires' (*The
Mill on the Floss*, book 1, chapter 3). No group of people in Eliot's
fiction, it should be said, is more given to convenience—doing harm
to no one, just doing the best for themselves—than her egoistic
landowners (think of Arthur Donnithorne, Harold Transome, Mr
Brooke). That is why, in a number of novels, Eliot explores versions
of a partnership or association between local landed interests and
socially mobile artisans for the ultimate betterment of society. Thus,
Adam Bede is good for Arthur Donnithorne; and Caleb Garth is
good for Sir James Chettam and, especially, Mr Brooke. More
broadly, she imagines in her social plots forms of interaction between
leisured and productive 'classes' (in the generic sense of that word):
Godfrey Cass and Silas Marner; the Transomes and Felix Holt; and
later, more boldly still, Deronda and the Mallinger-Grandcourts.

In these plots individuals from different social groups are brought
into contact with each other, or more usually brought to the per-
ipheries of each other's lives, in 'the stealthy convergence of human
lots' (*Middlemarch*, chapter 11): most social relationships, Eliot

shows, are latent. The unseen interdependence of individuals and groups is therefore represented in ways that suggest that the local-ized milieux of her fiction are paradigmatic of larger social realities. The 'Address to Working Men, by Felix Holt' frames this in terms of class responsibility: when all the 'various parts' of the human body depend on one another, they are 'likely all to feel the effect if any of them goes wrong' (*Essays*, p. 420). But it applies equally to local communities, where obscure actions are shown to have far-reaching consequences—consequences, Eliot even suggests, of national significance. This is the meaning of the web in *Middlemarch*, the most explicit of the (aesthetic) organizing structures Eliot super-imposes on social actuality to make sense of it. Middlemarch society is not English society; but it stands in for English society. It is only one small part of it—resembling the larger entity closely in many ways (it includes, for instance, 'representatives' of the various ranks and occupations of English society, and of the English 'character'). But it is itself: it has its own particularities, which deter the narrator, a thoroughgoing empiricist, from the temptations of a lazy, falsifying social allegory:

I . . . have so much to do in unravelling certain human lots, and seeing how they were woven and interwoven, that all the light I can command must be concentrated on this particular web, and not dispersed over that tempting range of relevancies called the universe. (*Middlemarch*, chapter 15)

Society, in this image, is a fabric, woven from different thread-lots. The use of the word 'lots' suggests destinies and conditions, but it also has overtones of merchandising—(appropriate, perhaps for this 'story of their coming to be shapen after the average and fit to be packed by the gross', chapter 15). Middlemarch society is, the narrator says elsewhere, a *sample*—again, a scientific or social-scientific test group, but also, in the commercial sense, a sample of the whole product. Many critics have observed, however, that the web also has 'predatory overtones'.[20] Characters, like Lydgate, who arrogantly believe themselves to be self-sufficient are caught up in its sticky threads of social interdependence, and consumed.

The function of the web in *Middlemarch* is also to represent histor-ical processes—in this case, the process of parliamentary reform—simultaneously in space and time. In this novel, human actions are conceived as 'preparations'—the 'slow preparation of effects from one life on another' (chapter 11): they are, in its scientific parlance, 'subtle actions inaccessible by any sort of lens', 'minute processes which prepare human misery and joy' (chapter 16). Those actions may have a profound effect on our unborn descendants, but also on our 'unintroduced neighbour' (chapter 11). The events of *Middlemarch*, which span two-and-a-half years from September 1829 until May 1832, are shaped by the evolving debates and decisions that will culminate, in the immediate aftermath of the novel, in the passing of the Reform Bill. Those debates and decisions are not centred on London, however; reform is a vast historical process centred nowhere. This is sometimes explicitly political. When Lydgate impatiently curses Bulstrode and the infirmary committee over Tyke vs. Farebrother—' "Confound their petty politics!" ' (chapter 18)—he little knows how deeply he has become embroiled in those politics, nor how deeply involved local politicking is with the national scene (Brooke's 'electioneering intentions' (chapter 18) are implicated in his vote against Farebrother, which forces the casting vote on Lydgate). Yet the meaning of that national-historical event, the passing of the Reform Bill, is not isolated to the novel's political plot. Its impetus is felt in Lydgate's passion for medical reform, and in Dorothea's passion for landlord reform. Resistance to it is felt everywhere, not only in those opposed to progress, but in those, like Lydgate himself, whose 'little local personal history [is] sprinkled with small temptations and sordid cares, which made the retarding friction of his course' towards real change (chapter 15). Change is not imposed on Middlemarch from without, by legislators, therefore, but is in the hands of Middlemarchers themselves. The Reform Bill promised a decentring of sovereignty; *Middlemarch* offers a decentring of history itself, involving individuals and communities at the level of their most personal choices.

This is also what Eliot meant when she wrote in *Felix Holt, the Radical* that 'there is no private life which has not been determined by the wider public life' (chapter 3). The implications of that claim are worked through with mixed success in *Felix Holt* (superbly in the Transome plot, awkwardly in the Felix plot), which involves its readers in a conspiracy of Byzantine legal complexity as a dramatic vehicle for her ethical conservatism. Felix is the mouthpiece for that conservatism (he is, as Raymond Williams puts it, less a character than 'a physical appearance and a set of opinions'[21]), but Eliot dubs him a 'radical' out of more than just a desire to provoke. Like Theophrastus Such, who satirizes those northern manufacturers that called themselves political radicals but 'never went to the root of anything' (*Impressions of Theophrastus Such*, 'A Political Molecule'), Eliot's aim is to return radicalism to the skilled artisans who were its originating force. Felix is, belatedly, one of those. Politicized by the recent Reform Act (the novel is set in a Midlands town in 1832–3), he chooses not to enter the family business peddling quack medicines when he returns home, but to go back to his artisan roots, training as a watchmaker and living and working among the poor. When he becomes aware that candidates in the forthcoming post-Reform election are engaging in bribery and corruption, he implores voters to act responsibly. Ultimately, however, he finds himself embroiled in an election-day riot, and wrongly charged with the manslaughter of a policeman. Eliot achieves a number of objectives through this narrative. By returning to the root of radicalism, as it were, she rehistoricizes it, claiming it back from those opportunists, as she characterizes them, who would promote radical politics for their own ends: members of the landed establishment, such as Harold Transome, and later Mr Brooke in *Middlemarch*, who choose to stand as Radicals; and the trade-union rabble-rousers out to exploit the workers. She is also able to differentiate the 'authentic' radicalism of men, like Cobbett, 'who have worked with their hands', and would not destroy any useful thing,[22] and the 'selfish radicalism and unsatisfied, brute sensuality' (*Letters*, i. 254) of the populace. In doing so, Eliot claims the radicalism of the artisans for the conservative politics underwriting her realist aesthetic: the sacred task of the artist in undertaking to paint the life of the People. Felix's politics also dissociate radicalism from democratic politics: ' "The way to get rid of folly" ', he speechifies in the novel, ' "is to get rid of vain expectations, and of thoughts that don't agree with the nature of things" ' (*Felix Holt, the Radical*, chapter 30).

Blackwood was, to say the least, sympathetic to these politics—'I suspect I am a radical of the Felix Holt breed, and so was my father before me', he wrote to Eliot warmly (*Letters*, iv. 246). Eager for more, he pressed her to distil Felix's ideas into a polemical piece for *Blackwood's Edinburgh Magazine*. The 'Address to Working Men, by Felix Holt' is Eliot's most direct statement of her own beliefs about the nature of society and the nature of citizenship (to distance Eliot from it, however little, by insisting that it represents only Felix's views is surely to cavil). Society, she writes, is a 'fine widespread network' in which individuals are 'fast meshed' (*Essays*, p. 419), held together by their dependence on each other 'and the sense they have of a common interest in preventing injury' (*Essays*, p. 421). For any individual or social group to claim more for themselves is to 'tug' at the network and risk unravelling the whole. Curiously, Felix appeals to the principle of unionism in asking the working men he is addressing to consider the common good; but in doing so he appeals to what he perceives is at the bottom of unionism, sectional self-interest: 'it is our interest to stand by each other'; thus, our 'common interest' prevails. The wider and stronger the union, the 'stronger and surer' its good effects. So, society is a very wide union. Having made this rhetorical point, Felix retreats from it, admitting 'no society is made up of a single class', and that 'Class Interest' must be done away with (*Essays*, p. 420).

The question of sectional interest does not go away, however. In the past, Felix admits, existing political privileges may well have been abused by those groups that stood to benefit from them to the exclusion of other members of the society. But that is no justification for selfishly demanding a share of those benefits. The institutions themselves, though their existence is historical ('the wonderful slow-growing system of things' (*Essays*, p. 421)) and their operation is historical (they act for the gradual betterment of human life), are in a crucial way *ahistorical*. They transcend the very interests they serve: they 'express and carry into practise the truth, that the highest interest of mankind must at last be a common and not a divided interest' (*Essays*, p. 420). This is not to say that Felix believes things should stay as they are: rather, that the 'old' political and social institutions should be left alone. He carefully casts those institutions in ways that show them to be part of the lives of artisans and labourers:

in our old society, there are old institutions, and among them the various distinctions and inherited advantages of classes, which have shaped themselves along with all the wonderful slow-growing system of things made up of our laws, our commerce, and our stores of all sorts, whether in material objects, such as buildings and machinery, or in knowledge, such as scientific thought and professional skill. (*Essays*, p. 421)

Clearly the abolition of class is impossible (Eliot's one clear admission of this fact). How, then, are we to do away with class interests yet not do away with class distinctions? How share in a common interest without sharing in common lives and enjoying common advantages? In answer to this, Felix proposes a new definition of class: not as a division of different competing interests but an apportionment of different *responsibilities*.

It soon becomes clear that what is important to Felix is the 'preservation of order' (*Essays*, p. 425). There were many peaceful demonstrations in favour of electoral reform through the 1860s but they were overshadowed by the 1866 Hyde Park riots, which precipitated a middle-class panic at the prospect of political violence which was hardly consistent with the history of working-class protest in Britain. In this the 'Address' reflects its times. It echoes, in particular, the argument Matthew Arnold was making in *Culture and Anarchy*, published as a book in 1869, but as a series of magazine articles contemporary with Eliot's Felix Holt texts. Social chaos, Arnold argued, could only be forestalled by culture. We can awaken our 'best self', as he called it, by being exposed to 'the best that has been thought and written in the world'. For Arnold, the State, through compulsory education, would provide that exposure; but Eliot does not think of cultivation in that way. Felix describes the new voters as 'a class whose wants have been of a common sort'— 'food, clothing, shelter, and bodily recreation'—and who have been for the most part shut out from the 'treasure of refined needs' (*Essays*, p. 426): 'knowledge, science, poetry, refinement of thought, feeling, and manners, great memories and the interpretation of great records, which is carried on from the minds of one generation to the minds of another' (*Essays*, p. 425). But he offers no working men a pathway to those refinements. High culture is simply what must be preserved; the coming men know or care nothing about such things. Democracy promises a fairer share of power and wealth, but—and here there are faint echoes of Mill and the tyranny of the majority, as well as Carlyle and the tyranny of Mammon—power and wealth will 'at last debase the life of the nation' (*Essays*, p. 426).

Citizenship entails much more than the right to participate in the political life of the nation; it entails a *duty* to participate. To be a citizen means that your existence is defined by your relationship to the State. Eliot rejects this equation of society and the State, and rejects the social contract at the base of liberal civil society which depends upon a reciprocal exchange between entitlements (civil, political, and social rights) and obligations. Obligation cannot, she insists, be bestowed by the vote, but can only be gradually and organically developed. In *Romola*, the novel in which she first ventures beyond the remembered social landscapes of her childhood, turning to politics and the nature of political life, Eliot lays out what she believes the responsibilities of citizenship entail. 'Citizen' is not a word much used in her fiction, but in *Romola* she means to refer specifically to the inhabitants of a city-state, Florence in 1492. Because the conventions of the historical novel permit her to integrate fictional characters and fictionalized figures from history, and because she can turn for a moment from the nation-state, where political life is stratified and diffuse, to the city-state, where it is enclosed and intensified, this is Eliot's one opportunity to examine the relationship between private experience and 'the wider public life' from *inside* a political culture. Her later novels are more ambitious because they approach the same problem, but from within private life, which is conferred with the status of history. But *Romola* is *all* politics—all its talk is political talk. The expulsion of the secular Medici and the rise of what we would now call a fundamentalist religious party headed by the charismatic Prior of San Marco, Savonarola,[23] allow Eliot to bring to the forefront the meaning of citizenship, which was 'strongly forced even on the most indifferent minds' by events in the city (*Romola*, chapter 39). As Romola learns, civic responsibilities and personal responsibilities are indistinguishable. In the central scene, she resolves to leave Florence and her unfaithful husband, Tito, and is turned back by Savonarola, who inspires her to throw 'all the energy of her will into renunciation' (chapter 41), teaching her that she is bound by 'ties of marriage, the state, and religious discipleship' (chapter 69). What Romola sees in Savonarola is not a dangerous ideologue. Rather, it is what Daniel Deronda also sees in Mordecai: 'the complete ideal shape of that personal duty and citizenship which lay in his own thought like sculptured fragments certifying some beauty yearned after but not traceable by divination' (*Daniel Deronda*, chapter 41). Where Deronda connects duty and citizenship with beauty, Romola connects it with *piety* (*Romola*, chapter 42). But they are, finally, both expressions of what Eliot puts into

Wordsworthian terms in the epigraph to chapter 18 of *Felix Holt* (from 'Tintern Abbey'): 'The little, nameless, unremembered acts | Of kindness and of love.'

That largely uneventful chapter is barely four pages long. In it Jermyn extracts information from Mr Lyon, Esther wonders whether she will have an opportunity to hear Transome's election speech, and her father proposes they visit Mistress Holt (and, hopefully, Felix), which Esther is prevented from doing by Jermyn, who runs across her on the way and asks her to join his daughters at the candidate's speech. Much of the chapter is spent dwelling on a 'trifling act' of kindness and love—Esther brushing her father's hair—which, however, 'meant a great deal in [her] little history'. Esther has been awakened (by Felix) to tenderness and, more importantly, to a kind of piety for ordinariness. Her attraction to Felix breeds some 'unsatisfied resentment' at his dismissive and scornful treatment of her triviality, but it is beginning to be 'mixed with some longings for a better understanding'—an understanding of the immense significance of such 'trifling acts'. The chapter concludes, again in organicist Wordsworthian terms, that 'in our springtime every day has its hidden growths in the mind, as it has in the earth when the little folded blades are getting ready to pierce the ground'. The moral growth that occurs below the surface of the polity, hidden, is the cultivation Felix calls for in his speech: the accretion of knowledge and understanding through that same piety for anonymity: living faithfully the hidden life (*Middlemarch*, Finale).

When Felix addresses Britain's new political 'masters', therefore, exhorting them, in strongly Carlylean terms (Eliot had read his *Chartism*), to the 'right use of power' now that they have the power they desired, he makes it perfectly clear that authentic social change can only come about through the right use of *powerlessness*. Eliot's fiction as a whole may also be described in just those terms. Her plots punish those corrupted by power: the lawyers Dempster ('Janet's Repentance'), Wakem (*The Mill on the Floss*), and Jermyn (*Felix Holt*); Bulstrode the banker in *Middlemarch*; and most of all, Tito Melema in *Romola* and Henleigh Grandcourt in *Daniel Deronda*. They also punish, in one degree or another, or at least chasten, those (especially women) who are tempted by power: from Hetty Sorrel to Maggie Tulliver, Rosamond Vincy, and Gwendolen Harleth. More particularly, post-*Romola* Eliot brings to the front earlier concerns with the distinction between power and energy, most notably in the languid droit de seigneur of Arthur Donnithorne and the purposeful energy of Adam Bede. The opposition is intensified in Harold Transome and Felix Holt's driven nature, and reaches its climax in *Daniel Deronda*, in the many subtle contrasts between languor and energy—most extremely realized in the contrast between the menacing indifference of Grandcourt's level drawl and the consuming force of purpose in Mordecai.

Increasingly, too, Eliot's fiction hinges on the relationship between the 'ardent public man' who aspires to political leadership or is thrust into a political role, and the ardent private woman, from whom the life of politics is shut off. This is not an invariable or symmetrical situation, but what is plotted out in the triangular relationship between Tito, Savonarola, and Romola, is repeated in the figures of Felix, Harold Transome, and Mrs Transome; Lydgate, Ladislaw, and Dorothea; and Daniel and Gwendolen. It is no wonder, then, that Eliot's women—who are made to learn, time and again, the right use of powerlessness—'for all their rebelliousness, never take part in politics' but rather 'retreat from strong, political positions into the realm of psychology and domesticity'.[24] This is not because 'women's political opinions did not yet signify' (because they did not have the vote) but because real political action, Eliot believed, took place precisely in the 'social unproductive labour' (*Letters*, iv. 425) being undertaken anonymously in the realm of psychology and domesticity (see Chapter 5, below).

Money

The Victorians were the first to concern themselves with a problem which has occupied modern societies ever since the age of capital began in earnest a century and a half ago: that social relationships are not primarily human relationships at all, but *economic* relationships. Few middle-class social and cultural critics in Britain believed capitalism was intrinsically harmful (unlike Karl Marx, who lived in exile in London for thirty years and observed the workshop of the world first hand). In general, they prospered from significant economic growth and rising living standards between 1800 and 1870. But those standards could only be achieved by an increasing degree of state intervention to control working conditions, institute public health and education measures, and remove inequities from the legal system. A regulatory social policy came squarely into conflict with economic theories which tended to favour unrestrained capitalist expansion. The best known of these was the principle of 'laissez-faire'—the belief that, left to itself, the economic system would tend naturally to bring prosperity because it is based on competition.[25] Laissez-faire economics were driven by an intense individualism, a conviction that the welfare of individuals surpassed any other consideration. What social critics feared was that society would become synonymous with the market, and that human relations would be debased into 'exchange relations': formalized exchanges to the mutual benefit of involved parties (where wage labourers exchange their labour for wages, for example, and exchange their wages for goods and services).

This was a contradiction at the heart of Victorian society—hard work, prudent investment, and the acquisition of wealth were valid expressions of human progress, but the pursuit of wealth degraded and dehumanized individuals—and it was very strongly felt among the leading social and cultural critics. Thomas Carlyle, most famously, vehemently attacked market capitalism and what he memorably called 'the cash-payment nexus' (the idea that the only real contact human beings have with each other is at the point of exchange of money) for its deleterious social and moral consequences. John Ruskin's first venture into social criticism in *Unto this Last* (1860)—a series of essays so controversial they were withdrawn from publication in the *Cornhill* mid-series—also attacked the values of political economy, arguing among other things that 'the essence of wealth consists in its authority over men'[26] and urging far higher levels of state intervention in matters of education and training, unemployment relief, and care of the aged. For Matthew Arnold, too, the Philistines—the English middle classes, to which he belonged himself—were reduced to machines by fetishizing the economic mechanisms of 'trade, business, and population . . . as ends precious in themselves'.[27] Only culture can look beyond machinery, he wrote, because it has a passion for disinterested, useless knowledge—what he called 'sweetness and light':

Never did people believe anything more firmly than nine Englishmen out of ten at the present day believe that our greatness and welfare are proved by our being so very rich. Now the use of culture is that it helps us, by means of its spiritual standard of perfection, to regard wealth as but machinery, and not only to say as a matter of words that we regard wealth as but machinery, but really to perceive and feel that it is so. If it were not for this purging effect wrought upon our minds by culture, the whole world, the future as well as the present, would inevitably belong to the Philistines.[28]

The Victorian novel also offered a forceful and frequently influential critique of the market system. But although mainstream novelists routinely condemned the incompatibility of mechanistic economic values and human values, none went so far as to suggest that the capitalist system itself was at fault, or offer any alternative to it. Rather, they offered the novel itself as a remedy for the regrettable side effects of an otherwise beneficial system. Of course, the novel was a product of that same system, and benefited from a modernizing and expanding book trade and an exponential growth in the educated reading public, which made it necessary for novelists to conceal or explain away the relationship of their art to commerce. In *Hard Times*, for example, Dickens satirizes the effects of utilitarianism and political economy in the mechanistic, inhuman regime of Gradgrindery, and represents the salient humanizing influence of culture—the work of the novel itself—in Sleary's circus, which symbolizes, in Walter Allen's words, 'poetry, the life of the imagination . . . freedom and generosity of mind, . . . the truth of natural feelings'.[29]

In George Eliot's case, this problem necessitated a certain awkward self-consciousness about the profitability of her fiction. From the beginning, the success of *Adam Bede* prompted her to write:

I don't know which of those two things I care for most—that people should act nobly towards me, or that I should get honest money. I certainly care a great deal for the money, as I suppose all anxious minds do that love independence and have been brought up to think debt and begging the two deepest dishonours short of crime. (*Letters*, iii. 69)

Eliot's dealings with Blackwood were similarly complicated by the assumption that art transcended all money-grubbing: although she had 'the strongest distaste for the odour of mere money speculation about [her] writing', she wrote of *The Mill on the Floss*, it was nevertheless her 'duty to seek not less than the highest reasonable advantage' from her work (*Letters*, iii. 219). This was also part of the difficulty with the Liggins affair. Eliot was infuriated that Liggins claimed '*he gets no profit out of "Adam Bede," and gives it freely to Blackwood*':

Conceive the real George Eliot's feelings, conscious of being a base world-ling—not washing his own slop-basin, and *not* giving away his M.S.! Nor even intending to do so, in spite of the reverence such a course might inspire. (*Letters*, iii. 44)

When Eliot embarked on *The Spanish Gypsy* in 1868, moreover, she wrote to Cara Bray:

Don't you imagine how the people who consider writing simply as a money-getting profession will despise me for choosing a work by which I could only get hundreds where for a novel I get thousands? I cannot help asking you to admire what my husband is, compared with many possible husbands—I mean, in urging me to produce a poem rather than anything in a worldly sense more profitable. (*Letters*, iv. 438)

Eliot's abhorrence of penury and debt, respect for thriftiness, and veneration of the self-helpful independent small business that profits from careful housekeeping, hard work, and enterprise, are amply expressed in her fiction. The pressure of money difficulties is every-where felt by good people. Eliot's realism dwells affectionately on Milly Barton's unceasing rounds of mending and making-do in 'Amos Barton' and the shabby gentility of the Farebrothers in *Middlemarch*. She creates the legend of Mrs Poyser's household lore and its vital contribution to the economy of the farm in *Adam Bede*; anatomizes the intimidating domestic proficiency of the Dodson sisters in *The Mill on the Floss*; and takes pleasure in the happy self-sufficiency of the Garths in *Middlemarch*. But Eliot's plots do not turn on thrift but on profligacy, poor financial judgement, and debt. The Tullivers lose everything in *The Mill on the Floss* because Tulliver goes indiscriminately to law and is defeated, and because he guarantees a loan to his brother-in-law Moss, which is called in. The Cass brothers squander their income and borrow on their expect-ations, as Fred Vincy does in *Middlemarch*, losing the Garths' small savings along the way. The ramifications of money troubles in *Middlemarch* are extensive: Mayor Vincy's social climbing leads him into difficulties when there is a downturn in the ribbon trade, which compromises him with his brother-in-law Bulstrode, affects Fred's chances, and cultivates in Rosamond a habit of living beyond her means, which in turn precipitates Lydgate's downfall. In *Daniel Deronda*, similarly, Mrs Davilow invests her entire fortune in Grapnel and Co., which collapses and leaves the family in ruin, forcing Gwendolen to marry Grandcourt.

Eliot's most important treatment of the theme of money is *Silas Marner*. In this short novel she explores the debasing influences of exchange relations and 'the remedial influences of pure, natural human relations' (*Letters*, iii. 382). *Silas Marner* is not a social-problem novel but a fable of the interpenetration of social and economic relations in mid-Victorian Britain. As a fable it is also a critique. But what is this fable about? What is it criticizing? The market economy and the nature of industrial labour relations? Eliot wrote *Silas Marner* when she was also trying to write *Romola*, a novel deeply concerned with the character of Victorian society. By choosing to cast a critique of contemporary social concerns in a fabular form, she was attempting to suggest, as Dickens had in *Hard Times*, the value of the imagination—the simple made-up tale—in overcoming Mammon. But in this context *Silas Marner* perhaps owes more to Ruskin than to Dickens. Eliot is usually characterized as an admirer of Ruskin's art criticism who found his social criticism fatuous and disagreeable because she believed in laissez-fairism and thought Ruskin's vigorous and impassioned pleas for state social intervention to be simple-minded. The evidence for this lies in a letter to Sara Hennell in 1858 about Herbert Spencer's laissez-fairist article in the *Westminster Review*, 'State Tamperings with Money and Banks', best known for the much-quoted maxim: 'The ultimate result of shielding men from the effects of folly is to fill the world with fools.' A closer reading of this letter reveals that Eliot was, however, only (at best) hesitantly in agreement with Spencer against state interference in financial institutions: a dinner with him to discuss the article 'inclined me to think that he must be in the right. But I have not time at present to think of the subject except in a scrambling way'. On the other hand, she has just read Ruskin's *Political Economy of Art* and found in it

some magnificent passages, mixed up with stupendous specimens of arrogant absurdity on some economical points. But I venerate him as one of the great Teachers of the day—his absurdities on practical points do no harm, but the grand doctrines of truth and sincerity in art, and the nobleness and solemnity of our human life, which he teaches with the inspiration of a Hebrew prophet, must be stirring up young minds in a promising way. (*Letters*, ii. 422)

Her interest in the question of intervention in a society driven by market forces and reduced to economic relations informs *Silas Marner*, which she began writing in 1860. Silas is the anti-artisan: he is the opposite of Adam Bede, or Felix Holt, whose craft of watch-making is the very antithesis of Silas's disembodied weaving. Deprived of faith in God (by his betrayal in Lantern Yard) and deprived of the affection of family and community, he is stripped down to *homo economicus*—a man whose only interaction with the world is through pure economic relations. His is not a life of stultify-ing wage labour, however; he is less the labourer than the machine. He represents the convergence of the 'cash-payment nexus' and (another of Carlyle's objects of critique) the mechanization of human activities: 'Not the external and physical alone is managed by machinery, but the internal and spiritual also. Here too nothing fol-lows its spontaneous course, nothing is left to be accomplished by old, natural methods'.[30] At the same time, Silas seems to represent the pure market economy itself: a machine-like system for capital accumulation, which has no human dimension. But that is an illu-sion. The trouble with Silas is that he is no capitalist: he makes £272 in fifteen years, which is never going to buy out the Casses. His is not self-expanding capital; and he is not motivated by self-interest, but by the need to fill his days with some activity. Silas is unworldly and unmaterialistic: he is corrupted not by the desire to possess but only the desire to accumulate coin. These are not tokens: part of his irresponsibility concerns his refusal to enter into any kind of rela-tions at all, so that the coins do not stand in for anything that they could be exchanged for—possessions, status, or greater wealth.

Is Eliot criticizing the market here? *Silas Marner* seems to suggest that work done for purely commercial or economic motives is innately morally contaminating. Silas's contamination is expressed as an inexplicable sickness he is struck down with—the cataleptic trances. In one sense these are a representative symbol of the neg-ation of his will, the absenting of a whole ethical dimension from his life. Silas is carried along passively by the highly deterministic rituals and dogmas of Lantern Yard. There and later the plot is driven forward by crucial acts from which he is momentarily absented. Yet at the same time the trances suggest an other-worldliness. Their very emptiness is suggestive: to the Lantern Yarders he is a conduit of spiritual messages, to the Raveloe people a kind of demonic figure. The only cure is intervention—not of the state but a miraculous child. The quasi-religious nature of this act takes us back to the climax of *Romola* and the fundamental importance of intercession in Eliot: the importance of individual acts of kindness and love.

CHAPTER 5

ELIOT AND THE WOMAN QUESTION

'BUT "what am I to do with my life?" . . . herein lies the momentous question.'[1] No question is more momentous to George Eliot's heroines, or more urgent to the mid-Victorians. What is a middle-class woman to do with her time, and how can she plan a future for herself? What is her proper social role? How is that role defined by her nature, and how does it differ from a man's nature and role? What work can women do, and what sort of education do they need? What is the special character of their social power, and how might that be compromised by the extension of the franchise, the removal of legal disabilities, and the acknowledgement of women's claims to social equality? And what would *happen* if women took charge of their lives, and articulated their ambition, or anger, or drive for power: what would happen, that is to say, to England as a civil society, as a nation? These were questions of vital importance, not just to a small number of feminist women and their supporters and opponents, but to the whole mid-Victorian reading public, which engaged in or followed the intense discussion and debate known as the 'woman question' (see Chapter 2, above). These concerns also found expression in the stories women were told, and told themselves, about their lives—in daily conversation, and in magazine articles, statutes, sermons, treatises, advertisements, novels, plays, and poems: in every kind of discourse, public and private. In Eliot's fiction, they are sometimes put explicitly, in the impassioned outbursts of her female protagonists. But more often they are implicit in the stories themselves, and in plots that cross back and forth between women's and men's lives, drawing out analogies and contrasts. Deeply embedded assumptions about what women were and did—what they were expected to be and do—are carried through into those plots. At every point in their development, and especially in their unsettled and often troubling resolutions, they register the complexities and contradictions of the woman question, and the final impossibility of unravelling those complexities. Assumptions about women's nature and vocation are also carried through into the language of the fiction, where a woman's very authority to speak must constantly be justified. It is at these levels, of character, plot, and language, and not at the level of explicit debate, that the woman question makes its presence most profoundly felt in Eliot.

Consider what happens in the major novels. When Dinah Morris is introduced in the opening chapters of *Adam Bede* she has solemnly elected not to marry and have a family, but to live, work, and preach among the desperately poor villagers of Snowfield in neighbouring Stonyshire. But from the moment she is alone with Adam in chapter 11, and for the first time in her life blushes with 'painful self-consciousness' at 'the dark penetrating glance of this strong man', she is marked out for the greater vocation of wife and mother. She duly marries Adam, and in the final chapter of the novel, when the Wesleyan Conference outlaws women preachers, she happily submits, knowing, Adam says, that ' "she's not held from other sorts o' teaching" ' (Epilogue).

Felix Holt, the Radical repeats this pattern, although Esther Lyon, of whose inner life we know very little, is no Dinah. Socially ambitious and pleasure-loving, Esther is affronted early on by Felix's arrogant challenge that she ' "show her power of choosing something better" ' than the petty life of a ' "lower kind of being" ' who would ' "hinder men's lives from having any nobleness in them" ' (chapter 10). Eventually, though, when a plot of Dickensian perplexity gives her what she most wants—the luxury of the Transome estate—and Felix's misfortune urges her to plead on his behalf, she does choose something better: she chooses Felix as her husband.

By contrast, in *The Mill on the Floss*, Maggie Tulliver's education prepares her only for a respectable young woman's ' "dull, wearisome life" ', so that she must suppress 'the intense and varied life she yearned for' (book 6, chapter 2). Without an education beyond the requirements of female accomplishments, and without opportunities for work, Maggie's passionate nature is channelled into a violent internal struggle between competing forms of desire—intellectual, spiritual, and sexual. In a small provincial town a woman's passion, however noble its nature or object, is morally dangerous. Maggie's life is accordingly reduced to a cramped cycle of temptation and renunciation, played out in the two stages of the fateful event which takes the novel towards its climax: the languid eroticism of her tidal journey downriver with Stephen Guest; and her cold reawakening to her obligations and emotional attachments to St Ogg's. It is a cycle which can only be disrupted by the intervention of a catastrophic natural occurrence—the flood.

There is a very similar homecoming scene—or rather, two scenes—in *Romola*. The first describes its heroine being sternly turned back by Savonarola on the road just outside Florence. Dressed as a nun, she has taken flight from her corrupt husband, Tito Melema, and is intent on pursuing the life of an ascetic intellectual woman alone in Venice. Passionately committed to this new life, she nevertheless obeys him—'a strong being who roused a new strength within herself'—by throwing 'all the energy of her will into renunciation' (*Romola*, chapter 40). Later, when she learns of Tito's treachery and unfaithfulness, she leaves again, drifting away, as Maggie does, in a boat, until she reaches a plague village, where she tends the sick and is worshipped as a visitation of the Madonna. When Tito dies and Savonarola is executed, Romola returns to Florence and, in one of Eliot's most intriguing endings, sets up house with two other women—her cousin, Monna Brigida, and Tessa, her late husband's mistress, a simple-minded milkmaid who had been tricked into a mock marriage with Tito, and borne him two children.

In *Middlemarch*, Dorothea Brooke is also providentially released from a suffocating life, not by a flood but by the death of her husband, Casaubon. It was a life she stubbornly chose for herself, of course, against all advice; but only because, like the childish St Teresa of the novel's Prelude, she was blinded to Casaubon's real nature by her own 'ardently willing soul' (Prelude), and by her desperation to escape the narrow provincialism of Middlemarch and the 'toy-box' learning (chapter 10) expected of a gentry lady. Like Maggie, Dorothea's 'ardent nature turned all her small allowance of knowledge into principles' (chapter 20), and her version of Mulock's question—'What could she do, what ought she to do?' (chapter 3)— goes right to the heart of Eliot's double concern in the novel with aspiration and moral conduct. To demand a fuller, more consequential life is not in itself a good, especially if it means neglecting or disdaining ordinary responsibilities. This principle holds for Lydgate and Bulstrode, whose lives end miserably, as well as for Dorothea, whose life (we are meant to see) ends happily. Ironically, though, it is Casaubon's reactionary and unconsidered view of woman's nature—the ' "great charm of your sex is its capability of an ardent self-sacrificing affection, and herein we see its fitness to round and complete the existence of our own" ' (chapter 5)—that is endorsed in Dorothea's melancholy destiny as the self-sacrificing wife of a rising parliamentarian.

Gwendolen Harleth in *Daniel Deronda* is not afflicted by any such conflicts between worldly duties and higher duties—at least not at first. Returning penniless to Offendene, she resolves with magisterial self-belief, ' "I will do something. I will be something" ' (chapter 21), as if resolution and self-belief were enough. Like Hetty Sorrel, however, Gwendolen has no 'shape for her expectations' (*Adam Bede*, chapter 13), no very clear sense of what it might mean to 'be something'. Unshakeably confident in her powers, only the 'clear-seeing Klesmer' tells her the truth of the matter: ' "you have not been called upon to be anything but a charming young lady," ' he tells her, ' "whom it is an impoliteness to find fault with" ' (*Daniel Deronda*, chapter 23). As the story unfolds, Deronda is called upon to lead his people into the promised land. Gwendolen is not called upon to do anything.

From these examples, Eliot's narratives appear to share a common trajectory. They begin by challenging conservative ideas of femininity and women's roles, only to end up reinforcing those ideas (as the ending of *Middlemarch* reinforces the same values it had earlier mocked in Casaubon), or at best evading their real consequences (as in the fantasy ending of *The Mill on the Floss*). The greater the heroines' ordeals, the more inexplicable these ultimate celebrations of orthodoxy or evasions of social reality seem. 'Save for the supreme courage of their endeavour,' Virginia Woolf remarked, 'the struggle ends . . . in tragedy, or in a compromise that is even more melancholy'.[2] Many of the generation of feminist readers drawn to Eliot in the 1960s and 1970s by the courage of these passionate heroines were likewise deterred by Eliot's dispiriting endings, and by her failure to offer positive role models for women. For some, it was nothing short of a betrayal. They felt, as Kate Millett did (writing in 1970, at the height of second-wave feminism), that Eliot had 'lived the revolution' but 'refused to write of it'.[3] After all, it was not as though there were no contemporary mid-Victorian models: foundresses of *something*, such as Florence Nightingale; and serious women writers with a wide readership who did write about strong, independent women daring to pursue independent livelihoods and lives: Lucy Snowe in Charlotte Brontë's *Villette* (1853), for example, or the heroine of Elizabeth Barrett Browning's *Aurora Leigh* (1857). Why not Eliot?

In the years following, however, feminist critics began to question many of these assumptions, which had been guided by the initial (and essential) feminist project of recovering a genuinely alternative foundational tradition of radical women's writing. Referring back to Woolf, who had been among the first to recognize the murkiness of Eliot's attitudes to women and the complexity of her position as a successful woman who lived openly with a married man, feminists in the 1980s moved to reclaim her for feminism. Her ambivalence was forgiven and celebrated (for Elaine Showalter, Eliot was no longer 'a distant and powerful mother' but 'an imperfect, impulsive, and attractive sister whose conflicts and choices prefigure modern women's emergent selves'[4]); and her work was reclaimed from criticism which was judged by Penny Boumelha to have been 'damagingly author-based'. It confused Eliot's life and work in ways that only served to 'shore up and validate those biographical and confessional models of writing produced by women that have so often served to limit and trivialize it'.[5] This kind of 'recycled intentionalism' was deeply misguided, Boumelha argued, because it denied 'textual production' by assuming that 'we should seek and can find in or through a work of fiction the consciously or unconsciously held views of its writer'.[6] This more politically and linguistically sophisticated approach had the advantage of releasing feminist critics from the vexed business of having to decide whether Eliot was or was not a feminist by proposing rather to appropriate her work *for* feminism. It is indicative of the dominance of this approach that few readers would now claim that gender readings should take Eliot's consciously or unconsciously held views about women's rights and disabilities as their cardinal point of reference; or that those views make very much difference to the meaning of the work, which was produced within 'historical and generic constraints' quite independent of its author's situation, and continues to be produced within the changing cultural contexts of its readings.[7] It could be argued, however, that—in Eliot's particular case, I mean—feminist critics in the 1980s were so adamant in asserting the primacy of textual production over biographical evidence, of work over author, precisely because Eliot's strongly held views were both insistent and unpalatable. We simply cannot ignore them: not because they tell us unequivocally what Eliot's opinions were, or because they offer us a 'key' to the ideologies of gender in the writing, but because they do help us to understand why Eliot chooses as she does among the range of possible destinies for her heroines, and why her narrators explain or comment upon those destinies in the ways they do. These heroines *are* constrained by the collision of the 'historical and formal possibilities of writing and reading' (the possibilities and limits set by realism, most obviously), and by the historical context of 'the woman question'. But they are also constrained by the ideological possibilities and limits set by Eliot's specific intellectual project.

As we have already seen, that intellectual project was deeply rooted in a conservative social ideology, which was essential to the originality of Eliot's insights and formal experimentation. In keeping with this, she takes a conservative view of the woman question, but at the same time her fiction is passionately, angrily sympathetic with women's struggles against the forces of tradition and social convention. This inconsistency cannot be explained away. Eliot's women are torn by unconventional ambitions and yet revert to the convention which has become ingrained in them; and Eliot's fiction is torn by a constant struggle to reconcile the irreconcilable. Consider briefly, first, the context in which she wrote. Women's nature and role was the subject of fierce debate when Eliot and Lewes left England to live together in Germany in 1854. That year Britain declared war on Russia and invaded the Crimea, and the debate turned on the nation's future and the role of the 'Englishwoman' in that future. The ideal Englishwoman (for the middle classes, who controlled the debate) was represented as a sexless helpmate of men: no longer an aberration of the male—the temptress, the Eve—but his opposite: his moral hope and guide, the Madonna. This can partly be explained by the parallel ascendancy of puritan evangelicalism and capitalism in Victorian England. Capitalist individualism, sanctified as self-help and progress, also encouraged aggressive competition and inequality, which called for a redemptive space outside the marketplace. At the same time, biological proofs for profound sexual difference (not just in reproductive function) reinforced this view, claiming to refute scientifically the old arguments for the essential sameness of the sexes. Not only were women

intended above all for childbearing and motherhood, their physiological and psychological make-up fitted them to preserve the most
precious values of the society, symbolized by the home. But ironically enough, as Mary Poovey has argued, 'when it was given one
emphasis, woman's reproductive capacity equaled her maternal
instinct; when given another, it equaled her sexuality'. As a result
'the contradiction between a sexless moralized angel and an aggressive, carnal magdalen was . . . written into the domestic ideal as one
of its constitutive characteristics'.[8] The womanly domestic woman
therefore depended for her very existence on the existence of her
opposite, the prostitute: not a woman who sold sex for money, it
should be said, but 'any woman who deviated from the feminine
ideal and lived outside middle-class codes of morality'.[9] Driven by
the zeal of evangelicals and the intense nationalism generated by the
war, it became a middle-class mission to reform these 'fallen
women', thereby constantly reinforcing a normative femininity.
Fallen women were accordingly treated not with hostility but pity, as
lost innocents. When Eliot chose to live outside middle-class codes
of morality, therefore, she was not simply spurned by respectable
women, but pitied as a magdalen figure. 'I can only pray, against
hope,' John Chapman wrote to a friend in the highly topical language
of the fallen women debates, 'that [Lewes] may prove constant to
her; otherwise she is *utterly* lost' (*Letters*, viii. 126).

The year 1854 was also a turning point in the debates on the
woman question because it was the year that the representation of
the fallen woman moved from the periphery to the centre of mainstream literary and visual culture. It was the year Elizabeth Gaskell's
controversial novel, *Ruth*, was published. This was not the first novel
by a major novelist to depict the plight of the fallen woman sympathetically; but it was the first in which she was the heroine. It was
also the year the Pre-Raphaelite painter William Holman Hunt
exhibited his difficult and highly contentious picture *The Awakening
Conscience* in the ultra-conservative Royal Academy summer exhibition. Viewers were shocked by this image of the 'dark and repulsive
side of modern domestic life', which represented 'the momentary
remorse of a kept mistress, whose thoughts of lost virtue, guilt,
father, mother, and home have been roused by a chance strain of
music'.[10] However shocking, Hunt's painting proved to be the first of
many with this theme which featured in the RA over the following

decade. In countless iconic images, as in *The Awakening Conscience*, a dense symbolic narrative unites angel and whore in the same woman, her self-destructive sexual passion threatening domesticity itself as it threatens her ruination.

In fiction, however, the two interlocked forms of femininity—the sexless moralized angel and the aggressive, carnal magdalen—had to be assigned to complementary pairs of female characters. The pattern for this pairing was already available to novelists in romances like Sir Walter Scott's *Ivanhoe* (1819), in which the comely, docile, blonde-haired English heroine, Rowena, competes for the hero's love with the sensual dark-haired Jewess, Rebecca. Eliot experimented extensively with this positive–negative typology of feminine definition (see below). Only in her first story, 'Amos Barton', does a highly conventionalized figure of womanliness feature on her own. Milly Barton is 'a lovely woman' who 'supersedes all acquisitions, all accomplishments', and whose 'presence' is 'imposing in its mildness'. In terms that recall the popular women's conduct manuals of the day, Eliot writes of the triumph of Milly's 'serene dignity of *being*' over 'the assiduous unrest of *doing*' (chapter 2), and intones the inviolable middle-class doctrine of the separate spheres of men and women: 'a loving woman's world lies within the four walls of her own home; and it is only through her husband that she is in any electric communication with the world beyond' (chapter 7). In keeping with all this, the story ends with a situation worthy of hundreds of unremarkable, sentimental mid-Victorian paintings of 'woman's mission': Amos's eldest daughter, Patty, who looks exactly like her dead mother, remains by her father's side to make 'the evening sunshine of his life' (Conclusion).

Milly Barton is far from typical of Eliot's women, as we shall see, but the tension between the 'assiduous unrest of doing' and the 'serene dignity of being' remained absolutely central in Eliot's thinking. Not that she embraced the ideal of respectable femininity at the core of middle-class domestic ideology; she rejected it out of hand, but did not do so in favour of the political, legal, and social measures, radical and moderate, being put forward by the Victorian women's movement. Rather, Eliot's aim was to undermine the fundamental binary opposition in mid-Victorian sexual ideology between womanliness and unwomanliness, and in doing so cut right across the claims of organized feminism and its reactionary opponents. This aim underlies her tentative and often contradictory remarks about women and reform; and underlies plots which are kept in motion by women's unhappiness and restlessness, and reach closure only when they arrive at the compromise that was, as Woolf observed, more melancholy even than tragedy.

Eliot only extremely cautiously gave out her opinions about women's nature and role, the efficacy and value of franchise and law reform, educational reform, and the reform of the professions to admit women. The early essays are equivocal. 'Woman in France: Madame de Sablé' (October 1854) is a meditation on 'womanly intellect' (*Essays*, p. 55) and the social and historical conditions favouring its development in France, in which Eliot provocatively claims (given her own situation) that 'laxity of opinion and practice with regard to the marriage-tie', had 'tended to bring women into more intelligent sympathy with men' (*Essays*, p. 56) in the aristocratic France of the seventeenth and eighteenth centuries. That did not necessarily hold for ordinary Englishwomen, however. In a review of the American feminist Margaret Fuller's *Woman in the Nineteenth Century* a year later, Eliot maintained, as she would continue to do throughout her life, that the 'thorough education of women . . . will make them rational beings in the highest sense of the word' (*Essays*, p. 203). She also upholds (in passing) the argument made by both Fuller and the English pioneer feminist Mary Wollstonecraft that women ' "need, especially at this juncture, a much greater range of occupation than they have, to rouse their latent powers" ' (Fuller): they could be doctors or enter business, and ' "would not then marry for a support" ' (Wollstonecraft) (*Essays*, p. 204). Only in the closing paragraphs, however, does Eliot venture to speak her own mind on the subject:

On one side we hear that women's position can never be improved until women themselves are better; and, on the other, that women can never become better until their position is improved—until the laws are made more just, and a wider field opened to feminine activity. But we constantly hear the same difficulty stated about the human race in general. There is a perpetual action and reaction between individuals and institutions; we must try and mend both by little and little—the only way in which human things can be mended. (*Essays*, p. 205)

Here are the two central tenets of Eliot's thinking about women: the woman question is a human question, and not a special case; and the struggle for women's social equality is being carried out, as the struggle for the extension of the franchise was being carried out, by people who already believed in their 'actual equality—nay, even their moral superiority to men'. This, Eliot cautions, is a 'false position'. Abstract ideals of equality are harmful, and neither Fuller nor Wollstonecraft, to their credit, allowed their 'ardent hopes of what women may become' to 'prevent them from seeing and painting women as they are' (*Essays*, p. 205). With a conservative's pragmatism, Eliot too was committed to seeing and painting women as they were. Realism is 'the practice of regarding things in their true nature and dealing with them as they are' (as the *Oxford English Dictionary* defines it), and Eliot's realism constantly reminds us that the way ' "to get rid of folly is to get rid of vain expectations, and of thoughts that don't agree with the nature of things" ', as Felix Holt puts it (chapter 30).

As we saw in Chapter 4, this idea belongs in the tradition of British conservative thought beginning with Edmund Burke. Eliot had faith in the possibility of historical betterment through 'perpetual action and reaction' between individuals and historically authenticated institutions, so that both may be improved 'by little and little'. As Cross put it in his biography, Eliot's 'great hope for the future' was 'the improvement of human nature by the gradual development of the affections and the sympathetic emotions, and "by the slow stupendous teaching of the world's events"—rather than by means of legislative enactments' (*Life*, p. 624). Understandably, therefore, when Eliot was asked (as she was in 1869) why she did not support most of the practical expedients favoured by the women's movement, she replied that it was because she felt 'too deeply the difficult complications that beset every measure likely to affect the position of women' and felt 'too imperfect a sympathy with many women who have put themselves forward in connexion with such measures' (*Letters*, v. 58).[11]

Eliot was equally reluctant to support feminist campaigns for labour market reform. Her friend Barbara Bodichon, a leading feminist in London, 'did [her] the honour', she wrote to Charles Bray, 'to copy out a passage' from a letter of hers for the pamphlet *Women and Work*, which Bodichon published in 1857. The quote—'Ill-done work seems to me the plague of human society. People are grasping after some grandiose task, something "worthy" of their powers, when the only proof of capacity they give is to do small things badly' (*Letters*, ii. 396 n. 7)—is actually attributed to Anna Jameson in the pamphlet. It is significant that Eliot should claim it, however, and continue in the letter to Charles Bray: '"Conscience goes to the hammering in of nails" is my Gospel. There can be no harm in preaching *that* to women, at any rate' (*Letters*, ii. 396). In a letter to Bodichon herself in 1868, Eliot lamented 'the great amount of social unproductive labour which needs to be done by women, and which is now either not done at all or done wretchedly':

No good can come to women, more than to any class of male mortals, while each aims at doing the highest kind of work, which ought rather to be held in sanctity as what only the few can do well. I believe—and I want it to be well shown—that a more thorough education will tend to do away with the odious vulgarity of our notions about functions and employment, and to propagate the true gospel that the deepest disgrace is to insist on doing work for which we are unfit—to do work of any sort badly. (*Letters*, iv. 425)

'A more thorough education': this was the one feminist reform issue that Eliot strongly supported—but only, as this letter makes clear, because she believed it would lead to women abandoning any delusions about their right to demand equal opportunities in the workplace. For Eliot men and women were intended for different kinds of work because they were physically and psychologically different. A few months after writing to Bodichon, Eliot put this argument to Emily Davies, who was leading the campaign for women's higher education. These differences, Eliot wrote, 'lie on the surface and [are] palpable to every impartial person with common sense' (*Letters*, iv. 467), but they also have 'deep roots' in the unique 'psychological development' of different women. What ensued, Eliot pointed out, was a profound difference in 'the *proportion* of feeling and all mental action, in the given individual', man or woman. But the difference of gender remained, and 'the difference of function' that 'lies in woman's peculiar constitution for a special moral influence':

And there lies just that kernel of truth in the vulgar alarm of men lest women should be 'unsexed.' We can no more afford to part with that exquisite type of gentleness, tenderness, possible maternity suffusing a woman's being with affectionateness, which makes what we mean by the female character, than we can afford to part with the human love, the mutual subjection of soul between a man and a woman—which is also a growth and revelation beginning before all history. (*Letters*, iv. 468)

Women's education was therefore no threat to men because it was intended to promote 'the mutual delight of the sexes', Eliot argued: 'complete union and sympathy can only come by women having opened to them the same store of acquired truths or beliefs as men have, so that their grounds of judgment may be as far as possible the same' (*Letters*, iv. 468), and so that their lives may be 'passed together under the hallowing influence of a common faith as to their duty and its basis' (*Letters*, v. 58).

Eliot was indeed out of sympathy with those of her women friends who put themselves forward in connection with reform measures. On occasions, she did claim affinity with feminist ideals, as in the letter to Bray and another of 1867 to Clementia Taylor, a strong supporter of women's rights. In the latter, Eliot sympathizes 'most emphatically in the desire to see women socially elevated—educated equally with men, and secured as far as possible with every other breathing creature from suffering the exercise of any unrighteous power' and concludes: 'on the whole I am inclined to hope for much good from the serious presentation of women's claims before Parliament' (*Letters*, iv. 366). What she doesn't say is that the 'much good' she hopes for is most decidedly not the vote. Writing to Sara Hennell shortly afterwards, and scolding her 'for undertaking to canvass on the Women's Suffrage question', she argued that it was in fact 'an extremely doubtful good', adding: 'I love and honour my friend Mrs Taylor, but it is impossible that she can judge beforehand of the proportionate toil and interruption such labours cause to women whose habits and duties differ so much from her own' (*Letters*, iv. 390).

Eliot was no doubt thinking of herself as one whose 'habits and duties' differed so markedly from those of the feminists. As an artist who held that the sacred function of art was aesthetic teaching—by which she meant the development of the affections and sympathetic emotions of her readers—Eliot was deeply committed to an alternative form of 'public action'. Art, she believed, was a better instrument of social change, which worked not through 'legislative enactments' but the gradual evolution of enlightened individuals and institutions. 'I . . . venerate those who are struggling in the thick of the contest' (*Letters*, ii. 396), she wrote; and saw herself as part of that same struggle to improve women's lives. But for her it was a struggle to perform adequately a woman's duty to others. She had felt this acutely as a young woman. Writing to the Brays from Geneva in 1849, where she was recovering from the ordeal of nursing her father through his last illness, she professed that 'the only ardent hope I have for my future life is to have given to me some woman's duty, some possibility of devoting myself where I may see a daily result of pure calm blessedness in the life of another' (*Letters*, i. 322). Eliot was deeply unhappy at this time, and full of self-doubt and guilt, but she remained faithful to this ardent hope. It shaped her artistic vocation and was the basis for the strong sense of kinship she felt with feminist friends whose aims were otherwise so different. 'The influence of one woman's life on the lot of other women is getting greater and greater with the quickening spread of all influences', she wrote in 1873 (*Letters*, v. 372): as women became more politically organized; and as they came to recognize themselves and their struggles.

Influence: this word is at the very centre of Victorian debates about women and power. The 'true secret of woman's political influence, the true object of her political enlightenment', Sarah Lewis wrote in the ultra-conservative *Woman's Mission* (1839), was as a 'moral agent' aloof from 'the actual collision of political contests, and screened from the passions which such engender'.[12] Significantly, when Eliot conceives of her art as at once ethical and autonomous—independent from sectarian, political, and market forces—she does so in terms which explicitly invoke the rhetoric of these conservative conduct manuals: art, like the womanly woman, is an 'active influence for good' (*Biography*, p. 463). Eliot's objective in this bold appropriation was not simply to offer a critique of conservative sexual ideology, however, but to show that the 'special moral influence' of women need be no poor substitute for political power if it could be seen to share something with the special moral influence of art. When Ladislaw impulsively calls Dorothea a poem in chapter 22 of *Middlemarch*, he rather too readily agrees that she could not be a poet (because she is a woman), and is ironized for it. But what he says precisely sums up the conjunction in Eliot's thought of femininity and culture—by which she meant the 'verbal equivalent for the

highest mental result of past and present influences' (*Letters*, iv. 395).
In this way, Eliot radicalizes conservative ideology. She is brutally
honest about the real conditions of women's power and powerlessness; at the same time she makes much larger claims for the influence
of women on the historical evolution of society and culture.

Even more radically, Eliot proposes that the motive force for this
influence is passion: that—to sexual conservatives—most dangerous
and unwomanly force. Her heroines, in 'the sway of a passion against
which [they struggle] as a trespass' (*The Mill on the Floss*, book 7,
chapter 2), must learn to find the right balance between the impulse
to power—always in conflict with 'a need of being loved' (book 1,
chapter 5)—and the impulse to self-abnegation. 'The great problem
of the shifting relation between passion and duty' (book 7, chapter 2)
does not set passion and duty in opposition to each other as *eros* and
ethos, or unwomanliness and womanliness. Rightly understood, they
are each part of the other; and it is not until they are rightly understood by Eliot's heroines that the narratives can reach a point of
closure. This process is so long and arduous because ambition is the
mark of all these heroines. It is also, paradoxically, the characteristic
by which they are most sharply distinguished. Women 'go in pairs in
George Eliot's novels', as one contemporary reviewer remarked
(*CH*, p. 239), and versions of the dark and light woman (Dorothea
and Rosamond) or the angel and the whore (Dinah and Hetty) are
constantly turning up. But Eliot also deliberately destabilizes these
oppositions, in superficial ways (Dinah and Rosamond are both
blonde, for example) and in more profound ways. Like Rebecca in
Ivanhoe, Maggie Tulliver is intelligent, unruly, and exotic-looking,
and is aware that the dark woman can never triumph because of her
essential unwomanliness. Blonde Lucy Deane, on the other hand,
represents order and stability—womanliness—and for all her
insipidity, is never satirized in the novel. Indeed, Maggie and Lucy
meet on terms of mutual understanding, as Rosamond and Dorothea
do in *Middlemarch*, and Gwendolen and Mirah in *Daniel Deronda*.
Eliot's aim is to break across the defining antitheses of the conservative sexual orthodoxy—the sexless 'womanly woman' of the
domestic ideal versus the dangerously sexualized 'unwomanly
woman' who demands to live outside that ideal—and across the
defining antitheses of the debates on the woman question: conservatism versus feminism; private sphere versus public sphere; education

for wifehood and motherhood versus education for work. To achieve this, Eliot reconfigures womanliness and unwomanliness as the opposition between a young woman who is passionate and intelligent, and who struggles 'towards a noble life' (*CH*, p. 109), and a young woman who is passionate and intelligent, and who strives for social advancement. Of the former, whom we might call the self-searching heroines, Maggie Tulliver, Romola Bardi, and Dorothea Brooke are the fullest expression. They are, as one contemporary reviewer said of Dorothea, 'full of nobility of the highest kind, but without a definite practical sphere, and compelled to lavish [their lives] on spiritual efforts to subdue [their] own enthusiasm, [their] throbbing, inward yearning for a higher life' (*CH*, p. 301). Of the latter, Hetty Sorrel, Esther Lyon (initially), and Rosamond Vincy are the most straightforward representatives. They are the pretty, 'pleasure-craving' (*Adam Bede*, chapter 31) women who are, for the most part, oblivious to the existence of any life more noble, more consequential, than their small lives. They are vain, selfish, and without the heightened moral consciousness or authentic refinement of their opposites. But they are just as full of longing and ambition, which is expressed as emotional manipulation and domination within their restricted sphere. And their massive moral unconsciousness, joined with an 'inborn energy of egoistic desire' and an intense sexuality, endows them with an 'iridescence of . . . character' (*Daniel Deronda*, chapter 4) that is as luminous in its own way as the wordy inner turmoil of their more earnest counterparts.

Eliot's self-searching heroine arrives, fully formed, with Maggie Tulliver, one of the most remarkable heroines in nineteenth-century fiction: as original as Jane Eyre, Emma Bovary, Anna Karenina, or Isabel Archer, and utterly unlike any other woman in the English novel. Maggie is ordinary, but beneath her ordinariness, Eliot shows us a powerful intellectual ambition gradually crushed by everyday struggles: what she calls the collision between 'the outward and the inward' life (*The Mill on the Floss*, book 3, chapter 5). These struggles are not solely women's struggles, however, as the narrative insists, but the struggles of every ordinary person (Mr Tulliver or Mrs Moss) to make sense of a world that flows on unthinkingly and destructively, whether in the form of powerful natural forces or crushing social conventions. The novel's exploration of 'the all important question of women's access to knowledge and culture and to the power that goes with them', is therefore embedded in an exploration of the wider conflict between subjective experience and objective knowledge.[13] To live is to be puzzled, as Mr Tulliver is, unable to understand one's own nature, let alone the nature of things. The novel's passionate critique of the inadequacy of women's education is therefore also situated in this wider context of individuals' yearning for 'some explanation of this hard, real life . . . some key that would enable her to understand, and, in understanding, endure' (book 4, chapter 3). All of Eliot's striving heroines are in search of this key, which is to be found, Eliot asserts, not in intellectual aspiration but in love:

It is a wonderful subduer, this need of love—this hunger of the heart—as peremptory as that other hunger by which Nature forces us to submit to the yoke, and change the face of the world. (book 1, chapter 5)

Maggie is indeed subdued by this 'strongest need in [her] nature' (book 1, chapter 5), and tormented by the restlessness of her striving consciousness.

Eliot continues to explore the idea of the woman who is 'essentially noble but liable to great error—error that is anguish to its own nobleness' (*Letters*, iii. 318) in Romola Bardi, who, like Maggie, seeks in 'the bonds of . . . strong affection' the 'deepest secret of human blessedness' (*Romola*, chapter 61). Disillusioned by Tito, she turns to Savonarola, whose extremist political reforms are driven by the union of religious fervour, intellect, and revolutionary idealism. But the Frate is as false as the arch-politicians he condemned. By the end of the novel, Romola is desperate: she wants 'any great purpose, any end of existence which could ennoble endurance and exalt the common deeds of a dusty life with divine ardours'. Disguised in her 'grey religious dress' (as Dorothea is in Rome), she abandons hope of finding any 'form of believing love' that would lead her to act as an 'inward constraining existence' and guide her into 'that supremely hallowed motive which men call duty'. What she is left with is what Maggie is left with: an unbearable 'burden of choice'. Like Maggie, Romola longs to fall asleep and, drifting in a boat on the tide, 'to commit herself, sleeping, to destiny' (chapter 61). When she wakes near a village where plague-infected Jews have been dumped, she also wakes to find her great vocation. Freed from the burden of choice in the 'village of the unburied dead' she becomes 'the blessed

Lady' who does 'beautiful loving deeds there, rescuing those who were ready to perish' (chapter 68).

   The image of Romola as Madonna calls up conventional Victorian images of femininity, but Eliot is looking far beyond that. To find the great purpose that will exalt the common deeds of a dusty life, Eliot's striving heroines must let go of their minds, and trust to what is essentially an anti-intellectual and a *feminine* vocation:

she had simply lived, with so energetic an impulse to share the life around her, to answer the call of need and do the work which cried aloud to be done, that the reasons for living, enduring, labouring, never took the form of argument. (chapter 69)

To live without the torment of consciousness is to give up aspirations to greatness, to recognize that she is not 'something higher' (chapter 69) but someone ordinary.

   Like Maggie and Romola, Dorothea is 'certainly troublesome—to herself chiefly'. She is 'a girl whose ardent nature turned all her small allowance of knowledge into principles, fusing her actions into their mould, and whose quick emotions gave the most abstract things the quality of a pleasure or a pain' (*Middlemarch*, chapter 20). This ardour encompasses both knowledge and an instinct towards sympathy and moral action. Yet Dorothea is ashamed of her own feelings, powerless to know what to do with them:

She was humiliated to find herself a mere victim of feeling, as if she could know nothing except through that medium: all her strength was scattered in fits of agitation, of struggle, of despondency, and then again in visions of more complete renunciation, transforming all hard conditions into duty. (chapter 20)

This is a typical crisis for Eliot's self-searching heroines. Dorothea, like Maggie and Romola, is afflicted with 'fits' of agitation and despondency, brief moments of passionate insight which burn out almost immediately because they can find no sustained expression in action—except, ultimately, in the very principle of renunciation itself: denying oneself delight, and making life bearable and meaningful by making an idol of duty.

   Set against the women who 'round and complete' men's existence are those who '"hinder men's lives"' (*Felix Holt, the Radical*, chapter 10). The model for these is Hetty Sorrel, whose originality as a fictional creation is sometimes overlooked. One contemporary reviewer of the novel observed that Hetty was 'one of those who are so much less than they seem to be, whose most significant acts mean so little, that it is not easy to fix upon any central principle in their nature, any strong point of thought, or word, or act which belongs to them' (*CH*, p. 82). Hetty is strongly defined against Dinah Morris: 'What a strange contrast the two figures made!' (*Adam Bede*, chapter 15). Dinah, in her mid-twenties, has 'pale reddish hair', one of those faces 'that make one think of white flowers with light touches of colour on their pure petals', and a 'total absence of self-consciousness in her demeanour' (chapter 2). Hetty is 17, with a 'cheek like a rose-petal', dark eyes and dark hair (chapter 7), and 'rounded neck' and 'dimpled arm' (chapter 33). Eliot complicates these oppositions, however, by having Dinah think of Hetty as a 'sister', and having Hetty dress up as Dinah at the Poysers' table. Hetty's very presence in the book, moreover, is framed by Dinah and by sinfulness. Dinah is the first to mention her, using familiar Victorian symbolism of the fallen woman, as ' "that poor wandering lamb Hetty Sorrel" ' (chapter 3); and almost the last to speak of her—again as the ' "foolish lost lamb" ' (chapter 35). Yet Dinah is a kind of wanderer too, ' "walking and preaching" ' (chapter 6); and she is also ' "a lovely young woman on whom men's eyes are fixed" ' (chapter 8). The structural relationship between Dinah and Hetty does not approach the complexity of the 'equivalent centre[s] of self' (*Middlemarch*, chapter 21) in later novels, but it sets the pattern for the relationships between Dorothea and Rosamond in *Middlemarch*, and Gwendolen and Mirah in *Daniel Deronda*.

In ways that look forward to Rosamond and Gwendolen, Hetty is distinguished from the grave and intense Dinah chiefly by the fact that hers is 'a luxurious and vain nature, not a passionate one' (*Adam Bede*, chapter 31). Yet, like her successors (*and* her apparent opposites—Maggie and Dorothea, for example), she is strongly associated with the symbolism of sexual passion—with music and animals particularly. The very potency of her sexuality in fact masks the superficiality of her character even from someone as insightful as Adam, who falls in love with her (as Lydgate later does with Rosamond) in complete ignorance of it. She is constantly associated with the misinterpretation of beauty as refinement and complexity of feeling:

Hetty's face had a language that transcended her feelings. There are faces which nature charges with a meaning and pathos not belonging [to them] . . . but speaking the joys and sorrows of foregone generations . . . just as a national language may be instinct with poetry unfelt by the lips that use it. (chapter 26)

That the body of a woman who is neither especially intelligent nor especially good might be an unconscious vehicle for such transcendent passions indicates once again how the feminine and the aesthetic are interlocked in her revisionary idea of the cultural power of a woman's influence:

For the beauty of a lovely woman is like music: what can one say more? Beauty has an expression beyond and far above the one woman's soul that it clothes, as the words of genius have a wider meaning than the thought that prompted them: it is more than a woman's love that moves us in a woman's eyes—it seems to be a far-off mighty love that has come near to us, and made speech for itself there; the rounded neck, the dimpled arm, move us by something more than their prettiness—by their close kinship with all we have known of tenderness and peace. (chapter 33)

Hetty's confession and repentance form the climax of *Adam Bede*, as Janet Dempster's do in 'Janet's Repentance'. Like Janet, Hetty has been ill-used by a man—not beaten, as Janet is, but seduced by Arthur Donnithorne. Where in the earlier story the plot anatomized the processes by which suffering is redemptive, and did so by showing how culpability and guilt are transferred from an irredeemably bad man to a woman whose only sin is to take refuge in alcoholism, in *Adam Bede* the iconic figure of the fallen woman is sufficient to encompass both victimhood and criminality. The plot therefore turns on an unspeakable act, a mother killing her own child, which is the evil consequence ' "folded in a single act of selfish indulgence" ' (chapter 41), a consequence visited too upon an innocent man, Adam, whose his 'unspeakable suffering' wakens him 'into a new state . . . [of] full consciousness' (chapter 42). For Hetty, it is also an awakening. The 'hidden dread' (chapter 36)—an unwanted pregnancy kept secret—brings down upon her the fate of the fallen woman:

hidden behind the apple-blossoms, or among the golden corn, or under the shrouding boughs of the wood, there might be a human heart beating heavily with anguish: perhaps a young blooming girl, not knowing where to turn for refuge from swift-advancing shame; understanding no more of this life of ours than a foolish lost lamb wandering farther and farther in the nightfall on the lonely heath; yet tasting the bitterest of life's bitterness. (chapter 35)

Hetty's pain rises up and takes over the last chapters, eclipsing Adam's righteous suffering and drawing the narrator out:

My heart bleeds for her as I see her toiling along on her weary feet, or seated in a cart, with her eyes fixed vacantly on the road before her, never thinking or caring whither it tends, till hunger comes and makes her desire that a village may be near. (chapter 37)

It does so, too, without ever succumbing to a sentimental reversal in which Hetty would be transformed from a 'lower nature' (chapter 15) to a higher nature. Her 'hard unloving despairing soul' (chapter 37) is transformed by confession, and she is freed from the dread that would condemn her to a ceaseless wandering in the wilderness, but Hetty never knows 'what it is to have suffered and be healed, to have despaired and to have recovered hope' (chapter 31). Like Arthur and Adam, Hetty has no vision of consequences, and must accept the punishment for her act. Limited to 'a narrow fantastic calculation of her own probable pleasures and pains' she leaps 'from a temporary sorrow into a life-long misery' (chapter 31).

In Rosamond Vincy, Eliot develops these aspects of Hetty's character and situation, incorporating muted features of the femme fatale (only fully represented in Eliot in the character of Bertha Grant in her short romance tale, 'The Lifted Veil'). Yet Rosamond is a far subtler creation than Hetty, to which Eliot brings a much greater degree of psychological penetration. She is clever, 'a sylph caught young and educated at Mrs. Lemon's' (*Middlemarch*, chapter 16):

Rosamond never showed any unbecoming knowledge, and was always that combination of correct sentiments, music, dancing, drawing, elegant note-writing, private album for extracted verse, and perfect blond loveliness, which made the irresistible woman for the doomed man of that date. Think no unfair evil of her, pray: she had no wicked plots, nothing sordid or mercenary; in fact, she never thought of money except as something necessary which other people would always provide. She was not in the habit of devising falsehoods, and if her statements were no direct clue to fact, why, they were not intended in that light—they were among her elegant accomplishments, intended to please. Nature had inspired many arts in finishing Mrs. Lemon's favourite pupil, who by general consent (Fred's excepted) was a rare compound of beauty, cleverness, and amiability. (chapter 27)

Rosamond lives by stratagem. She is capable of a 'quiet gravity' when it is called for, which amounts to a talent for 'not showing her dimples on the wrong occasion' (chapter 12). Like Hetty, she is associated with music, and her accomplished piano playing seems to reveal hidden depths—a 'hidden soul seemed to be flowing forth from Rosamond's fingers'—so that Lydgate is 'taken possession of, and began to believe in her as something exceptional' (chapter 16).

This is Rosamond's 'social romance' (chapter 12), constructed whenever she needs 'to vary the flatness of her life' (chapter 75). She has 'a great sense of being a romantic heroine, and playing the part prettily' (chapter 31). Lydgate too is under the illusion of Rosamond's sweet submissiveness:

his old dreamland, in which Rosamond Vincy appeared to be that perfect piece of womanhood who would reverence her husband's mind after the fashion of an accomplished mermaid, using her comb and looking-glass and singing her song for the relaxation of his adored wisdom alone. (chapter 58)

Lydgate is 'completely mastered by the outrush of tenderness at the sudden belief that this sweet young creature depended on him for her joy' (chapter 31). But her submissiveness is part of her cleverness, as he discovers:

He had regarded Rosamond's cleverness as precisely of the receptive kind which became a woman. He was now beginning to find out what that cleverness was—what was the shape into which it had run as into a close network aloof and independent. No one quicker than Rosamond to see causes and effects which lay within the track of her own tastes and interests. (chapter 58)

With 'that victorious obstinacy which never wastes its energy in impetuous resistance' (chapter 58), Rosamond does what she likes, and keeps Lydgate 'under control' (chapter 64). Overcome by his 'anxiety about ways and means' (chapter 58), becoming entrapped in the Bulstrode scandal, and learning of her ill-advised secret letter to his cousin, Lydgate wants to 'tell her brutally that he was master, and she must obey . . . [but] he had a growing dread of Rosamond's quiet elusive obstinacy, which would not allow any assertion of power to be final' (chapter 64).

Late in the novel, Rosamond gains a dim, momentary insight into the insignificance of her power and the triviality of her life. She is made aware, as Gwendolen Harleth will be, of something much larger. Repulsed by Will Ladislaw, she finds herself 'almost losing the sense of her identity, and ... waking into some new terrible existence' (chapter 78). As in *Adam Bede*, the epiphany occurs in a sort of confession scene with her dark-haired counterpart, Dorothea, in which Rosamond is 'hurried along in a new movement which gave all things some new, awful, undefined aspect' (chapter 81):

she was under the first great shock that had shattered her dream-world in which she had been easily confident of herself and critical of others; and this strange unexpected manifestation of feeling in a woman whom she had approached with a shrinking aversion and dread, as one who must necessarily have a jealous hatred towards her, made her soul totter all the more with a sense that she had been walking in an unknown world which had just broken in upon her. (chapter 81)

But Rosamond is not 'alone in that scene'. In the previous chapter, after a night of despair, Dorothea had undergone her own epiphany. In 'the chill hours of the morning twilight', she had gone back over every moment of a scene she thought she had witnessed (Will and Rosamond in love with each other). Finally, she asks herself: 'Was it her event only? She forced herself to think of it as bound up with another woman's life'. She vows to '"clutch"' her own pain and '"compel it to silence"' (chapter 80), and decides to visit Mrs Lydgate. Dorothea, 'pale and changed', stands opposite Rosamond, who looks 'like the lovely ghost of herself' (chapter 81); together they reach a common understanding about suffering and resignation. This is a remarkable moment, this coming together of the vain, empty-headed woman and the self-searching, ardent, intellectual woman.

In the configuration of its female protagonists, *Daniel Deronda* more closely resembles *Adam Bede* than *Middlemarch*. The womanly Mirah Cohen is consigned to the margins of the novel, as Dinah Morris (whose name is faintly echoed in Mirah's) had been. Gwendolen Harleth, however, although she is in a direct line of descent from Hetty Sorrel, is the first of Eliot's vain, ambitious, pleasure-seeking heroines to be given room to grow, and given an inner life on the scale of a Maggie or a Dorothea. This presents enormous challenges to the analysis of women and power Eliot had pursued up to that point—not just in the major protagonists, but in the minor characters. (Eliot's middle-aged and older women, for example, married or widowed, are portraits of female power. Those like Mrs Poyser, Mrs Glegg, and Mrs Cadwallader, who are 'confident first in the superiority of the female sex' (*CH*, p. 102), are balanced by those women whose real superiority is thwarted, and who suffer: Janet Dempster, Mrs Moss, Harriet Bulstrode, and above all Mrs Transome in *Felix Holt, the Radical*.) Gwendolen's story takes off, in a way, from Rosamond's. She is, quite explicitly, the 'spoiled child': the beautiful, accomplished, clever young woman who wields absolute power in her tiny social circle. Where Rosamond is polished and brittle, however, Gwendolen is spirited and imperious, with 'a certain fierceness of maidenhood in her' (*Daniel Deronda*, chapter 7) which is pointedly associated with the goddess Diana. She feels an over-powering physical repulsion to men, and is a supreme hunter (in the archery contests) and horse-rider, whose 'inborn energy of egoistic desire' (chapter 4) is like an 'animal stimulus', unchecked until she is married. Much of the first half of the novel is given over to an exploration of the power promised by maidenhood, which allows women (in Gwendolen's mind) to ' "do what they like" ' (chapter 7). Gwendolen's great ambition is to be powerful in spite of marriage:

her thoughts never dwelt on marriage as the fulfilment of her ambition; the dramas in which she imagined herself a heroine were not wrought up to that close. To be very much sued or hopelessly sighed for as a bride was indeed an indispensable and agreeable guarantee of womanly power; but to become a wife and wear all the domestic fetters of that condition, was on the whole a vexatious necessity. Her observation of matrimony had inclined her to think it rather a dreary state, in which a woman could not do what she liked, had more children than were desirable, was consequently dull, and became irrevocably immersed in humdrum. Of course marriage was social promotion; she could not look forward to a single life; but promotions have sometimes to be taken with bitter herbs—a peerage will not quite do instead of leadership to the man who meant to lead; and this delicate-limbed sylph of twenty meant to lead. (chapter 4)

In *Daniel Deronda*, power is represented as the power to choose (and the novel's ethical dilemmas similarly revolve around the fact that no choices are without consequences). As in earlier novels, Gwendolen is overwhelmed by circumstances (the financial collapse of Grapnell and Co.) from which her own nature cannot retrieve her (she will not take a position as a governess), and for which her limited education and accomplishments are useless. Eliot deliberately draws a parallel between her situation and Mirah's (both audition for Herr Klesmer, for instance), in order to set up a contrast between the destinies of ordinary and exceptional women:

[Gwendolen] rejoiced to feel herself exceptional; but her horizon was that of the genteel romance where the heroine's soul poured out in her journal is full of vague power, originality, and general rebellion, while her life moves strictly in the sphere of fashion; and if she wanders into a swamp, the pathos lies partly, so to speak, in her having on her satin shoes. Here is a restraint which nature and society have provided on the pursuit of striking adventure; so that a soul burning with a sense of what the universe is not, and ready to take all existence as fuel, is nevertheless held captive by the ordinary wirework of social forms and does nothing particular. (chapter 6)

Daniel Deronda is the one novel of Eliot's to focus on the figure of the exceptional woman—the woman of great gifts who chooses to pursue those gifts in preference to wifehood and motherhood. Unknown to him, Daniel's mother is the Princess Halm-Eberstein, once known as the famous singer Alcharisi. Nearing death, she summons him to Genoa to reveal to him his Jewish identity and explain why she left him to Sir Hugo's care—not just because she wanted him to have the advantages of an English gentleman, but because she simply did not want him:

'Every woman is supposed to have the same set of motives, or else to be a monster. I am not a monster, but I have not felt exactly what other women feel—or say they feel, for fear of being thought unlike others. When you reproach me in your heart for sending you away from me, you mean that I ought to say I felt about you as other women say they feel about their children. I did *not* feel that. I was glad to be freed from you.' (chapter 51)

The Princess is, as Gillian Beer points out, a significant figure in Eliot's work: 'the passional, declarative woman, essentially creative, and freed from the ordinary conditions of living as a woman'.[14] ' "You are not a woman," ' she exclaims to Deronda. ' "You may try—but you can never imagine what it is to have a man's force of genius in you, and yet to suffer the slavery of being a girl"' (chapter 51). But she is not, of course, an Englishwoman, and it may be argued that Eliot is able to explore this dangerous ground—the woman of genius who rejects maternity: a woman somewhat like herself—through an exotic and safely remote figure. But the novel is elsewhere just as candid about the slavery of being a girl and the taboos surrounding it: in particular, in its representation of sexual cruelty and rape in marriage. Gwendolen's is more than just an unhappy marriage. It is where she learns that there are only those with power and those who suffer under those with power; where all actions are motivated only by will or fear:

Gwendolen's will had seemed imperious in its small girlish sway; but it was the will of a creature with a large discourse of imaginative fears: a shadow would have been enough to relax its hold. And she had found a will like that of a crab or a boa-constrictor which goes on pinching or crushing without alarm at thunder. Not that Grandcourt was without calculation of the intangible effects which were the chief means of mastery; indeed he had a surprising acuteness in detecting that situation of feeling in Gwendolen which made her proud and rebellious spirit dumb and helpless before him. (chapter 35)

Eliot draws on the topical language of imperialism to describe Gwendolen's maidenly power over her 'domestic empire' (chapter 4), and again to describe the devastating loss of that power in her 'husband's empire of fear' (chapter 35). (At another point Grandcourt is described as a 'white-handed man' who, if he had been sent 'to govern a difficult colony' would have exterminated the 'superseded proprietors' (chapter 48).) This rhetoric also has the effect of putting Gwendolen's narrowly localized experience into the much wider contexts of the novel—the outside world, the world of human history:

Could there be a slenderer, more insignificant thread in human history than this consciousness of a girl, busy with her small inferences of the way in which she could make her life pleasant?—in a time, too, when ideas were with fresh vigour making armies of themselves, and the universal kinship was declaring itself fiercely: when women on the other side of the world would not mourn for the husbands and sons who died bravely in a common cause, and men stinted of bread on our side of the world heard of that willing loss and were patient: a time when the soul of man was waking to pulses which had for centuries been beating in him unheard, until their full sum made a new life of terror or of joy.

What in the midst of that mighty drama are girls and their blind visions? (chapter 11)

This is not a rhetorical question. The narrator answers: 'They are the Yea or Nay of that good for which men are enduring and fighting. In these delicate vessels is borne onward through the ages the treasure of human affections' (chapter 11). This rousing affirmation of femininity—a conventional defence of the very oppressions the novel is criticizing—returns to a theme we found earlier at the heart of *Adam Bede*: women as bearers of the whole culture. Deronda, whose life has been a 'meditative yearning after wide knowledge' (chapter 16), discovers and embarks upon his epic enterprise—the founding of a Zionist state. Gwendolen, unlike Dorothea before her, experiences the presence of a wider knowledge not as yearning but as terror:

What she unwillingly recognized, and would have been glad for others to be unaware of, was that liability of hers to fits of spiritual dread, though this fountain of awe within her had not found its way into connection with the religion taught her or with any human relations. She was ashamed and frightened, as at what might happen again, in remembering her tremor on suddenly feeling herself alone, when, for example, she was walking without companionship and there came some rapid change in the light. Solitude in any wide scene impressed her with an undefined feeling of immeasurable existence aloof from her, in the midst of which she was helplessly incapable of asserting herself. The little astronomy taught her at school used sometimes to set her imagination at work in a way that made her tremble; but always when some one joined her she recovered her indifference to the vastness in which she seemed an exile; she found again her usual world in which her will was of some avail. (chapter 6)

Eliot makes the point in *Daniel Deronda* that lives 'are enlarged in different ways' (chapter 36), and it is significant that Gwendolen's enlargement entails her being left with nothing at the end of the novel. Nothing, that is, except a reassertion of her transformed will: ' "I mean to live" ', she assures her mother (chapter 69).

Yet this gesture also releases Gwendolen, as Maggie, Romola, and Dorothea had been released, from 'the assiduous unrest of doing' into the 'serene dignity of being', returning us to the problematic question of women's influence: that imagined power—'incalculably diffusive', as the *Middlemarch* Finale puts it—that Eliot's women radiate beyond their lives and beyond the texts they inhabit. We cannot, I would suggest, fully understand the force of these endings if we fall into the trap of thinking of these women as just women. To some extent Eliot's richly grounded realism encourages us to do this. But it is far from being a naively reflectionist realism, and we are never allowed to forget that they are characters, whose influence in the world is incalculably diffusive precisely because they are characters—literary creations. They exist as part of a complex and contradictory discursive exploration of femininity and its possibilities and limitations; and what happens to them happens inside that discursive context. This was recognized by Richard Simpson, who, in a contemporary review that was both astute and hostile, accused Eliot of a 'misconception' of the relations between the sexes which led to 'an error in the essence of things':

Women work more by influence than by force, by example than reasoning, by silence than speech: the authoress grasps at direct power through reasoning and speech. Having thus taken up the male position, the male ideal becomes hers,—the ideal of power,—which, interpreted by the feminine heart and intellect, means the supremacy of passion in the affairs of the world. (*CH*, p. 241)

We should not lose sight of the fact that the self-effacing destinies of Eliot's heroines were invented and analysed and celebrated in narratives which also seize the 'direct power' of 'reasoning and speech' from the world of men and interpret it with 'feminine heart and intellect: they declare 'the supremacy of passion in the affairs of the world'. But nor should we attempt to resolve the contradictions that lie at the heart of Eliot's representation of women. In their very oppression women embody Eliot's ideal state of moral being—the 'growing moral force to lighten the pressure of hard non-moral outward conditions' (*Letters*, viii. 402–3). From one point of view, they have carried 'the evangelical faith in duty and renunciation' from the age of belief into the agnostic age, as G. M. Young recognized, astutely calling Eliot's ethic 'a woman's ethic';[15] and they have learned in the process 'the great amount of social unproductive labour which needs to be done' (*Letters*, iv. 425) to achieve social advancement. But Eliot also believed that a 'thorough recognition' of women's 'worse share in existence' should be the basis not for resistance or reform but for 'a sublimer resignation in woman' (*Letters*, viii. 402). She did not, I believe, choose that word—

sublimer—offhandedly. She means, precisely, a *passionate* resignation, one that is more exalted and noble (than that of men); but also one that is unsettling, that is associated with terror as well as beauty, and with the infinite, and with that characteristic of art to elevate its readers.

CHAPTER 6

ELIOT AND RELIGION

WRITING to her former teacher and spiritual mentor Maria Lewis in 1840, the 20-year-old Mary Ann Evans, then a fervent evangelical Anglican, remembered the shock of reading Edward Bulwer-Lytton's novel *Devereux* (1829) several years earlier. She was 'considerably shaken', she confessed, to find that the novel included a 'very amiable atheist' (*Letters*, i. 45), an Italian named Bezoni, who for all his 'dark doctrine' lived a virtuous life and died 'attending the victims of a fearful and contagious disease' (*Letters*, i. 45 n. 8). This character left her with the impression that 'religion was not a requisite to moral excellence', she wrote, and that atheism could seem 'wonderfully calculated to promote social happiness' (*Letters*, i. 45). Seventeen years later few readers of *Scenes of Clerical Life* could have identified the unknown 'George Eliot'—apparently a clergyman himself—as an atheist who was to become 'the first great *godless* writer of fiction' in England (*CH*, p. 453). Like *Devereux*, Eliot's fiction was 'wonderfully calculated' to promote the idea that religion was not a requisite to moral excellence and that unbelief was indeed a powerful agent of social happiness. Yet there are no avowed or dogmatic atheists of Bezoni's kind in *Scenes of Clerical Life*—or in any of Eliot's novels. On the contrary, there are a great many Christians: most of them undogmatic middle-of-the-road Anglicans; and some of them devout evangelical Protestants, both Low Church Anglicans and Dissenters of various sects, the best of whom Eliot treats with love and reverence (such as Dinah in *Adam Bede*), and the worst with deep compassion (such as Bulstrode in *Middlemarch*).

Of course this goes without saying. Eliot was a realist, and committed to the representation of things as they were: even in an era of such profound crisis in religious faith, most provincial English men and women would have professed themselves believers, notwithstanding that it was belief of an easygoing untheoretical kind. Nor should it surprise us that Eliot would privilege the unselfconscious loving-kindness of those people in her liberal humanistic atheism.

She felt deep emotional bonds with the orthodox Tory Anglicanism of her 'earliest associations and most poetic memories' (*Letters*, iv. 214), much more than with the exacting Calvinist faith of her youth, whose values and symbols were, however, so thoroughly absorbed into her thought and art. But Eliot went further than this. She refused to indulge in 'negative propagandism' (*Letters*, iv. 64–5):

Pray don't ever ask me again [she wrote to her good friend Barbara Bodichon] not to rob a man of his religious belief, as if you thought my mind tended towards such robbery. I have too profound a conviction of the efficacy that lies in all sincere faith, and the spiritual blight that comes with No-faith. (*Letters*, iv. 64)

Eliot felt 'no antagonism towards any religious belief, but a strong outflow of sympathy'[1] towards communities meeting to 'worship the highest Good (which is understood to be expressed by God)' (*Letters*, v. 448). At the same time she was highly critical of the many ways that worship—the affirmation of sacredness in daily observances—had become corrupted by zealotry, chicanery, and arid institutional habits and formulas. *Silas Marner* offers a deeply felt critique of such corruptions: Silas is exiled from the fanatical Dissenting sect which is his whole life by a drawing of lots, and is saved only by 'the remedial influence of pure, natural human relations' (*Letters*, iii. 382) embodied in people who know 'nothing of abstractions' (*Silas Marner*, chapter 2)—who practise only undoctrinal parish Anglicanism. Eliot was also critical of the rise of populist evangelicalism: the 'superficial, Grocer's-back-parlour view of Calvinistic Christianity' (*Letters*, v. 121) peddled by celebrity evangelical preachers. Her (unsigned) 1855 *Westminster Review* essay, 'Evangelical Teaching: Dr Cumming', represents her most sustained and hostile attack on the inhumanity and narrowness of fundamentalism, with its 'confused notions' of 'biblical interpretation' (*Essays*, p. 177). This essay also foreshadows Eliot's own characteristic humanism, locating 'the idea of God' in human sympathy:

But Dr. Cumming's God . . . is a God who instead of sharing and aiding our human sympathies, is directly in collision with them; who instead of strengthening the bond between man and man . . . thrusts himself between them and forbids them to feel for each other except as they have relation to Him. (*Essays*, p. 188)

The Cumming essay shows the importance of Eliot's early evangelical Protestant faith—she was a fervent Calvinist from 1830 until 1841—to her secular humanism. It also shows how important she believed atheistic rationalism was to the survival of Christian ethics after Christianity—an ethics under siege by industrial modernity. She rejected Christianity, but 'the poetry of the old faith'[2] had 'soaked itself too deeply into the fibre of her thought and feeling for her to give it up as well'.[3] That is the common view of the origin of Eliot's 'seriousness, her moral insistence, her presentation of the law of consequences and of determinism (clearly related to the doctrine of the "wages of sin" and predestination), and notably . . . the notion that "Work is worship"'.[4]

It would be wrong, though, to think that Eliot experienced a last-minute failure of rationalist nerve; that, finding herself unable to face the consequences of her own scepticism, she took shelter again in the underlying ethos of her abandoned faith. The atheistic humanism she conceived in the 1840s and 1850s *was* profoundly Christian, a reaching towards what she called a 'religion of the future' (*Letters*, vi. 216): the 'new religion of humanity' (*CH*, p. 456). But this can be viewed in two quite different ways. For the conservative polemical satirist W. H. Mallock, Eliot's novels were 'without God, not against Him. They do not deny, but they silently and skilfully ignore Him. . . . The glory and devotion that was once given to God is transferred silently to man' (*CH*, p. 454). On the other hand, we should recognize that Eliot was not simply fudging the issue. She was doing what Cumming and his followers would not do: 'honestly and seriously endeavouring to meet and solve what he knows to be the real difficulties' with religious belief (*Essays*, p. 174). Viewed thus, Eliot's humanism was not a nostalgic secularization of anachronistic beliefs and cultural orientations—fragments of a lost faith held over against modern moral ruin. Christianity was its foundational condition. Eliot may have been an instinctive conservative, and her reverence for the cultural past certainly contributed to her desire to reshape Christian culture for an age of advancing scientific discovery. But it was rather her unshakeable faith in human advancement and secular reason that led her to follow progressive thinkers in Germany and England in discarding primitive Christian superstitions that did not stand up to rational scrutiny: the existence of a divine supernatural being; the immortality of the soul; the

Godhead of the historical Jesus. But that same progressivism informed her essentially Christian ethical humanism. If for many readers Eliot was, as Mallock contended in 1878, 'a suppressed theist' and 'a person intoxicated with God',[5] she was also a person deeply imbued with the secularist intellectual tendencies of her age. Theism is not suppressed in Eliot: as a notebook entry in 1862 reveals, she believed in the 'Necessity of strong theistic feeling as a preparation for the Religion of Humanity'.[6] Strong theistic feeling is precisely what characterizes her atheistic humanism, formed as it is from the 'inner substance' of Christianity, which, as Richard Simpson observed in 1863, 'having ever existed as a germ within the shell . . . will be displayed in all its fresh ripeness when the dead husk drops away' (*CH*, p. 224).

Sometimes in Eliot theistic feeling is vested in strong individuals who act as ethical touchstones for the rest of the characters: Deronda, most obviously, stands 'in the stead of God' (*Daniel Deronda*, chapter 64) to Gwendolen (Grandcourt, Deronda's obverse, is also a kind of god, a vestige of the absolutist gods of pagan belief). Eliot's narrators, too, have a godlike omniscience. But more often, the idea of God—godliness—is transposed into Eliot's idea of a 'higher life' or 'Higher Good'. The 'spiritual blight that comes with No-faith' is therefore not the blight that comes with the loss of Christian faith but the blight that comes with the loss of faith in the existence of this higher life—all too likely in an age of rationalism and materialism which disproves the existence of a supernatural being and renounces religious belief. But what did Eliot mean by the higher life? First of all, she meant that 'vivid sympathetic experience' that exists in the here and now: not the promise of some transcendent or visionary realm beyond the everyday, but the transcendence that comes from relinquishing the comforts of such a realm. But the here and now is, of itself, meaningless; for vivid sympathetic experience is not possible without a strong sense of the past and vision of the future. The higher life is accordingly what we would now describe as 'culture': not literature and art but 'common memories and habits of mind' (*Impressions of Theophrastus Such*, 'The Modern Hep! Hep! Hep!'). In the earlier novels these memories and habits are laid down in local communities. They are 'the loves and sanctities of our life' which have their 'deep immovable roots in memory' (*The Mill on the Floss*, book 2, chapter 1). By the end of her career, however, Eliot recognized that one of the defining conditions of modern social life was the absence of an early home to foster those loves and sanctities. In its place she offered another organicist myth, of the whole cultural and spiritual memory of the West—a homeland which is no longer a nation-state but a state of culture. That homeland lay in Judaism and the Jewish people.

If for many readers Eliot represents 'a generation distracted between the intense need of believing and the difficulty of belief' (*CH*, p. 463), she was not altogether an exemplar of the mid-Victorian 'crisis of faith' herself. She lost her faith suddenly and completely sometime in 1841, the year she and her father moved to Foleshill near Coventry, and she met the Bray and Hennell families. From that moment she was untroubled by agnosticism: ultimately, the truth or otherwise of religions became unimportant to her. She was, however, deeply troubled by the implications of her own disbelief. She became what Basil Willey (describing Strauss) called a 'devout sceptic', rejecting traditional religion because she was 'too earnest to accept it'.[7] Later she would confide that this period, for all that its exhilarating rationalism liberated her soul 'from the wretched giant's bed of dogmas' (*Letters*, i. 162), also caused her a great deal of pain: 'for I had given up the form of Christian belief, and was in a crude state of free-thinking' (*Letters*, iii. 176). In this letter to Sara Hennell, she is referring playfully to Charles Bray and the radical freethinkers of the Rosehill circle in Coventry, including Sara's brother Charles Hennell, whose *An Inquiry Concerning the Origin of Christianity* (1839) she read in November 1841. This book was profoundly influential in the development of Eliot's ethical humanism. It was nothing less than 'a conjectural natural history of Christianity'[8] based upon 'a true account of the life of Jesus Christ, and of the spread of his religion' which found that the Gospels contained 'no deviation from the known laws of nature, nor to require, for their explanation, more than the operation of human motives and feelings'.[9] Hennell was among the first in England to question the historical accuracy of the Gospels, to assert that the miracles of Jesus did not deviate from the known laws of nature, and that the narratives of Jesus's life and teachings were combinations of myth and topical Jewish political history. Hennell was a Unitarian and did not believe in the divinity of Christ, but his research led him far beyond that issue. If Christianity was not 'divine revelation', then what was it? He concluded that it was 'the purest form yet existing of natural religion' which 'need no longer appeal for its support to the uncertain evidence of events which happened nearly two thousand years ago ... but ... will rest its claims on an evidence clearer, simpler, and always at hand,—the thoughts and feelings of the human mind itself'.[10]

When George Eliot was reading Hennell's *Inquiry* in the early 1840s, it was also coming to the attention of the leading German 'Higher Critic' of the Bible, David Friedrich Strauss, whose *Das Leben Jesu* (*The Life of Jesus*) had appeared in Germany three years earlier. *Das Leben Jesu* has been described as 'one of the landmarks and turning-points of nineteenth-century religious thought'.[11] It was considered to be an extremely dangerous book in England—'a book which a person can hardly read without being more or less hurt by it', Archdeacon Hare declared in 1839[12]—and when Mary Anne Evans began the work of translating it in January 1844, it was known only to a few readers. Strauss's critical method was historical and dialectical.[13] He laid out each and every event in Jesus's life as it was reported in the Four Gospels, and presented systematically the assertions of two opposing approaches to interpretation: that of the orthodox theologians, who viewed the Gospels as divine histories; and that of the rationalists, who sought to reconcile divine events with their natural explanations. Neither was satisfactory to Strauss, who proposed a third way, the mythical-poetical interpretation of each episode, which explained it in terms of earlier Old Testament myths or Hebrew poetry. Thus, Strauss looked at key episodes in the Gospels which required a suspension of ordinary physical laws (raising the dead, healing the blind, walking on water) and argued that they were not historical events or events that could be explained naturalistically.

Strauss's conclusions were radical and controversial.[14] They implied that it was necessary to replace Christian deism with a metaphysical system in which God and humanity were united not in Christ but in humanity itself. Men and women were the incarnation of God. Like Hennell, therefore, Strauss reframed religious experience as inward experience: God was not transcendent, but immanent. And, again like Hennell, he stopped short of seeing religious experience as a human psychological need, concluding that the 'supernatural birth of Christ, his miracles, his resurrection and ascension, remain eternal truths, whatever doubt may be cast on their reality as historical facts'.[15] The paramount importance of Strauss's work to nineteenth-century thought, and to Eliot, lies in the fact that he set out to write a destructive critique of the biblical and doctrinal views of Christ, which would enable him to abstract the true essence of Christian faith from the religious imagery with which it had been entangled.[16] Insight brought despair, however, for this 'alienated theologian': Strauss was 'not an atheist, but he was unable to believe in a transcendent, personal God who intervenes supernaturally in the course of nature and history'.[17]

Eliot was strongly sympathetic to Strauss's despair. The 'highest "calling and election"', she later wrote, 'is to *do without opium* and live through all our pain with conscious, clear-eyed endurance' (*Letters*, iii. 366). Yet she could not sympathize with Strauss's method, nor accept the consolations of metaphysics as an adequate substitute for religion. She was one of the foremost intellectuals to introduce German thought into England, and was an advocate for the 'truly philosophic spirit' (*Essays*, p. 36) native to Germany and sadly absent in England. But as an Englishwoman she was also resistant to the 'system-mongers' (*Essays*, p. 149) of German metaphysics, and found 'the greater solidity and directness of the English mind' (*Essays*, p. 30) more agreeable.[18] The relentless march of Strauss's crushing logic, and his tendency to displace the poetry and beauty of religious experience with an exhaustive metaphysical system ('the deepest philosophic truth'): all this was deeply uncongenial. In her first essay in the *Westminster Review* in 1851—a review of Robert Mackay's study of the religious mythologies of the Greeks and Hebrews, *The Progress of the Intellect* (1850)—Eliot was guarded about the positivist assumption that 'theological and metaphysical speculation have reached their limit, and that the only hope of extending man's sources of knowledge and happiness is to be found in positive science' (*Essays*, p. 28). This may look like a defence of Strauss's metaphysical speculation, but her remarks are squarely directed at the Comtean law of the three stages of knowledge (see below) which, she wrongly assumed, ignored the past and its 'practical bearing on the present' (*Essays*, p. 28). Later in the same essay, however, she writes:

it would be wise in our theological teachers, instead of struggling to retain a footing for themselves and their doctrine on the crumbling structure of dogmatic interpretation, to cherish those more liberal views of biblical criticism, which, admitting of a development of the Christian system corresponding to the wants and the culture of the age, would enable it to strike a firm root in man's moral nature, and to entwine itself with the growth of those new forms of social life to which we are tending. (*Essays*, p. 42)

Here are the beginnings of Eliot's conception of a post-Christian ethics and post-Christian culture. At its heart is an idea of progress: the progress of religion in step with the progress of the intellect and the society. Eliot's whole thought tends towards 'the development of the Christian system' (not its rejection), not just for the sake of reconciling it to inconvenient modern realities; but in order to secure it from anachronism and assure its universality and durability. Eliot's instinctively historical, organic, and scientific modes of thought underlie her conception: that 'divine revelation' is 'co-extensive with the history of human development, and is perpetually unfolding itself to our widened experience and investigation' (*Essays*, p. 30). How Christianity was actually to 'develop' to meet 'the wants and the culture of the age' and withstand the 'widened experience and investigation' of the nineteenth century remained an open question; one Eliot referred to the work of three very different philosophers—Comte, Spinoza, and Feuerbach.

The most important influence on Eliot's 'religion of humanity' was undoubtedly Ludwig Feuerbach's *The Essence of Christianity*. But as the (capitalized) phrase 'Religion of Humanity' more usually refers to the positive philosophy of Comte—and indeed Comtean positivism was not just a philosophy but a comprehensive social and religious system—it is important to examine Comte's less dramatic but no less important influence first, to avoid any confusion. In his *Cours de philosophie positive* (*Course in Positive Philosophy*) (1830–42) Comte traced the historical development of Western philosophy from its theological and metaphysical origins to its culmination in observational science, and especially a science of society: the discipline of sociology, of which he was a founder (see also the discussion of Comte in Chapter 7, below).[19] The *Cours* is therefore a historical study of the progress of the human mind, which Comte traced through three phases: the theological; the metaphysical; and the positive. The immature theological phase (the medieval period), was characterized by beliefs in gods and spirit forces. The succeeding metaphysical phase (between the Reformation and the failure of the French Revolution) was characterized by a misplaced faith in political, social, and philosophical abstractions. Finally, the positive phase evolved to a purer form of understanding, in which all phenomena were verifiable and measurable.

To Comte, Humanity—the 'Great Being . . . constituted by the beings, past, future, and present, which co-operate willingly in perfecting the order of the world'—was designed 'to meet men's religious needs and to replace God'.[20] The problem with Christian religion, Comte argued, was its encouragement of a selfish investment in personal immortality and its social irresponsibility in duping the poor with the promise of compensation in eternity. Religious experience was, in any case, the expression of an immature phase of human development. Eliot employs the language of Comtean positivism when she writes to Harriet Beecher Stowe in 1869:

I believe that religion too has to be modified—'developed,' according to the dominant phrase—and that a religion more perfect than any yet prevalent, must express less care for personal consolation, and a more deeply-awing sense of responsibility to man, springing from sympathy with that which of all things is most certainly known to us, the difficulty of the human lot. (*Letters*, v. 31)

Appropriately enough, Eliot's poem, 'O May I Join the Choir Invisible' (1867), was taken up as a positivist prayer in her friend Richard Congreve's Church of Humanity. Its cardinal sentiments—that the dead achieve immortality by living on in 'minds made better by their presence' and in thoughts that 'urge man's search | To vaster issues', contributing to 'the growing life of man' and the music that is 'the gladness of the world'—are sentiments expressed throughout the novels. As early as 1860 E. S. Dallas, reviewing *The Mill on the Floss* in *The Times*, recognized that in 'the highest sense we might call this a religious novel', even though religion 'is chiefly "conspicuous by its absence"' (*CH*, p. 136). The positivist Religion of Humanity is explicitly alluded to in *Romola*, in the late scenes in which the heroine, like a Renaissance Madonna, tends the plague-stricken villagers. More generally, Comtean positivism makes its most important contribution to Eliot's ethical humanism in the formulation of her notion of egoism. In keeping with the historical development of the mind, positivism stressed the progression of the ethical sensibility from a primitive phase of egoism (where personal needs and desires are foremost) to an advanced phase of altruism (where the needs and desires of the whole society are foremost). To be moral was consciously to minimize egoism and maximize altruism. This, in outline, is the trajectory of Eliot's moral plots. Gwendolen Harleth, for instance, is like a Comtean child, an egoistic primitive terrified by ghosts and thrown into 'fits of spiritual dread' by 'the vastness [of a universe] in which she seemed an exile' (*Daniel Deronda*, chapter 6). The closeted image of the death's head at Offendene, which springs open at the climax of her performance, signifies the harmfulness of repressing supernatural experience in a relentlessly materialistic advanced society. But it is also indicative of the 'puerile state of culture' to which Herr Klesmer adverts (chapter 5). In Comtean terms, the British conception of religious experience is fixed at an undeveloped stage: it has not moved on to that more enlightened conception of the higher life which Deronda will pursue. Having said that, so many other factors bear upon Eliot's plots and her notion of egoism (the passage from suffering to sympathy, the moral law of consequences), that it cannot be described as positivist in any straightforward way.

For example, Feuerbach, like Comte, believed that 'man can and should raise himself above the limits of his individuality, and not above the laws, the positive essential conditions of his species'.[21] Without God, enlightened individuals were isolated, and human power limited; but enlightened *societies* had the capacity for 'infinite' power.[22] To achieve this, human beings had only to recognize the sacredness of their own humanity. Feuerbach was influenced by Spinozan pantheism, which held that God cannot be distinct from his creation. But he was a Romantic, and went much further, proposing that God is a necessary fantasy of his creation's imagination. As Eliot wrote to Mrs Ponsonby in 1874, 'the idea of God, so far as it has been a high spiritual influence, is the ideal of a goodness entirely human (i.e., an exaltation of the human)' (*Letters*, vi. 98). This is Feuerbach's great idea: that God is nothing more than an exaltation of the human, the perfection of ourselves that we mistakenly alienate from ourselves. Religion, by extension, was the illusion of a belief system that did not 'admit that its elements are human'. The 'substance and object of religion is altogether human,' Feuerbach insisted: 'divine wisdom is human wisdom'; and theology, the study of religion, is really anthropology, the study of humankind. The essence of Christianity is 'the essence of human nature itself'.[23] The relation of man to God, therefore, 'is nothing else than his relation to his own spiritual good',[24] and the 'divine being is nothing else than the human being, or, rather, the human nature purified, freed from the limits of the individual man, made objective'.[25] The conclusion to Eliot's Cumming essay makes this point forcefully:

The idea of God is really moral in its influence—it really cherishes all that is best and loveliest in man—only when God is contemplated as sympathizing with the pure elements of human feeling, as possessing infinitely all those attributes which we recognize to be moral in humanity . . . The idea of a God who not only sympathizes with all we feel and endure for our fellow men . . . is an extension and multiplication of the effects produced by human sympathy. (*Essays*, pp. 187–8)

Eliot's conception of sympathy—'the one poor word which includes all our best insight and our best love' (*Adam Bede*, chapter 50)—is drawn from this strain in Feuerbach, although it also owes something to other Romantic thinkers, as well as to Comtean altruism, as we have seen, and Spinoza, whose thought informs Eliot's meliorism—the conviction that one must 'throw the whole force of one's soul towards the achievement of some possible better' (*Letters*, iv. 499), and the Eliotean dictum that 'the responsibility of tolerance lies with those who have the wider vision' (*The Mill on the Floss*, book 7, chapter 3). Eliot translated Spinoza's *Ethics* from medieval Latin after she finished the Feuerbach in 1855 (it was the first English translation, but remained unpublished because of a dispute between Lewes and its planned publisher). Although the roots of her ethical humanism were laid down by then, Spinoza's ideas clearly left their mark deeply in some of the most characteristic humanist moments of the fiction. Most famously, Dorothea's sudden intuition that Casaubon had 'an equivalent centre of self, whence the lights and shadows must always fall with a certain difference' (*Middlemarch*, chapter 21), owes its origin, as Rosemary Ashton has shown, to Spinoza's central idea that altruism begins only when self-interest is subjected to self-scrutiny.[26]

Eliot derived from Feuerbach her conviction of the divinity of human social relations, and the primacy of morality—the 'right, the true, the good'[27]—over religion. Religion 'is jealous of morality; it sucks away the best forces of morality',[28] so that wherever 'the right is made dependent on divine authority, the most immoral, unjust, infamous things can be justified and established'.[29] Eliot also recognized, with Feuerbach, that human love was 'the deepest, truest emotion'[30] and the supreme form of what he calls 'conscientiousness', beside which the self-consciousness of religious experience is primitive.[31] Yet if Feuerbach's aim was to see Christianity as it really is in 'essence', stripped of the illusions of a separate supernatural God, Eliot's aim was to penetrate to the essence of that distinctively *English* religion, Protestantism, stripped of centuries of theology and dogma, and decades of sectarian conflict and controversy, in search of 'the lasting meaning that lies in all religious doctrine from the beginning till now' (*Letters*, iv. 65). The values, practices, and ways of being that were central to her evangelical upbringing therefore remained central to her fiction because they were central to her atheism. At the heart of Calvinist self-examination (the idea that one continuously monitors one's thoughts and actions and searches one's motives), for example, the Feuerbachian Eliot finds the humanistic quality of moral self-consciousness. This gives her fiction its characteristic shape and feel: its distinctive rhythm of acts, events, and speech punctuated by a discourse of rigorous ethical analysis; its strong interest in the ironical space between false motives (what human beings believe about their own motives for action) and real motives; and its division of the world into self-searching and morally unconscious characters.

Eliot rejects, too, the deterministic Calvinist belief in predestination (that salvation was predestined for the elected few), but its nucleus remains as a determinism centred on human action and its moral consequences. The famous dictum from *Adam Bede*—'Our deeds determine us, as much as we determine our deeds' (chapter 29)—sums up the dialectic of continuity and change, determinate conditions and free choices, informing Eliot's fiction, which owes as much to advanced scientific and social scientific thought as it does to Calvinism (see Chapter 7, below). History is made by human actions and choices, but those actions and choices take place within conditions set by actions and choices of the past: the past is a determinate force in human life, but it was also once a present: someone's present, in which actions were taken and choices were made which led to particular consequences. This necessary link between actions and consequences is vital in Eliot's work. History is therefore evolutionary and progressive, but only to the extent that the gradual development of human conditions as they are is due, in Eliot's view, to a keen sense of ethical responsibility for one's actions. By extension, a consciousness of the interplay between individual choices and historical forces is also necessary to the ethical advancement of a whole society.

The word 'determinism' therefore describes what Eliot called in her first essay, 'the presence of undeviating law in the material and moral world' which is an 'inexorable law of consequences' (*Essays*, p. 31); and what Felix Holt, in his 'Address to Working Men', calls 'the great law of inheritance' (*Essays*, p. 429), 'the law by which human lives are linked together . . . the law of no man's making': 'We who are living now are sufferers by the wrong-doing of those who lived before us; we are sufferers by each other's wrong-doing; and the children who come after us are and will be sufferers from the same causes' (*Essays*, p. 419). It is an invisible force which—and this is where its origins in evangelical Protestantism are most strongly indicated—is discernible only to a virtual elect: those with the 'practised vision' who see 'the true bond between events' (*Daniel Deronda*, chapter 21). They are also those who see rightly the difference between what is changeable and what is fixed, and can therefore make a realistic choice between resignation and action. It was Eliot's maxim, she wrote to a correspondent, 'Never to beat and bruise one's wings against the inevitable but to throw the whole force of one's soul towards the achievement of some possible better' (*Letters*, iv. 499).

Likewise the pietistic temper of evangelicalism—its suspiciousness of worldliness and pleasure—is removed from an illusory Christian context of sinfulness and piety in Eliot's fiction and placed in the context of a human moral failing. Worldliness for Eliot takes the form of a sensual complacency (think of Arthur Donnithorne's love of ease, or Nicholas Bulstrode's or Fred Vincy's blithe self-satisfaction), and piety gives way to the high seriousness of everyday life. Similarly, the Christian notion of conscience remains central. Conscience is not 'an inner deliverance of fixed laws' but 'the voice of sensibilities as various as our memories' (*Daniel Deronda*, chapter

41); and that voice may be external to us, in the voices of those we form intimate relationships with (as Deronda becomes 'a part of [Gwendolen's] conscience' (chapter 35)). Beneath the evangelist's missionary purpose, too—the conversion of non-believers to the faith—lies a humanistic mission to guide others into the clear light of moral consciousness. The conversion experience is central to evangelical Protestantism. Converts become conscious of their sin, are awakened to grace, and become committed to Christ. This is the 'justification by faith' that Lawyer Dempster so abhors in the Reverend Tryan in 'Janet's Repentance' (in opposition to the idea of justification by good works, in which religion is essentially an outward, social experience, not an inward, spiritual, personal experience). As a girl Mary Ann/e Evans had been struck 'suddenly and hard' by 'the conviction that one was utterly sinful and could be saved from hell only by accepting the atonement of Christ' (*Biography*, p. 19). In Eliot's atheistic humanism the conversion experience remains powerful: its essence is that 'change of mental poise' which happens when another person touches us 'with a peculiar influence, subduing [us] into receptiveness' (*Daniel Deronda*, chapter 35). We cannot be changed, in other words, by ideas, doctrines, or institutions. The evangelical emphasis on personal spriritual experience remains paramount in Eliot.

In much the same way, the artistic vocation is for Eliot a secular variation on the evangelical mission:

the inspiring principle which alone gives me courage to write is, that of so presenting our human life as to help my readers in getting a clearer conception and a more active admiration of those vital elements which bind men together and give a higher worthiness to their existence; and also to help them in gradually dissociating these elements from the more transient forms on which an outworn teaching tends to make them dependent. (*Letters*, iv. 472)

Here Christianity is a 'transient form', the 'vital elements' of which are conveyed in what Eliot hoped was a more permanent form of teaching: aesthetic teaching.

Where Eliot's aesthetic teaching departs most radically from evangelical Protestantism is in its Feuerbachian rejection of the essential sinfulness of humanity. When contemporary readers of the early novels, unaware of Eliot's atheism, felt them to be irreligious it was most often because they seemed to propound a dangerously unorthodox idea of sin. The Feuerbachian psychology presumes the essential goodness of human beings, and it forms the basis of Eliot's faith in the 'good within them' (*Letters*, v. 448). In this, her position has certain affinities with Comtean positivism, which 'founds its hopes on benevolent human instincts',[32] and with Spinoza. Uniquely, however, Eliot replaces the Christian notion of original sin with a notion of 'the difficulty of the human lot'—'that which of all things is most certainly known to us' (*Letters*, v. 31). Her novels are narratives of the fall and redemption: they trace the 'beginning of hardship' (*Adam Bede*, chapter 36), 'the first arrival of care' (*Daniel Deronda*, chapter 16). Hardship and care are echoes of original sin in that they arise directly out of human failings. In one direction this leads to narratives that trace 'the process of moral defeat' in her characters.[33] These are among her most profound and original stories. Adumbrated in Amos Barton's paltry selfishness, and given substance in the effortless, sliding moral negligence of Arthur Donnithorne and Godfrey Cass, these stories form the greatest parts of her greatest novels: the compelling story of Tito Melema's decline, the story of 'a man falling into falsehood' (*CH*, p. 211), in *Romola*; the stories of Lydgate's defeat, Casaubon's defeat, and Bulstrode's defeat in *Middlemarch*, all stories of 'the moral chaos that takes possession of the mind after wrong has been done';[34] and the extraordinary story of Gwendolen Harleth's coming to moral consciousness in *Daniel Deronda*. In another direction it leads to narratives of suffering. Humans 'have to suffer for each other's sins', she wrote in *The Mill on the Floss*; each and every wrong action sends out 'pulsations of unmerited pain' to others (book 3, chapter 7). Suffering is at the centre of Christianity, and for that reason Feuerbach (for whom the suffering God of Christianity was an expression of the human ideal that 'it is divine to suffer for others'), and Eliot after him, place it at the centre of their atheistic humanism. Eliot had suffered, and felt instinctively the importance of suffering. Grieving for the death of her father in 1849, she wrote: 'the worship of sorrow is *the* worship for mortals' (*Letters*, i. 284). She urged, W. H. Mallock wrote, 'with a solemn eloquence . . . in a solemn ecstasy, that a man's highest life is to be found in sorrow, borne for the sake of others' (*CH*, p. 455). This is first worked through fully in *Adam Bede*, where sorrow is 'an indestructible force . . . passing from pain to sympathy' (chapter 50). The deep 'unspeakable suffering' that Adam endures becomes 'a baptism, a regeneration, the initiation into a new state':

he had only now awaked to full consciousness. It seemed to him as if he had always before thought it a light thing that men should suffer, as if all that he had himself endured and called sorrow before was only a moment's stroke that had never left a bruise. Doubtless a great anguish may do the work of years, and we may come out from that baptism of fire with a soul full of new awe and new pity. (chapter 42)

In *The Mill on the Floss*, too, Philip Wakem feels himself, Tom, and Maggie 'being drawn into a common current of suffering and sad privation' (book 2, chapter 6) and Tom feels 'that new sense which is the gift of sorrow—that susceptibility to the bare offices of humanity which raises them into a bond of loving fellowship, as to haggard men among the icebergs the mere presence of an ordinary comrade stirs the deep fountains of affection' (book 2, chapter 7).

The 'full consciousness' that comes with sorrow is closely related to the idea of duty in Eliot, with its deep evangelical roots. Duty is 'that recognition of something to be lived for beyond the mere satisfaction of self'.

No man can begin to mould himself on a faith or an idea without rising to a higher order of experience: a principle of subordination, of self-mastery, has been introduced into his nature; he is no longer a mere bundle of impressions, desires, and impulses. ('Janet's Repentance', chapter 10)

As Mallock put it, 'transcendent morality' for Eliot meant 'shar[ing] willingly in the common lot' and not seeking to escape from ties ' "after those ties have ceased to be pleasant" ' (*CH*, p. 455).

But this does not mean that Eliot propounds a dourly Calvinistic idea of duty—she is deeply conscious of the perilous attractions of renunciation, for example, that seductive culture of self-denial. Rather, her insistence that we share willingly in the common lot draws her imagination away from evangelical enthusiasm towards an ethical humanism that seems closer in practice to the sociable undogmatic Tory Anglicanism of her father. On the face of it this is inconsistent: the Evangelical Revival (which led to the breakaway Methodism of the mid-1700s and the infiltration of the Church of England by evangelicals in the 1790s) was in every way socially and ideologically opposed to easygoing establishment Anglicanism. This apparent inconsistency confused readers of *Scenes of Clerical Life*:

some objected because the stories seemed to approve 'indiscriminately every school of religious opinion'; others pointed out that Eliot's aim was 'to bring into vivid light the fundamental agreement underlying all these differences' (*CH*, p. 222). If Dorothea Brooke's journey from 'excessive Evangelical piety to a wider view of human destiny'[35] mirrors Eliot's own journey from Calvinism to atheistic ethical humanism, therefore, it is also a journey towards the reconciliation of a seriousness of purpose that belongs to evangelicalism and a deeply ingrained ethical sensibility that Eliot cherished in undogmatic Tory Anglicanism.

Eliot's fictional career begins with evangelicalism at its heart because, like Feuerbach, she sets out to 'anthropologize' it. In 'Silly Novels by Lady Novelists' she had argued for the dramatic potential of middle- and lower-class English social life which was evangelical to the core, and demanded: 'Why can we not have pictures of religious life among the industrial classes in England, as interesting as Mrs. Stowe's pictures of religious life among the negroes?' (*Essays*, p. 319). Evangelical Protestantism is, in effect, the founding spirit of her fiction, for 'are not Evangelical opinions understood to give an especial interest in the weak things of the earth, rather than in the mighty?' (*Essays*, p. 318). Eliot's commitment as a realist to representing the weak things of the earth, signalled in the character of Amos Barton in her very first story, drives her commitment in the early stories and novels to the evangelical classes. This is also why Eliot's English pastoral fiction is characteristically set in an evangelical golden age between Wesley's death (1791) and the institutionalization (and perceived decline) of evangelicalism after 1833. By setting *Adam Bede* in 1799 Eliot is placing Dinah Morris's career in a very specific context. Her vocation is in the Wesleyan spirit of practical piety and vigorous individualistic preaching. 'Janet's Repentance', on the other hand, is set in the early 1830s. Tryan is therefore in many ways exceptional to the general drift of evangelicalism at this time ('Perhaps Milby was one of the last spots to be reached by the wave of a new movement' ('Janet's Repentance', chapter 2)). Although an Anglican, he embodies the same spirit of uninstitutionalized evangelicalism. The central conflicts of the novel revolve around this very issue. The townspeople of Milby are quick to institutionalize Tryan, however, dividing themselves into sects (Tryanites and anti-Tryanites). Eliot's aim is to show how individuals transcend the institutions that 'represent' them.

Eliot was convinced that the moral life was possible outside Christian morality, however, because she saw people living such lives every day. That is why the 'lasting meanings' of Christianity are not to be found in the evangelical Christians in her fiction. Their lives of intense belief are invariably on the margins of the real world (as Dinah is for much of *Adam Bede*, and Rufus Lyon for much of *Felix Holt*); or they undertake a long journey away from evangelicalism towards secular humanism (as Silas does, and Dorothea). The essence of Christianity for Eliot is rather to be found in the undogmatic gentry churchmen in her novels, and their undogmatic parishioners: they represent the authority of tradition which is needed to endorse the post-Christian humanism expressed in the novels. At first Eliot explicitly sought a reconciliation between evangelicalism, which has the intensity and force to carry its strength of purpose beyond religious orthodoxy, and those people of 'no very lofty aims, no theological enthusiasm' (*Adam Bede*, chapter 5). In 'Janet's Repentance', the everyday loving-kindness of Milby's undoctrinal churchgoers (such as Mrs Pettifer) mingles with Tryan's ardent evangelicalism. In *Adam Bede*, too, Dinah's Methodism is 'liberal, eclectic, enlightened, independent, and therefore unreal', Anne Mozley thought (*CH*, p. 95); but for those very reasons it is strongly approved of by the Reverend Irwine, the 'good, easy-going rector ... not fervent in doctrinal controversies, and given to a little quiet sporting' (*CH*, p. 76). Clergymen like Irwine abound in Eliot. They are men of 'large, tolerant, charitable character, with no great belief in dogma' (*CH*, p. 299): Dr Kenn in *The Mill on the Floss*; Farebrother in *Middlemarch*; and (much more problematically) Mr Gascoigne in *Daniel Deronda*. In *Silas Marner*, too, Eliot traces the reconciliation of the best aspects of evangelical puritanism stripped of its corrupting institutional organization (embodied in the social isolation of Silas) and the best aspects of undoctrinal parish Anglicanism; not this time in a clergyman, but in Dolly Winthrop, 'with her quaint kindness, her simple piety, and her good sense' (*CH*, p. 173).

Eliot's novels are records of spiritual struggles: not struggles against the nineteenth-century drift of unbelief, but struggles conducted on the other side of belief, where 'the working-out of higher possibilities' (*Letters*, iii. 366) is a task that must fall to everyone, every day. For that reason her contemporaries thought of her as an atheistic writer of religious novels (not simply because by the time the pseudonym was revealed, her 'teaching had been dubbed clerical, and it was too late in the day to turn upon her and call her an atheist' (*CH*, p. 225)). It is also why she came to believe that all the great religions were 'rightly the objects of deep reverence and sympathy' because they are 'the record of spiritual struggles which are the types of our own' (*Letters*, v. 448), a belief which is the organizing principle of her last and most ambitious work of fiction, *Daniel Deronda*. In that novel Eliot takes a story such as Hennell or Strauss might have found buried among ancient Hebrew myths, and with astonishing assurance interweaves it with a story more modern than anything else she wrote, a story of post-religious culture and post-national economics. *Daniel Deronda* is in many ways a revision of *Romola*, which had drawn an implicit parallel between late fifteenth-century Florence and mid-Victorian Britain in its critique of those, like Tito, who represent 'culture cut adrift from all vestige of moral or religious faith' (*CH*, p. 202). Eliot had always been interested in what was common to Christian spirituality and secular liberalism, and her purpose in *Romola* was, as Richard Holt Hutton recognized, 'to trace out the conflict between liberal culture and the more passionate form of the Christian faith in that strange era' (*CH*, p. 200), 'a mental struggle exactly similar . . . to what might occur today between the claims of a sublime faith appealing to the conscience, and a distaste for miracle or vision in its prophet' (*CH*, p. 203). If we abandon Christianity and strive towards a wholly secular politics and culture, how can we protect ourselves against evil? How can we protect ourselves against religious fundamentalism? Eliot pursues these questions through the overlapping of Tito's Machiavellian career and the meteoric rise and fall of Savonarola's religious fanaticism. The solution is ethical humanism.

It is not until *Daniel Deronda* that Eliot at last sets her post-Christian ethical humanism directly against the God she had so 'silently and skilfully' ignored (*CH*, p. 454) until then. It turns out not to be the God of evangelical Christianity, however, but the God of Judaism. In an early letter to John Sibree (written in 1848), Mary Ann Evans had betrayed the conventional anti-Semitism of a fervent Christian who shared a God, and the ceremonies, scriptures, and culture of that God, with a reviled race:

My Gentile nature kicks most resolutely against any assumption of
superiority in the Jews . . . I bow to the supremacy of Hebrew poetry, but
much of their early mythology and almost all their history is utterly revolt-
ing. Their stock has produced a Moses and a Jesus, but Moses was
impregnated with Egyptian philosophy and Jesus is venerated and adored
by us only for that wherein he transcended or resisted Judaism. The very
exaltation of their idea of a national deity into a spiritual monotheism
seems to have been borrowed from the other oriental tribes. Everything
specifically Jewish is of a low grade. (*Letters*, i. 246–7)

In 1876, George Eliot declared in a letter to Harriet Beecher Stowe:

There is nothing I should care more to do, if it were possible, than to rouse
the imagination of men and women to a vision of human claims in those
races of their fellow-men who differ most from them in customs and
beliefs. But towards the Hebrews we western people who have been reared
in Christianity, have a peculiar debt and, whether we acknowledge it or
not, a peculiar thoroughness of fellowship in religious and moral sentiment . . . To my feeling, this deadness to the history which has prepared
half our world for us, this inability to find interest in any form of life that
is clad in the same coat-tails and flounces as our own lies very close to the
worst kind of irreligion. (*Letters*, vi. 301–2)

Over the course of nearly thirty years, and under the influence of
Lewes and others, Eliot developed a profound sympathy with and
understanding of the historical and contemporary struggles of Jews
in England and Europe, and an equally profound interest in Jewish
thought and culture. Yet it could be argued that, although Eliot
completely overcomes her earlier prejudices, she never completely
moves away from the assumptions informing them. For her, specifically Jewish culture and thought is of a very high grade indeed, and
does not require the transcendent culture of Christianity to redeem
it. But Eliot's interest in Judaism is nevertheless an interest in the
moral condition of her own culture and the best way to redeem it.
Anti-Semitism was to her the ultimate expression of a moral vulgarity disfiguring British culture in the 1860s (Dickens had earlier
called this moral vulgarity 'Podsnappery' in *Our Mutual Friend*, after
the character of Mr Podsnap who incessantly trumpets the prejudices of the smugly superior, insular Englishman). What she was
trying to do in *Daniel Deronda*, Eliot explained to Blackwood, was 'to
widen the English vision a little . . . and let in a little conscience and
refinement' (*Letters*, vi. 304).

This involves her in a critique of her own realism. In what seems like a calculated rebuttal to the universalist ambitions of the earlier fiction, the narrator of *Daniel Deronda* muses early in the novel on the significance to the buzzing neighbourhood of Grandcourt's imminent arrival at Diplow. In a mildly ironic tone reminiscent of *Pride and Prejudice*, s/he pauses for a moment to put things into perspective—to remind us that 'nothing is here narrated of human nature generally: the history in its present stage concerns only a few people in a corner of Wessex' (chapter 9). *Daniel Deronda* has other ideas about 'human nature', urging us, as its history duly progresses to other, higher stages, to see that, in literary realism at least, what is given as 'human' actually represents the limited and confined life worlds of very specific communities, societies, and (especially) nations. Eliot was taking an enormous risk with this novel, pushing past the limits of her earlier fiction, developing or undermining its insights. Just as she had exposed the pastoral solutions of *Adam Bede* to the most searching critique in her next novel, the claustrophobic *Mill on the Floss*, for example, so in *Daniel Deronda* she set about interrogating *Middlemarch*'s foundational assumptions about society and its representation. What resulted was a narrative in two halves: an English 'realist' half, dominated by the psychological struggles of densely imagined characters (the Gwendolen–Grandcourt plot); and a 'typological' Jewish half, dominated by a non-realist narrative in which characters are one-dimensional 'types' whose complexity and motivation originate not in psychology or environment but in ancient epic narratives which are replayed in modern dress (as Jesus was, typologically speaking, the second Adam). If this bold experiment failed, it was largely because the forms of Victorian fiction could not bear the strain of such incompatible modes, and Eliot was unable to integrate them successfully as Joyce was later able to integrate Homeric epic, realist description, journalese, and countless other modes of language in *Ulysses*. The novel remains obstinately in two halves, their failure to coalesce embodied in Eliot's failure to bring fully to life the character of her eponymous hero. Once we realize, however, that Deronda has to be both kinds of character at once—liberal English gentleman and the new Moses—we begin to see Eliot's difficulty, and to see just how radical a creation he is.

They are not separate stories, however, for Jewish culture effectively takes the place of the English Midlands past in Eliot's imagination in *Daniel Deronda*. Like Eliot, Deronda was 'loath to part with long-sanctioned forms which, for him, were quick with memories and sentiments that no argument could lay dead' (chapter 32). Those forms are the forms of Western culture itself—the common memories and habits of mind transmitted through the whole culture of Europe from their 'birthplace'—Israel (*Impressions of Theophrastus Such*, 'The Modern Hep! Hep! Hep!'). Judaism, or rather Zionism, is a project to revive 'the organic centre', and illuminate the 'great facts which widen feeling, and make all knowledge alive as the young offspring of beloved memories' (*Daniel Deronda*, chapter 42). The Zionists represent for Eliot a new kind of universalism transcending the national life that was the basis for the Protestant Christianity underpinning her earlier work.

If Eliot's ethical humanism is fundamentally concerned with what makes us human, Judaism represents for her the influences which *first* 'made us human' ('The Modern Hep! Hep! Hep!'). As Richard Holt Hutton put it, reviewing *Daniel Deronda*, Eliot's ethical humanism is 'a purified Judaism,—in other words, a devout Theism, purged of Jewish narrowness, while retaining the intense patriotism which pervades Judaism' (*CH*, p. 366). Take for example the key notion of sympathy. In *Daniel Deronda* the 'many-sided sympathy' of the hero's character shrinks from the insincerity of 'strong partisanship' in any form. This is partly a sign of his liberalism; but it also shows how that liberal ideal of sympathy, without something of a strong partisanship, risks turning into a form of moral-intellectual cosmopolitanism—a 'yearning disembodied spirit, stirred with vague social passion, but without fixed local habitation'. Deronda is awakened to that by Mirah, through whom he comes to the recognition that Judaism was not 'an eccentric fossilized form' of religion, but 'something still throbbing in human lives'. Visiting the Jewish synagogue at Frankfurt, his thought begins to connect the worshippers 'with the past phases of their race', which stirs the 'fibre of historic sympathy' in him (chapter 32).

The language of *Daniel Deronda* is the language of 'enlargement': of a 'widening vision', on the one hand, and a growing sense of one's place in the world—and 'the future widening of knowledge'. As with other Eliot novels, that widening of knowledge is only really possible when it is 'rooted' in an 'early home' in 'some spot of a native land' (*Daniel Deronda*, chapter 3). However, in this novel Eliot confronts an English society for whom the organicist ideology of earlier novels is now meaningless. These are people without a rooted past (Gwendolen has no father and no stable home; the Meyricks have no father; Daniel has no father). There are undoubtedly problems with this appropriation of Judaism by an English liberal cultural ideology intent on replacing one form of organicism with another, and intent on widening its domain (the colonial overtones of that project are self-evident). Eliot is able to reconcile the Zionist separatism of the Jewish plot with the novel's emphasis on the importance of a vision that is wider than the national vision because the assimilation of Judaism into British culture is kept firmly in the past. Eliot goes on believing that 'there is a national life in our veins' (as she wrote in 'The Modern Hep! Hep! Hep!'), 'something specifically English . . . supremely worth striving for, worth dying for', and that the national spirit is a 'spirit of separateness' of which the English are 'perhaps' the principal example, and which, 'like the Muses, is the offspring of memory'. Judaism is part of the race memory of Britons, in other words; who, in forgetting the fact, have ironically become—as the world of *Daniel Deronda* is—the rootless cosmopolitans. What Eliot proposes is that the British acknowledge the heritage which has its roots in Jewish culture and follow the Jewish lead of sustaining their culture as 'something still throbbing in human lives' (chapter 32). The responsibility for that sustenance still falls, in a godless world, on mutual relations of sympathy; but in *Daniel Deronda* it is also a responsibility in the hands of a moral elite. The liberal gentleman— another version of the Protestant elect—reclaims the great world-historical mythology of the Jews from the fringes of mystical fanaticism (represented in the weakening and dying-off of Mordecai's race).

The England of *Daniel Deronda* is a place devoid of religious observance. It lacks the communal rituals of earlier religious belief, and the sense of moral attentiveness to self and society that went with those rituals. George Eliot's realism, which had always inhabited and affirmed the here and now, was also dedicated to finding new forms of observance for a post-Christian society. It is in this sense an existential mode: it holds that truth and meaning are to be found only by living authentically, not by seeking out the essence of life in doctrines, dogmas, or philosophies. There are difficulties and dangers in the here and now, however. For it is also that 'dread present' into which so many of her characters are sucked, ensnared and paralysed by the ' "inclination of the moment" ' (*The Mill on the Floss*, book 6, chapter 14): by impulses and desires, habit, chance. All human existence, according to Eliot, is a struggle to overcome that state: at the end of the day, art, culture, society, are all part of that same 'longing to acquire the strength of greater motives and obey the more strenuous rule' (*Felix Holt, the Radical*, chapter 27). Eliot's fiction is therefore religious in the sense that it is in pursuit of the sacred—it enacts a form of observance: a self-questioning, a voluntary subjection to the higher duties which are immanent in everyday life. It is an act—willed and felt—of sympathetic magic.

Yet from another point of view Eliot's atheistic ethical humanism might seem more like an excuse to hand over Christianity to an easygoing liberal Protestantism, unafraid of irrationality and evil, and joined to a self-surveillant Nonconformist conscience, obsessed with social control and economic expansion. This is why, raging against the outmoded and false values of the educated middle class, the German philosopher Friedrich Nietzsche singled out George Eliot for attack in *Twilight of the Idols* (1888):

G. Eliot.—They are rid of the Christian God and now believe all the more firmly that they must cling to Christian morality. That is an ENGLISH consistency; we do not wish to hold it against little moralistic females à la Eliot. In England one must rehabilitate oneself after every little emancipation from theology by showing in a veritably awe-inspiring manner what a moral fanatic one is. . . . We others hold otherwise. When one gives up the Christian faith, one pulls the right to Christian morality from under one's feet.[36]

But Eliot was not a moral fanatic with an easy conscience who smugly took for granted the survival of Christian morality, and her continuing right to that morality. Religious belief did not bear up under rational scrutiny, and had to go; but rationality was not the essence of religion. As Adam Bede puts it in Eliot's first novel: ' "religion's something else besides notions. It isn't notions sets people doing the right thing—it's feelings" ' (*Adam Bede*, chapter 17). And as Daniel Deronda puts it in her last, 'affection is the broadest basis of good in life':

'Do you think so?' said Gwendolen, with a little surprise. 'I should have thought you cared most about ideas, knowledge, wisdom, and all that.'

'But to care about *them* is a sort of affection,' said Deronda, smiling at her sudden *naïveté*. 'Call it attachment, interest, willingness to bear a great deal for the sake of being with them and saving them from injury. Of course it makes a difference if the objects of interest are human beings; but generally in all deep affections the objects are a mixture—half persons and half ideas—sentiments and affections flow in together.' (*Daniel Deronda*, chapter 35)

CHAPTER 7

ELIOT AND VICTORIAN SCIENCE

WRITING to a correspondent a few weeks before the first book of *Daniel Deronda* appeared early in 1876, George Eliot described her fiction as 'simply a set of experiments in life',

an endeavour to see what thought and emotion may be capable of—what stores of motive, actual or hinted as possible, give promise of a better after which we may strive—what gains from past revelations and discipline we must strive to keep hold of as something more sure than shifting theory. I become more and more timid—with less daring to adopt any formula which does not get itself clothed for me in some human figure and individual experience, and perhaps that is a sign that if I help others to see at all it must be through the medium of art. (*Letters*, vi. 216–17)

As we have seen in previous chapters, this is a very characteristic statement of the moral-aesthetic programme of Eliot's fiction and its 'sympathy with the historical life of man which is the larger half of culture' (*Letters*, iv. 97). Human advancement depends on 'past revelations and discipline', and the word 'discipline' is crucial because Eliot means us to reject, as she has done in her writing, seductive abstract systems and structures which falsely promise a key to understanding. Rather, we must endeavour to *see*. That, for Eliot, is real mental discipline: we must confront the harder truths that lie within our own lived experience, deeply rooted as that experience is in the lives and 'unhistoric acts' (*Middlemarch*, Finale) of other people, known and unknown, alive or long dead. Only then can we hope to add in our turn to what she calls (in the last sentence of *Middlemarch*) 'the growing good of the world'.

At the same time this letter reveals something of the complex relationship between Eliot's moral-aesthetic fiction, the dominant historical mode, and Victorian scientific thought and methods. Eliot first came into contact with advanced scientific thought through her Unitarian friends, the Brays and Hennells, in Coventry, but it was not until she met and fell in love with Lewes that her intellectual life became deeply and permanently involved with science, and especially with Lewes's 'favourite work' (*Letters*, ix. 10), the physiological foundations of psychology. It is not surprising, then, that her fiction should be engaged in a vital and ongoing dialogue with science: from 'Amos Barton', with its self-conscious biological metaphors—the 'delicate visitation of atoms', the 'capillary vessel' of gossip (chapter 6)—which caused some readers to speculate that George Eliot was 'very possibly a *man of Science*' (*Letters*, ii. 291); to the dense, intimidating language of astronomy and physics in *Daniel Deronda*, which caused Henry James to wonder (in the person of 'Theodora') if it were 'too scientific' (*CH* p. 427). Yet in calling her fiction 'a set of experiments in life' through which to see and help others to see, Eliot is indicating that it intersects with science in other more fundamental ways than its scientific metaphors and language. The whole process of moral education is an empirical—a scientific— process, Eliot seems to imply, in the very fact of being based in experience; and when that process is traced through the medium of narrative fiction, the methods of experimental science become essential.

In all the novels George Eliot's narrators adopt a broadly scientific approach, at once practising and enjoining their readers to practise empirical techniques such as close observation, comparison, and prediction, and applying forms of reasoning more usual in the laboratory. Moreover, scientific methods are even more deeply embedded in narrative structures which typically stress the value of learning for oneself, by experience: what in scientific language was called the *heuristic* method. Heuristic principles contributed to the extraordinary growth of popular science in Victorian Britain because they had a moral dimension and a civic function, actively promoting the values of mental discipline and self-reliance. For Eliot, the novel performed a similar function. All her protagonists search for a principle to guide them towards an unknown goal, in plots that resolve themselves into a celebration of the self-knowledge won by the ordeal of an often futile searching. These plots honour and memorialize the struggle to *make meaning*, and reach a point of closure only when desire and duty finally (if sometimes unconvincingly) coincide in the recognition of the higher worth of heuristic endeavour. Eliot's heroines are exemplary in this regard, from Maggie Tulliver, whose 'troublous life' (*The Mill on the Floss*, book 1, chapter 6) is an

arduous cycle of trial and error, to Gwendolen Harleth, whose dim
sense of the existence of bigger things as she stumbles in the dark is
intended to be a heroic counter-plot to Deronda's visionary awakening. In the same way, the Eliotean novel, by its very length and
density, can shape the moral and intellectual habits of its readers,
transforming novel reading itself into a heuristic experience.

Eliot's plots are also shaped by the play of counterbalancing forces
from the past and present that advance and impede their protagonists' progress—'the inexorable law of consequences'—and this is a
scientific law. It takes its legitimacy from the 'presence of undeviating
law' in nature: 'that invariability of sequence which is acknowledged
to be the basis of physical science, but which is still perversely
ignored in our social organization, our ethics, and our religion'
(*Essays*, p. 31). The fact that Eliot wrote this as early as 1851, in 'The
Progress of the Intellect', shows that by then she had already formu-
lated a theory—a scientific theory—to explain how determinism
without God might actually work. To understand human experience
historically, she argued, as we must, is to understand it scientifically.
There is a fundamental unity between the laws governing the physical
world and the underlying historical logic of society, ethics, and
religion:

every past phase of human development is part of that education of the
race in which we are sharing; every mistake, every absurdity into which
poor human nature has fallen, may be looked on as an experiment of
which we may reap the benefit. (*Essays*, p. 31)

Twenty years later, the Prelude to *Middlemarch* begins in these same
terms, by addressing those who care 'much to know the history of
man, and how the mysterious mixture behaves under the varying
experiments of Time'. To conceive of humanity, in the fullest sense
of human social, cultural, and psychological existence, as a 'mysterious mixture', shadows forth that novel's underlying concern with
the material physiological basis of human life—the biochemistry of
human behaviour which Lydgate seeks in his experiments with the
primitive tissue—and its simultaneous concern with the arcane,
semi-sacred nature of that physiology. In doing so, *Middlemarch* also
presents the physical world, governed by the laws of 'Time', as an
arch-experimenter, slowly and inexorably bringing about reforms
undreamt of by worldly social experimenters—those involved in

parliamentary and institutional reform in the late 1820s (and in the late 1860s, which the novel obliquely addresses).

Two interlocked ideas in *Middlemarch*—that human life and behaviour have a physiological basis, and (therefore) that human societies are natural structures and operate according to natural laws—form the basis of Eliot's social, moral, and artistic thought, and are developed in complex ways throughout her fiction. They are essentially ideas about the nature of the individual and the nature of society, and have their point of reference in the convergence of three different sciences: *physiology* (in the *Oxford English Dictionary*, 'the science of the functions and phenomena of living organisms and their parts'); *psychology* ('the science of the nature, functions, and phenomena, of the human soul or mind'); and *sociology* ('the science of the development and nature and laws of human society'). Eliot draws different elements from these three sciences in her fiction, developing what amounts to a distinctive theory of organicism which comprehends all psychological, social, ethical, and religious phenomena as necessary and interdependent elements in a dynamic living system regulated by consistent physical laws. What had previously been the province of metaphysics—nothing short of the human struggle for transcendence—is reconceived within a new paradigm. Before turning to a discussion of Eliot's organicism it may be useful to contextualize this new scientific paradigm and note certain tensions in her work between the relative strengths and weaknesses of art and science in the search for meaning. To begin with, an over-arching 'scientific paradigm' depended upon the notion of a unified 'scientific methodology', which only came to define the common practices of the different natural sciences (astronomy, chemistry, biology, and so on) at about the time Eliot was growing up. (The word 'scientist', in fact, was first used only in 1834.)[1] An important consequence of this unification was the growing conviction in the nineteenth century that scientific methods could be equally transferred to other disciplines—a conviction Eliot clearly shared.

Influenced, as we saw in Chapter 6, by the ideas of Comte, Eliot envisaged the progress of the intellect as, in one sense, the extension of rationalism into all intellectual fields. Comte was a system builder, who sought to move beyond empirical methods of observation and experiment to a rigorous deductive science which would allow the unified study of all phenomena. Comtean positivism sought to discover general principles in nature from which universal laws could be educed and explained in terms of their relationship to one another, with the aim of arriving at a General Law from which all others are derived. 'Science', in such a massive unified system of thought, is intended to encompass, or rather to subsume, everything, including art, in its shared aims of intellectual, moral, and social advancement.

Eliot's positivism was of a more moderate kind, however, retaining a strong conviction of the efficacy of empiricism—a conviction founded on the thriving tradition of natural history in Britain, a tradition of independent amateur observation and experimentation—and an equally strong conviction of the efficacy of art. Deduction, the logical process of drawing conclusions strictly from a set of given premises, is never as congenial to her as its opposite, induction (the logical process of drawing general principles from the observation of particular actions). Eliot reflected on the value of induction in her first review for the *Westminster* in 1851, 'The Progress of the Intellect':

A correct generalization gives significance to the smallest detail, just as the great inductions of geology demonstrate in every pebble the working of laws by which the earth has become adapted for the habitation of man. (*Essays*, p. 31)

This became the dominant habit of thought of Eliot's fictional narrators, who move comfortably between observable particulars and general principles. Indeed, as Henry James put it,

Nothing is finer, in her genius, than the combination of her love of general truth and love of the special case; without this, . . . we should not have heard of her as a novelist, for the passion of the special case is surely the basis of the storyteller's art. (*CH*, p. 498)

Only in the later novels (*Middlemarch* and especially *Daniel Deronda*) did Eliot adopt the rigorous and challenging modes of scientific reasoning that came to prominence after 1850: what scientists called 'hypothetico-deductive' modes, the discovery of what is unknown and, even to the microscope, unknowable, by presenting a hypothesis which can be tested and verified.

At the same time, the tension between these two tendencies— towards an accessible empiricism and its inductive procedures, which had so much to offer an ethical literature; and a more abstract, less accessible deductive science—became more pronounced as Eliot's career progressed. By 1870, science and literature had begun to diverge, breaking into the 'two cultures' of the twentieth century, and the humanistic bias and inclusive culture of early nineteenth-century science gave way to an increasingly professionalized and restricted scientific culture. Methodologically more unified, it was also increasingly characterized by theory, especially in the wake of the sensational and controversial mid-century developments in evolutionary biology and physics. Gradually, rationalism came to be annexed by theoretical science, and literature went on to claim for itself a quite different kind of cultural authority. In disapproving of the scientism of *Middlemarch*, therefore, James was actually protesting that *not* all true knowledge was scientific: literature produced its own knowledge, on its own terms. As the 1876 letter quoted at the head of the chapter reveals, Eliot too came to recognize the limits of pure rationalism. By then she was 'less daring to adopt any formula which does not get itself clothed . . . in some human figure and individual experience, and perhaps that is a sign that if I help others to see at all it must be through the medium of art' (*Letters*, vi. 216–17). Although she managed to exploit the emerging cultural authority of science to raise the status of the novel as an intellectual form, she also held to the ideal that art, not science, was the best medium for a comprehensive, fully human rationalism.

Eliot's fiction was therefore shaped by a more complex and competitive relationship between experimental science and the humanities in mid-Victorian Britain than is often recognized. If she believed there could be no social progress without art because art was the cultivator of moral sentiment, many Victorian scientists believed there could be no social progress without science, which saw itself as the pre-eminent cultivator of moral discipline. The scientist Karl Pearson, looking back on the period from the 1890s, recalled the time when it was assumed that 'inculcating scientific habits of mind' in the general populace would not only assure 'the spread of scientific knowledge' but also lead 'to more efficient citizenship and so to increased social stability': 'Minds trained to scientific methods are less likely to be led by mere appeal to the passions or by blind emotional excitement to sanction acts which in the end may lead to social disaster.'[2] With this aim in mind, T. H. Huxley, the biologist who became the most forceful advocate of Darwinism (he was dubbed 'Darwin's bulldog'), began teaching at the Government School of Mines in London in 1854. His classes included a series of lectures aimed at instructing working-class men in proper scientific methods. In one of the most influential of those lectures, 'On the Educational Value of the Natural History Sciences' (1854), Huxley told his listeners that his aim was to consider the 'position and scope' of physiology 'as a branch of knowledge', its 'value as a means of mental discipline', its 'worth as practical information', and 'at what period it may best be made a branch of Education'.[3] Huxley argued that science was 'nothing but *trained and organized common sense*',[4] the practical benefit of which, he told them in a later lecture, was to effect 'a revolution in their conceptions of the universe and themselves' and profoundly alter 'their modes of thinking and their views of right and wrong'.[5]

Huxley was a leading promoter of the mid-Victorian assumption that science was 'accessible, single, and transferable', meaning that it 'could be understood and practiced by a large number of people; that there was a single method common to all branches of science; and that this method could be extrapolated from natural science to other subjects'.[6] The increasing emphasis on proper standards of scientific training and accreditation, however, challenged the dominance of the untrained amateur and in practice made science much less accessible as it became 'more securely institutionalized'.[7] The aim of Huxley's lectures was not to train scientists at all but to train lay people in scientific methods 'as a means of mental discipline'. Ironically, then, scientific method grew in status just as the Baconian tradition of inductive science was giving way to a more conjectural, more abstract science based around mathematical constructs, 'unobservable entities and theoretical assumptions'.[8]

In the process, science became more professionalized and more exclusive, leaving behind the generalist tradition in which non-specialist intellectuals like Eliot could participate. This shift, in the mid-1850s, had a profound impact on Eliot, because it occurred just as she was launching her career as a novelist, and because at that time Lewes was one of its most public victims. He was then a busy journalist who could claim expertise in areas as diverse as the contemporary theatre and the history of philosophy, and who had just written the first English biography of Goethe. His only major work touching on science to that date had been a book popularizing Comte's philosophy of the sciences (1853). Significantly, Lewes's book drew a hostile and scornful response from Huxley—who was, in his lectures, claiming back the role of scientific educator and popularizer for the specialist scientist—in the *Westminster Review* in January 1854. (Eliot, becoming intimate with Lewes, had tried to suppress the piece as it was going through the press in late 1853.) In the article Huxley accused Lewes of being a 'mere book-scientist'.[9] Stung, Lewes resolved to borrow a microscope and train himself as a practical scientist. Eliot's first story began in *Blackwood's Edinburgh Magazine* alongside the first of Lewes's 'Sea-Side Studies' in 1857. In 1859–60, the years of *Adam Bede* and *The Mill on the Floss*, Lewes's *The Physiology of Common Life* established his reputation as something more than a book-scientist, and something more than the amateur naturalist of the gentlemanly *Sea-Side Studies* (published as a book in 1858). In 1858 and 1859 papers of his were read at a meeting of the British Association for the Advancement of Science, and duly praised by Huxley. His scientific output remained consistent until 1866, when he embarked on what his biographer describes as 'a comprehensive study of the human organism, physiological and psychological'.[10] The five-volume *Problems of Life and Mind* would occupy him until he died in 1878, by which time only three volumes had been published. The following year, the final two volumes, *The Study of Psychology* and *Mind as a Function of the Organism*, were finished by Eliot and published.

Although scientific method was central to Eliot's fiction, therefore, she was by no means unambivalent about the directions Victorian science took, or the wider implications of these changes for the 'scientific' fiction to which she was committed. As we know from 'The Progress of the Intellect', this commitment had its roots in her long-standing conviction, derived from Comte, that scientific rationalism would lead a revolution in the human sciences. Whether modern literature was to be regarded as one of the advanced human sciences remained a matter of doubt, however. Comte's positivist calendar, published in the *Cours de philosophie positive* (1830–42), traced in its thirteen months the evolution of human social development from a primitive religious stage to the intermediate metaphysical stage and finally to the scientific or positive stage. No literary figure features after Shakespeare (see pp. 198 and 199). By

This is the Positivist Calendar (Calendrier positiviste).

		PREMIER MOIS. **MOÏSE.** LA THÉOCRATIE INITIALE.	DEUXIÈME MOIS. **HOMÈRE.** LA POÉSIE ANCIENNE.	TROISIÈME MOIS. **ARISTOTE.** LA PHILOSOPHIE ANCIENNE.	QUATRIÈME MOIS. **ARCHIMÈDE.** LA SCIENCE ANCIENNE.	CINQUIÈME MOIS. **CÉSAR.** LA CIVILISATION MILITAIRE.	SIXIÈME MOIS. **SAINT-PAUL.** LA CATHOLICISME.	SEPTIÈME MOIS. **CHARLEMAGNE.** LA CIVILISATION FÉODALE.
Lundi.	1	Prométhée.	Hésiode.	Anaximandre.	Théophraste.	Miltiade.	Saint-Luc. . . . *Saint-Jacques.*	Théodoric-le-Grand.
Mardi.	2	Hercule. . . . *Thésée.*	Tyrtée. . . . *Sapho.*	Anaximène.	Hérophile.	Léonidas.	Saint-Cyprien.	Pélage.
Mercredi.	3	Orphée.	Anacréon.	Héraclite.	Érasistrate.	Aristide.	Saint-Athanase.	Otton-le-Grand. *Henri-l'Oiseleur.*
Jeudi.	4	Ulysse.	Pindare.	Anaxagore.	Celse.	Cimon.	Saint-Jérôme.	Saint-Henri.
Vendredi.	5	Lycurgue.	Sophocle. . *Euripide.*	Démocrite. . . *Leucippe.*	Galien.	Xénophon.	Saint-Ambroise.	Villers. . . . *La Valette.*
Samedi.	6	Romulus.	Théocrite. . *Longus.*	Hérodote.	Avicenne. . . *Averrhoès.*	Phocion. . . *Épaminondas.*	Sainte-Monique.	Don Juan de Lépante. *Jean Sobieski.*
Dimanche.	7	**NUMA.**	**ESCHYLE.**	**THALÈS.**	**HIPPOCRATE.**	**THÉMISTOCLE.**	**SAINT-AUGUSTIN.**	**ALFRED.**
	8	Bélus. . . . *Sémiramis.*	Scopas.	Solon.	Euclide.	Périclès.	Constantin.	Charles-Martel.
	9	Sésostris.	Zeuxis.	Xénophane.	Aristée.	Philippe.	Théodose.	Le Cid. . . . *Tancrède.*
	10	Menou.	Ictinus.	Empédocle.	Théodore-de-Byzance. *Trédzine.*	Démosthènes.	Saint-Chrysostôme. *Saint-Basile.*	Richard. . . . *Saladin.*
	11	Cyrus.	Praxitèle.	Théognis.	Héron.	Ptolémée Lagus.	Sainte-Pulchérie. . *Marcien.*	Jeanne-d'Arc.
	12	Zoroastre.	Lysippe.	Archytas.	Pappus.	Philopœmen.	Saint-Martin-de-Tours.	Albuquerque. . *Walter-Raleigh.*
	13	Les Druides. . . *Ossian.*	Apelles.	Apollonius de Tyane. *Philolaüs.*	Diophante.	Polybe.	Saint-Grégoire-le-Grand.	Bayard.
	14	**BOUDDHA.**	**PHIDIAS.**	**PYTHAGORE.**	**APOLLONIUS.**	**ALEXANDRE.**	**HILDEBRAND.**	**GODEFROI.**
	15	Fo-Hi.	Ésope. . . . *Pilpaï.*	Aristippe.	Eudoxe.	Junius-Brutus.	Saint-Benoît. . *Saint-Antoine.*	Saint-Léon-le-Grand. . *Léon IV.*
	16	Lao-Tseu.	Plaute.	Antisthène.	Pythéas. . . . *Néarque.*	Camille.	Saint-Boniface. . *Saint-Austin.*	Gerbert. . . *Pierre Damien.*
	17	Meng-Tseu.	Térence. . *Ménandre.*	Zénon.	Aristarque. . . *Béroze.*	Fabricius. . . *Cincinnatus.*	St-Isidore-de-Séville. *St-Bruno.*	Pierre-l'Ermite.
	18	Les théocrates du Tibet.	Phèdre.	Cicéron. . . *Pline-le-Jeune.*	Érastosthène. . *Sosigène.*	Annibal.	Lanfranc. . . *Saint-Anselme.*	Suger. . . . *Saint-Éloi.*
	19	Les théocrates du Japon.	Juvénal.	Épictète. . . *Arrien.*	Ptolémée.	Paul-Émile.	Héloïse. . . . *Béatrix.*	Alexandre III. . *Thomas Becket.*
	20	Manco-Capac. . *Tamehameha.*	Lucien.	Tacite.	Albategnius. . *Nassir-Eddin.*	Marius. . . *Les Gracques.*	Les archit. du moyen-âge. *S.-Bernard.*	St-François-d'Ass. . *St-Dominique.*
	21	**CONFUCIUS.**	**ARISTOPHANE.**	**SOCRATE.**	**HIPPARQUE.**	**SCIPION.**	**SAINT-BERNARD.**	**INNOCENT III.**
Mardi.	22	Abraham. . . . *Joseph.*	Ennius.	Xénocrate.	Varron.	Auguste.	St-François Xav. *Ignace de Loyola.*	Sainte-Clotilde.
Jeudi.	23	Samuel.	Lucrèce.	Philon d'Alexandrie.	Columelle.	Vespasien. . . *Titus.*	St-Charles-Borrom. *Fréd. Borrom.*	St-Charlemagne. *Ste Math-de-Toscane.*
Vendredi.	24	Salomon. . . . *David.*	Horace.	Saint-Jean-l'Évangéliste.	Vitruve.	Adrien. . . *Nerva.*	St-Vincent-de-Paul. *l'abbé de l'Épée.*	St-Étienne-de-Hong. *Math-Corvin.*
Samedi.	25	Isaïe.	Tibulle.	Saint-Justin. . *Saint-Irénée.*	Strabon.	Antonin. . . *Marc-Aurèle.*	St-Fléch.-de-Paule. *L'abbé de l'Épée.*	Sainte-Élisabeth-de-Hongrie.
Dimanche.	26	Saint-Jean-Baptiste.	Ovide.	Saint-Clément d'Alexandrie.	Frontin.	Papinien.	Bourdaloue. . . *Claude Fleury.*	Blanche de Castille.
Mardi.	27	Haroun-al-Raschid. *Abd'erame III.*	Lucain.	Origène. . . *Tertullien.*	Plutarque.	Alexandre-Sévère.	W. Penn. . . *Ulfila.*	Saint-Ferdinand III. . *Alphonse X.*
Dimanche.	28	**MAHOMET.**	**VIRGILE.**	**PLATON.**	**PLINE-l'ancien.**	**TRAJAN.**	**BOSSUET.**	**SAINT-LOUIS.**

Comte's Positivist Calendar, 1830-42

		HUITIÈME MOIS. DANTE. L'Épopée moderne.	NEUVIÈME MOIS. GUTEMBERG. L'Industrie moderne.	DIXIÈME MOIS. SHAKESPEARE. Le drame moderne.	ONZIÈME MOIS. DESCARTES. La philosophie moderne.	DOUZIÈME MOIS. FRÉDÉRIC. La politique moderne.	TREIZIÈME MOIS. BICHAT. La science moderne.
Lundi.	1	Les Troubadours.	Marco-Polo. . . . . . Chardin.	Lope de Vega. . . . . Montalvan.	Albert-le-Grand, Jean de Salisbury.	Marie de Molina.	Copernic. . . . . . Tycho-Brahé.
Mardi.	2	Bocace.	Jacques Cœur. . . . Graham.	Moreto. . . . Guillen de Castro.	Roger Bacon. . . . Raimond Lulle.	Côme de Médicis l'ancien.	Kepler. . . . . . . Halley.
Mercredi.	3	Rabelais. . . . . Chaucer.	Gama. . . . . . . Magellan.	Rojas. . . . . Guevara.	Saint-Bonaventure. . . Joachim.	Philippe de Comines, Guicciardini.	Huyghens. . . . . Fortignen.
Jeudi.	4	Cervantes.	Neper. . . . . Briggs.	Otway.	Ramus. . . . Le cardinal de Cusa.	Isabelle de Castille.	Jacques Bernouilli, Jean Bernouilli.
Vendredi.	5	La Fontaine.	Lacaille. . . . . . Delambre.	Lessing.	Montaigne. . . . . . Erasme.	Charles-Quint. . . Sixte-Quint.	Volta. . . . . . . Rœmer.
Samedi.	6	Foé. . . . . . Goldsmith.	Cook. . . . . . . Tasman.	Goethe.	Campanella. . . . . Morus.	Henri IV.	Bradley. . . . . . Sauveur.
Dimanche.	7	ARIOSTE.	COLOMB.	CALDERON.	SAINT-THOMAS-D'AQUIN.	LOUIS XI.	GALILÉE.
Lundi.	8	Léonard de Vinci. . . Le Titien.	Benvenuto Cellini.	Tirso.	Hobbes. . . . . . . Spinosa.	Coligny. . . . . . L'Hôpital.	Viète. . . . . . . Harriott.
Mardi.	9	Michel-Ange. . . Paul Véronèse.	Amontons. . . . . W'heatstone.	Vondel.	Pascal. . . . . Giordano Bruno.	Barnevelt.	Wallis. . . . . . . Fermat.
Mercredi.	10	Holbein. . . . . Rembrandt.	Harrison. . . . . Pierre Leroy.	Racine.	Locke. . . . . . Malebranche.	Gustave-Adolphe.	Clairaut. . . . . . Poisson.
Jeudi.	11	Poussin. . . . . Lesueur.	Dollond. . . . . . . Graham.	Voltaire.	Vauvenargues. . . Mme de Lambert.	De Witt.	Euler. . . . . . . Monge.
Vendredi.	12	Velasquez. . . . Murillo.	Arkwright. . . . . . Jacquard.	Alfieri.	Diderot. . . . . . . Tucy.	Ruyter.	D'Alembert. . . Daniel Bernouilli.
Samedi.	13	Teniers. . . . . Vandyck.	Conté.	Schiller.	Cabanis. . . . . Georges Leroy.	Guillaume III.	Lagrange. . . . Joseph Fourier.
Dimanche.	14	RAPHAËL. . . . . Rubens.	VAUCANSON.	CORNEILLE.	Le Chancelier BACON.	GUILLAUME-LE-TACITURNE.	NEWTON.
Lundi.	15	Froissart. . . . . Joinville.	Stévin. . . . . . . Torricelli.	Alarcon.	Grotius. . . . . . . Cujas.	Ximénès.	Bergmann. . . . . Scheele.
Mardi.	16	Camoens.	Mariotte. . . . . . . Boyle.	Mme de Motteville, Mme Roland.	Fontenelle. . . . Maupertuis.	Sully. . . . . . Oxenstiern.	Priestley. . . . . . Davy.
Mercredi.	17	Les Romanciers espagnols.	Papin. . . . . . . Worcester.	Mme de Sévigné, Lady Montague.	Vico. . . . . Herder.	Colbert. . . . . . Louis XIV.	Cavendish. . . . . Geoffroy.
Jeudi.	18	Chateaubriant.	Black.	Lesage, Sterne.	Fréret. . . . Winckelmann.	D'Aranda. . . . . Mazarin.	Guyton-Morveau.
Vendredi.	19	Walter-Scott. . . . Cooper.	Jouffroy. . . . . . . Fulton.	Mme de Staël, Miss Edgeworth.	Montesquieu. . . d'Aguesseau.	Turgot. . . . . . Pombal.	Berthollet. . . . . Ritter.
Samedi.	20	Manzoni.	Dalton. . . . . . . Thénard.	Fielding, Richardson.	Buffon. . . . . . . Oken.	Campomanes.	
Dimanche.	21	TASSE.	WATT.	MOLIÈRE.	LEIBNITZ.	RICHELIEU.	LAVOISIER.
Maridi.	22	Pétrarque.	Bernard de Palissy. . . Riquet.	Pergolèse. . . . . . Palestrina.	Robertson. . . . . Gibbon.	Sidney. . . . . . Lambert.	Harvey. . . . . . Ch. Bell.
Patridi.	23	Thomas à Kempis, Louis de Grenade.	Guglielmini.	Sacchini. . . . . . Grétry.	Adam Smith. . . . Dunoyer.	Franklin.	Boerhaave. . . . . Stahl.
Flidi.	24	Mme de Lafayette. . . Mme de Staël.	Duhamel (du Monceau).	Gluck. . . . . . . Lulli.	Kant. . . . . Fichte.	Washington. . . . Kosciusko.	Linné. . . Bernard de Jussieu.
Fratridi.	25	Fénélon, Saint-François-de-Sales.	Saussure. . . . . . Bouguer.	Beethoven. . . . . Handel.	Condorcet. . . . Ferguson.	Jefferson.	Haller. . . . . Vicq-d'Azyr.
Domidi.	26	Klopstock. . . . . Gessner.	Coulomb. . . . . . . Borda.	Rossini. . . . . . Weber.	Joseph de Maistre. . . Bonald.	Bolivar. . . Toussaint-Louverture.	Lamarck. . . . . Blainville.
Mairidi.	27	Byron. . . . Elisa Mercœur.	Fauhon.	Bellini. . . . . . Donizetti.	Hegel. . . . Sophie Germain.	Francia.	Broussais. . . . . Morgagni.
Humainde.	28	MILTON.	MONTGOLFIER.	MOZART.	HUME.	CROMWELL.	GALL.

(Catéchisme Positiviste, page 332.)

Jour complémentaire. . . . . Fête universelle des MORTS.

Jour additionnel des années bissextiles. . . . . { Reproduction universelle des deux principaux rétrogradateurs (Julien et Bonaparte), mais seulement pendant la première demi-génération.

Après ces quatre célébrations initiales de la Fête des Réprouvés, ce jour exceptionnel prendra sa destination normale pour le culte abstrait.

1871–2, therefore, not only is 'the divorce between science and other forms of knowledge' well advanced;[11] by this time 'science and the rational form a single united domain' and literature has been effectively 'expelled from the field of reason'.[12]

The effects of this schism can be seen in Eliot's appropriation of advanced scientific thought for her own purposes. Moved to defend *Romola*'s minutely detailed representation of everyday life in Renaissance Florence, she declared that it was the habit of her imagination to 'strive after as full a vision of the medium in which a character moves as of the character itself' (*Letters*, iv. 97). Her use of the word 'medium' is telling here. It is not being applied in its usually loose figurative sense, as a synonym for 'social context' or 'conditions of life', but in a more precise scientific sense: as the element in which an organism lives. This is because Eliot's fiction comprehends the relationship between individuals and their physical and social environments over time as primarily a physiological one: that is, in terms of the functions of living systems. Individuals act according to their inherited natures, which have a physiological foundation: not just what we might now call their 'genetic predispositions' but their cultural predispositions. They also act according to their function within a larger complex whole which has the systematic unity of a single organism. Each individual exists only by virtue of his or her position in that organism, and the organism exists only by virtue of the internal relations of its constituent parts. An extremely complex structure such as an advanced industrial society is therefore conceived of as a living body, unified by its internal relations even as it changes over time. In Eliot's reformulation of the German sociologist Wilhelm Riehl's ideas in her essay 'The Natural History of German Life', she argued that the

external conditions which society has inherited from the past are but the manifestation of inherited internal conditions in the human beings who compose it; the internal conditions and the external are related to each other as the organism and its medium. (*Essays*, p. 287)

This idea—organicism—was a characteristic form of mid-nineteenth-century thought. Eliot's version of it was adapted not only from Riehl's sociology and Comte's positivism but from sources as diverse as Wordsworth's poetry, Burke's political philosophy, Carlyle's history, Sir Charles Lyell's geology, and, closer to home, the evolutionary sociology of Herbert Spencer and physiological psychology of Lewes, who in the 1853 study of Comte which so offended Huxley had defined society as an organism 'in which incessant movement accompanies constant stability of form'.[13] It might be expected that organicism was anti-rationalist, and in its earlier Romantic forms it was (most notably in Coleridge in England and Herder in Germany). But for Eliot, Spencer, Lewes, and other Victorians, advances in geology and biology, particularly the various theories of evolution coming to prominence in the 1850s, had demonstrated the essential unity of life forms and organic systems, and reconciled organicist and rationalist modes of thought. Most prominently, Darwin marvelled at 'the beauty and infinite complexity of the coadaptations between all organic beings, one with another and with their physical conditions of life'.[14] This is not to say that organicism was a single theory, however. As Sally Shuttleworth has argued, 'George Eliot structured all her fiction in accordance with organicist assumptions', but organicism was not so much an idea as a 'language': a shorthand for many different approaches to questions of the gradual development of social bodies, and the nature of social interactions and interdependence.[15]

Organic theory was important to Eliot for a number of reasons. First, like Comtean positivism, it stressed the supreme importance of *relationships*. After Comte it was widely held that the real nature and task of science was to explain causal relationships—how things relate to one another, not what they mean in themselves—and organicism is a fundamentally relational mode of thinking. In *On the Origin of Species*, for example, Darwin argued that 'all living and extinct forms can be grouped together in one great system . . . connected together by the most complex and radiating lines of affinities'. How misguided it was, he declared, to 'look to some unknown plan of creation' to explain this great system: the aim of science must be to disentangle the 'inextricable web of affinities between the members of any one class', however formidable that task may be.[16] *Middlemarch* is Eliot's most explicit treatment of this idea. Its multiple plots trace the 'new consciousness of interdependence' (chapter 11) between the old provincial gentry and the rising town bourgeoisie during the reform period. Radically decentred in its form (hence its own question: 'why always Dorothea?' (chapter 29)), the novel seeks to show that individual lives and life events are made meaningful only by the inextricable web of affinities connecting them to other lives and other events. We are blinded to those affinities by our own egoism. Like the lighted candle that produces 'the flattering illusion' that scratches on the mirror are arranged concentric circles around 'that little sun' (chapter 27), our egoism places us at the centre of our own stories, lending an illusory unity to everything that happens to us and those around us. If we were to see things as they really were, Eliot demonstrates, we would have to be able to see them just as the narrator sees them: as 'the stealthy convergence of human lots', the 'slow preparation of effects from one life on another, which tells like a calculated irony on the indifference or the frozen stare with which we look at our unintroduced neighbour' (chapter 11). That is why irony is the dominant mode of *Middlemarch*, a novel that dramatizes the stealthy convergence of the lives of its unintroduced (or at least uninterested) Middlemarch neighbours. It is a forgiving irony, however. Eliot was fully aware that it is in the nature of human existence to be blind to 'the suppressed transitions which unite all contrasts' (chapter 20) and the suppressed differences which constitute objective reality: the complex patterns of resemblance and diversity. *Middlemarch* is called a 'history of the lights and shadows' (chapter 20) partly to suggest the authentic humanity of its own imperfect vision, and partly because it is conscious (as in the candle metaphor) of the different ways lights and shadows fall: 'always . . . with a certain difference' (chapter 21).

This is brought home painfully to Dorothea when she recognizes that the Casaubon at 'the centre of his own world' (chapter 10) is not the same Casaubon at the centre of her world. Totally absorbed in his 'Key to All Mythologies', with its deluded aim of extrapolating from all Western myth systems a single arch-narrative of human cultural origins, Casaubon embodies the folly of aspiring after universal knowledge and the inadequacy of explanatory structures that privilege unity and universality over relation. This does not mean that such aspirations are foolish and vainglorious. Casaubon might have been heroic, even in failure, for Eliot's realism is keenly aware of the realistic limits of consciousness. The most famous passage from *Middlemarch* is sanguine about the coarseness of human emotion:

If we had a keen vision and feeling of all ordinary human life, it would be like hearing the grass grow and the squirrel's heart beat, and we should die of that roar which lies on the other side of silence. (chapter 20)

If we are lucky to be 'well wadded with stupidity', we are still capable of what Eliot calls in *The Mill on the Floss* a 'large vision of relations' (book 4, chapter 1): not by constructing massive abstract systems of relations, but by becoming sensitive to the web of intimate and distant relations in which our lives are enmeshed and through which all our thoughts and actions extend. Casaubon embodies the perils of a self-centredness and intellectual vanity that ignores everyday relations, but he is also an object-lesson for any reader who may be tempted to ignore the small pressures, the petty rivalries, the failures of nerve, that led to his downfall. We must constantly resist the lure of the universal:

I at least have so much to do in unravelling certain human lots, and seeing how they were woven and interwoven, that all the light I can command must be concentrated on this particular web, and not dispersed over that tempting range of relevancies called the universe. (*Middlemarch*, chapter 15)

There is no big story to bestow meaning on individual lives, nor any first cause, whether God or the 'primitive tissue' that Lydgate pursues. All meaning, and all mystery, is fully present in every interchange at every moment, not in some absent essence of being. Both Casaubon and Lydgate suffer because they neglect the trivial responsibilities that distract them from their great work, and in doing so underestimate the 'petty medium' (*Middlemarch*, chapter 18) in which they have their everyday existence.

Organicism was therefore vital to Eliot's formulation of a philosophically sustainable atheistic humanism because it enabled her to discard metaphysical and religious systems of explanation (preeminently Christianity) that were no longer tenable whilst retaining the commanding ethical dimension built into the very notion of an organism's interdependence. It was also inherently conservative, in the special sense of that '*social-political-conservatism* . . . of a thoroughly philosophical kind' she had so admired in Riehl. A species of gradualism, it held that 'development can take place only by the gradual consentaneous development' of both the organism and its medium (*Essays*, p. 287). Complex organisms like societies are the product of slow growth over a long period of time: hence the importance of maintaining traditions, and resisting sudden or traumatic changes, as Felix Holt asserts in his 'Address to Working

Men': 'society stands before us like that wonderful piece of life, the human body, with all its various parts depending on one another, and with a terrible liability to get wrong because of that delicate dependence'. Even when no 'seat' of disease can be found, every part 'is likely to feel the effect if any of them goes wrong' (*Essays*, p. 420). Consequently there is no room in this theory for rival explanatory models of social reality—models based on inequality, for example, such as the class system—and certainly no room for planned social change (parliamentary reform) that may arise out of immediate class interests and social compromises.

Nowhere in Eliot's fiction is organicism brought into the service of social-political conservatism more obviously than in the rural idyll of *Adam Bede*, with its vivid representation of an organic social order disrupted but never seriously threatened by the events of the plot. The novel's ideological landscape, like its action, is bounded and defined by the Donnithorne estate. Hayslope and its neighbouring farms and villages do not comprise a timeless pastoral community any more than Thomas Hardy's hamlets and parishes. This is a community shaped by the forces of social change quite as much as the forces of tradition. (We are reminded, for example, that the Poysers' Hall Farm was once a country squire's Hall, but is now subsumed into the Donnithorne land.) Here, '"lives are as thoroughly blended with each other as the air they breathe"', and interdependence implies social duty: every sin causes suffering '"to others besides those who commit it"' (chapter 41), and must be redeemed by suffering. Indeed the language of duty and suffering emphasizes the gravity, the sanctity, of social responsibility in *Adam Bede*. People of all ranks and classes must strive to preserve the delicate organism which yields so rich and plentiful a historical life.

Anyone who reads *The Mill on the Floss* directly after finishing *Adam Bede* is struck by the sudden change in mood and tone. At the very beginning of *The Mill on the Floss*, the idyllic mode with which *Adam Bede* had been suffused is self-consciously bracketed off from the rest of the novel by the narrator's dreamy reverie (in book 1, chapter 1, 'Outside Dorlcote Mill'). Eliot does not mean to discount its importance by this gesture. As we shall see, it sets a pattern of alternating realist and non-realist modes which is itself an acknowledgement of the multifold nature of reality. Nor is Eliot trying to demolish any expectation her readers might have had of another

Adam Bede; nor make her realism seem so much more realistic. Rather, this is a calculated strategy to advance her theory of organicism by exposing the idyllic as a literary mode, which can falsify experience by defining, and limiting, individuals' lives just as romance, for example, does, shaping and conditioning Maggie's life as inexorably as heredity. The effect of the first rough and ready exchange between Mr and Mrs Tulliver (in book 1, chapter 2) is immediately to relegate the narratorial reverie to a space outside the 'real' world of St Ogg's. Juxtaposed with the petty provincial ambitions and humiliations of a small town, and the hidden traumas of its children, the opening seems suddenly high-keyed and artificial: *literary*.

St Ogg's is 'a continuation and outgrowth of nature' (book 1, chapter 12), like *Adam Bede*'s Hayslope, but it is not a social organism in which interdependent parts harmoniously coexist. Both the plot and language of *The Mill on the Floss* take up instead a radically different vocabulary of the evolutionary development of an organism as it struggles for survival. This is the new vocabulary of Darwinism, and its incorporation into *The Mill on the Floss* testifies to the extraordinary and immediate impact of Darwin's *On the Origin of Species*, published in 1859 and read by Eliot when she was beginning work on the novel. Unlike Hayslope, the 'organic' community of St Ogg's is characterized by competition and struggle among stronger and weaker 'species', from families and family members to neighbours and rival lovers. These are forces of nature, often beyond the control of individuals, whose agency even in their own volitional acts is always open to question. Mr Tulliver cannot resist the irresistible forces of market competition and the law which threaten to ruin him, but he is just as surely ruined because he is powerless to control his own nature: he 'had a destiny as well as Oedipus, and in this case he might plead, like Oedipus, that his deed was inflicted on him rather than committed by him' (book 1, chapter 13). Lawyer Wakem is not a malicious man, just 'an ingenious machine, which performs its work with much regularity' (book 3, chapter 7). Tom gains mastery over the affairs of his family not because he chooses to but because, every bit a Dodson, he could not choose otherwise ('when he was a man he should be master of everything and do just as he liked' (book 2, chapter 1)). Mrs Tulliver, on the other hand, is a Dodson who struggles (and fails) to adapt successfully to the different conditions of her marriage: her sisters, all of them married, remain Dodsons even in the face of the extinction of the family line. By contrast the ungovernable Maggie—'the picture of her aunt Moss' (book 1, chapter 7)—is driven by 'the need of being loved, the strongest need in [her] nature' (book 1, chapter 5). Her deepest love, for Tom, is lost on the 'well-made barbarian' (book 2, chapter 3), who is locked by the events of the immediate past (Tulliver's ruination by Wakem) into a deadly rivalry with the deformed Philip—like Maggie, a 'mistake of nature' (book 1, chapter 3).

In *The Mill on the Floss* there are those whose nature equips them to comprehend and control the world and themselves (as the Dodsons do with their rigid sense of material duty), and those who are tormented by this imprisonment within the limits of their own natures (book 7, chapter 3). Maggie is desperate for a key to the meaning of 'this hard, real life' (book 4, chapter 3): desperate to understand herself and her own actions. But as Philip remarks,

'I don't think any of the strongest effects our natures are susceptible of can ever be explained. We can neither detect the process by which they are arrived at, nor the mode in which they act on us. . . . I think there are stores laid up in our human nature that our understandings can make no complete inventory of.' (book 5, chapter 1)

This is borne out by Tom's wasted education, which brings into question the value of learning when we cannot unlearn who we are, or change our essential nature. But what exactly does Eliot mean by an individual's 'nature'? Even in commercial St Ogg's, it is curious, first of all, that she should choose a mercantile metaphor in Philip's speech (and elsewhere: the word 'stores' turns up again in the 1876 letter quoted at the beginning of this chapter) to describe something like the irrationality and violence of 'the strongest effects' of our natures. It suggests that even the most irrational parts of the mind are, in essence, rational—and even moral. The mind is a storehouse, where provisions diligently 'laid up' for our future needs can be (mostly) classified and accounted for, even if the most vital aspects of our nature are sometimes overlooked in the stocktaking.

Eliot is describing the unconscious mind here—in *Daniel Deronda*, too, the narrator observes that there is 'a great deal of unmapped country within us which would have to be taken into account in an explanation of our gusts and storms' (chapter 24)—but in the pre-Freudian terms of Victorian rationalist psychology. Her central concern is with the physiological mainsprings of determinism: if we are to know how the past actually inhabits the human body, how an individual's personality may be counted among the consequences of someone else's past actions, we must have some conception of how external conditions are internalized by the mind and body, and passed on down the generations. Eliot first engaged with these ideas when she was introduced to the new science of phrenology in Coventry in the 1840s. Now discredited, phrenology theorized that the variable development of the different functional areas of the brain cortex was reflected in bumps on the skull, and claimed to be able to determine a person's character through the analysis of those bumps. It seems thoroughly unscientific now, but phrenology was an important moment in the history of psychology. It introduced the idea that brain functions were specifically localized; and more importantly that psychological and moral phenomena such as 'character' had some physiological basis. Eliot inevitably became suspicious of it under the influence of Lewes's experimental work in the mid-1850s. She fell out with Charles Bray as a result, but in defending her altered point of view, she insisted to Bray that she 'never believed more profoundly than . . . now that character is based on organization': in other words, that it has some physiological basis (*Letters*, ii. 210).

Lewes's *Physiology of Common Life*, begun when Eliot started writing novels in the late 1850s, offered a scientific explanation for this process. It proposed that the minds of individuals developed along pathways laid down by the history of the actions of the nervous system in its constant interactions with the external medium in which it has its existence. All our sensations (what we see, hear, know, feel) are therefore conditioned, physiologically, by the history of the whole organism of which we are a part, beginning with the ' "first ideas" ' of our identity and environment in early childhood (*The Mill on the Floss*, book 2, chapter 1). Lewes's psychology later influenced the Russian physiologist Pavlov, who put forward the theory of 'conditioned reflexes' to describe how the human temperament was formed by the organization of the nervous system under particular conditions. Eliot's conception of the 'process and unfolding' of character (*Middlemarch*, chapter 15) is not Pavlovian, however. It owes more to Herbert Spencer, who applied Darwin's evolutionary ideas to a laissez-faire theory of social development (Spencer coined the phrase ' the survival of the fittest'), and whose lifelong project to synthesize the natural and social sciences drew together physiology, psychology, ethics, metaphysics, and sociology. Like Spencer, Eliot saw in the organization of the nervous system of individuals a reflex of the organization of the physiological, social, and institutional systems (including systems of belief, kinship systems, and so on) in which those individuals were formed: a common deep history of physiological and psychological processes. For Eliot, the inward life is ineluctably historical: what is deep in our inward being is also deep in our past. This nexus of the psychological and the historical looks forward in some respects to Freud and the significance of narrative to psychoanalysis and the 'talking cure'. But in Eliot it has specific epistemological connotations. Fiction seeks to know not by observing the world under a microscope, but by observing it under the conditions of time. Every human act and event, every inconsequential life, 'suggests a vast sum of conditions' imperceptible to ordinary senses or not worthy of attention.

Eliot's task in *The Mill on the Floss* is not just to suggest the vast sum of conditions that shape the Dodsons and Tullivers, and especially Maggie, but to show how, in a provincial backwater, small-minded people preoccupied with their own petty concerns live insensible, materialistic, irreligious lives, yet continue to yearn after some form of transcendence and meaning. This becomes one of Eliot's greatest themes: the imperative of learning (the hard way) that transcendence is not elsewhere, but here and now, in the large vision of just such ordinary relations among just such small-minded people. It is a lesson learned, or not learned, by nearly every one of Eliot's major characters after Maggie Tulliver, who represents a first attempt at the sustained analysis of the collision between the irrational and unconscious dimensions of human existence and its ethical and spiritual dimensions. In *Adam Bede* Eliot had tentatively approached the problem of destructive energies released unconsciously (in both Hetty and Arthur). And in an important short story, 'The Lifted Veil', written while she was working on *The Mill on the Floss*, Eliot tried her hand at a 'sensational' romance centrally concerned with the nature of consciousness and the physiology of transcendence (this story is discussed below). In Maggie the struggle to grasp human existence intellectually comes into violent conflict with her daily struggles to live meaningfully in the face of her own volatile passions. One aim of *The Mill on the Floss* is to reconcile apparently irrational passions with their rational causes: again, only possible if we change the way we look at things. A mind equipped with a larger vision of relations will perceive that there is nothing *unnatural* even in the most chaotic and apparently senseless events. Indeed it is part of the function of art, which is the prime cultural medium through which we recognize the relatedness of unrelated phenomena, to reveal the meaningfulness, the naturalness of these events.

This returns us to the opening reverie in *The Mill on the Floss*. It seems that it is no longer possible for the leisurely narrator to be a licensed trespasser, as in *Adam Bede* (chapter 17): to be outside Dorlcote Mill is to be somehow outside nature. Or is it? The narrator's reverie is an aesthetic experiment—a kind of proem, like the opening of *Romola*—but Eliot is also encouraging us to interpret it as a *state of mind*. In an intense dream-state, the half-conscious narrator projects his own memories and desires onto the scenes he involuntarily conjures up. It is surely important that Eliot should psychologize her narrator's immersion in the past, not just for the symbolic integrity of water in the novel, but because it allows her to extend her realism to embrace another (non-realist) notation of individual subjectivity: the involuntary activity of consciousness. The extreme contrast Eliot sets up here between two radically different kinds of writing is meant to echo the perilous relationship between land and water in the novel. Dorlcote Mill is that problematic space where consciousness and unconsciousness intersect. The language of social realism in *The Mill on the Floss*, overbearing and unappealing after *Adam Bede*, is the language of consciousness: the surface world, where law and meaning predominate. But the novel is punctuated by another, non-realist language: the language of passion. Eliot's aim is to show that this language, too, is part of nature.

Her vehicle for this is the fastidiously planned, provocatively antirealist flood. It has been argued that the flood has the effect of neutralizing the novel's own commentary, contradicting or negating everything that comes before it and bringing the novel 'hard up against its own realism' by indulgently releasing Maggie from 'the narrow, unjust, oppressive world that social realism has to depict'.[17] It might also be objected that the flood thwarts, even undermines, the entire *intellectual* project of Eliot's realism. In the destruction of a moment it does away with all the ineffectual talk in the novel, achieving what no amount of impassioned discussion—and there is an awful lot of it here—can hope to achieve. Is this a crisis of reason, sweeping rational inquiry away 'into the same oblivion with the generations of ants and beavers' (*The Mill on the Floss*, book 4, chapter 1)? What happens to the novel's deep commitment to 'that complex, fragmentary, doubt-provoking knowledge which we call truth' (book 6, chapter 12)? Eliot herself claimed that the flood, like the plague village scenes at the end of *Romola*, belonged to her 'earliest vision of the story': both of them 'were by deliberate forecast adopted as romantic and symbolical elements' (*Letters*, iv. 104). But symbolical of what?

Eliot was undoubtedly alluding to the contemporary controversy over uniformitarianism and catastrophism in the flood. In his *Principles of Geology*, which appeared in the early 1830s, the geologist Sir Charles Lyell had hypothesized that rocks were formed by slow continual processes such as heat and erosion. By implication, the earth could not have been formed by any supernatural means within a matter of days. Although not the first to speculate on the extreme age of the earth, Lyell was the first to propose that 'since scientific geology should only work with observable causes, we must accept that we do not have access to any rocks formed under conditions differing significantly from those we observe today'.[18] Lyell's theory of uniformitarianism (which had a profound influence on Darwin's theory of evolution by natural selection) disposed of the rival theory of catastrophism, arguing that 'the earth has always been more or less the same, because the constructive forces of elevation which create mountains and continents are exactly balanced by the destructive forces of erosion'.[19] Although Eliot is obviously a uniformitarianist, her aim is not to enter the Lyell controversy. On the contrary, the flood is a reminder that natural catastrophes do still occur, and can seem, to less advanced societies at least, to be portents or signs of something else. In the distant past the Rhone 'rose, like an angry, destroying god sweeping down the feeble generations whose breath is in their nostrils and making their dwellings a desolation' (*The Mill on the Floss*, book 4, chapter 1). In the more recent past, the Floss also rose, destroying a generation of the Tullivers. But in doing so it only unleashed the same forces that had always acted in the world.

Sudden and apparently meaningless, floods can nevertheless be explained without recourse to an idea of providence. All we need is a fuller understanding of the operation of the uniform laws of nature: a larger vision of relations.

In the same way, catastrophic human passions only appear to be chaotic in nature, but are really subject to the same laws as any other psychological phenomena: the 'contrast between the outward and the inward', for example, that causes 'painful collisions':

A girl of no startling appearance, and who will never be a Sappho or a Madame Roland or anything else that the world takes wide note of, may still hold forces within her as the living plant-seed does, which will make a way for themselves, often in a shattering, violent manner. (*The Mill on the Floss*, book 3, chapter 5)

A contemporary critic of *The Mill on the Floss* observed that 'George Eliot, like Maggie, hungers and thirsts after a higher life' (*CH*, p. 143). The flood is the novel's attempt to find a potent symbol for that 'higher life', as potent as the angry, destroying god of earlier times, with the important difference that the St Ogg's flood is meant to testify to the existence of the higher life *as a fact of nature*: as much as those other hard facts of material existence, the fragments of wooden machinery that sweep Tom and Maggie to their deaths (*The Mill on the Floss*, book 7, chapter 5). If this ending fails to convince us, as it does, it is only because we are not actually convinced of its naturalness at all: it *is*, finally, a catastrophic intervention, against what realism prescribes as nature. Although we know that 'feeling, rising high above its average depth, leaves flood-marks which are never reached again' (book 5, chapter 4), the realist novel can make no complete inventory of feeling without betraying its positivist heritage.

At the heart of this problem, which haunts Eliot's fiction, is the nature of vision: the relations between imagination and rational analysis; and between subjective perception and objective vision. The narrator of *The Mill on the Floss*, very much a man of science, is also a part-time Wordsworthian visionary, whose eyes 'have dwelt on the past' (Conclusion) and for whom the flood is the one 'supreme moment' of ecstatic reunification (book 7, chapter 5): akin to what Wordsworth had called in *The Prelude* a 'spot of time'. How might these two figures be reconciled? Eliot explored that question in a short tale she wrote in 1859, when she was struggling with *The Mill on the Floss*. Like its sullen hero, Latimer, 'The Lifted Veil' is something of an aberration; 'a slight story of an *outré* kind', Eliot called it (*Letters*, iii. 41), written when her head was 'too stupid for more important work' (*Journals*, p. 77). It is, first of all, a commentary on *The Mill on the Floss*—it explores problems of identity and authorship raised by the Liggins affair—and on realism more generally. A cross between a Hawthornean metaphysical romance and a Gothic horror story, and anticipating 'sensation fiction' (about to come into vogue with Wilkie Collins's *The Woman in White* and Dickens's *Great Expectations*), 'The Lifted Veil' admits a range of melodramatic effects and sensational incidents prohibited by realism. It eschews psychological penetration for the vivid, even lurid, external manifestations of psychic states: appropriately enough for a tale examining the ethical implications of subconscious and unconscious experience.

The result is a strikingly modern allegory of insight and delusion. Latimer is a kind of mid-Victorian Faust, an over-reacher figure who craves the visionary powers of Homer, Dante, Milton, and the Romantics, but gets more than he bargained for: struck down suddenly with a strange disease, he is granted terrible powers of premonition and, in language that anticipates *Middlemarch*, a 'microscope vision' of the interior life of every person, important and unimportant, who comes into his horizon. The veil of other minds lifted, Latimer endures a painful (though fluctuating) din of hidden thoughts and feelings—all the 'vagrant, frivolous ideas and emotions' and 'petty promptings of . . . conceit' beneath the surface of good society, and the concealed 'vanity and love of power' motivating sexual relationships. Like a vivisector, he sees everything as it really is, in all its 'naked skinless complication' ('The Lifted Veil', chapter 1). He also suffers surreal visions of 'strange cities, of sandy plains, of gigantic ruins, of midnight skies with strange bright constellations, of mountain-passes, of grassy nooks' (chapter 2).

Self-confessedly a failure in everything, Latimer provides an interesting parallel to the dreary failings of the Dodsons and Tullivers in *The Mill on the Floss*. Significantly, too, his curse is associated with femininity. He is 'fragile, nervous, ineffectual' and 'held to have a sort of half-womanish, half-ghostly beauty' ('The Lifted Veil', chapter 1)—the obverse of Maggie's tomboyish energy and aspirations after the freedoms and opportunities of men—like the neurasthenic heroes of the *fin de siècle*. His powers of absolute insight are a salient counterpoint to the 'blind, unconscious yearning' of *The Mill on the Floss* (book 3, chapter 5). But if Maggie is enslaved by the incomprehensibility of life, Latimer is enslaved by its terrible lucidity. Eliot's aim in the story is to examine this enslavement, which comes when visionary power is literalized—turned into a fact of nature. In particular, 'The Lifted Veil' dramatizes the dire consequences of the poet's power of insight being exchanged for the scientist's power. Not that Latimer is any scientist, or any poet. Rather his is a cautionary tale about positive science and the poverty of imagination. Science may have the power to strip the world of all delusions—to see all things just as they are—but if there is nothing left for the imagination to do, then we are consigned to a hell of certainties. 'The Lifted Veil' makes a claim for the supreme value of uncertainty and ignorance in human existence; and a claim for the vital significance of art and literature as the supreme expression of the groping after truth:

Conceive the condition of the human mind if all propositions whatsoever were self-evident except one, which was to become self-evident at the close of a summer's day, but in the mean time might be the subject of question, of hypothesis, of debate. Art and philosophy, literature and science, would fasten like bees on that one proposition which had the honey of probability in it, and be the more eager because their enjoyment would end with sunset. Our impulses, our spiritual activities, no more adjust themselves to the idea of future nullity, than the beating of our heart, or the irritability of our muscles. (chapter 2)

'The Lifted Veil' is a defence of the imagination and a critique of the power of science—'*was* it a power?', Latimer muses; 'Might it not rather be a disease . . .?' (chapter 1).

Eliot revisits these problems of scientific knowledge, moral vision, and the higher life in *Middlemarch*, her most overtly scientific novel. This necessarily involves a closer critique of scientific method, the nature of vision, and the role of interpretation in meaning, for even

with a microscope directed on a water-drop we find ourselves making interpretations which turn out to be rather coarse; for whereas under a weak lens you may seem to see a creature exhibiting an active voracity into which other smaller creatures actively play as if they were so many animated tax-pennies, a stronger lens reveals to you certain tiniest hairlets which make vortices for these victims while the swallower waits passively at his receipt of custom. (*Middlemarch*, chapter 6)

Middlemarch is concerned with the difficulty of ensuring any kind of objective analysis in an unavoidably subjective, perspectival world—a world in which everything is always in flux, and change is always the 'double change of self and beholder' (chapter 11). This is also a question about the nature of vision. Lydgate chooses the medical profession because it gives him the opportunity to pursue scientific research of an experimental and highly theoretical nature—and Eliot means us to see that this research is important and original—in the course of his everyday practical doctoring. Lydgate means to be a man of science and a man of the people, to 'do good small work for Middlemarch, and great work for the world' (chapter 15). But he is what Eliot calls a 'little spotted with commonness' (this is nineteenth-century bourgeois realism's version of the fatal flaw of tragedy): he is conceited and arrogant, but almost imperceptibly so, especially to himself. His intellectual passion for microbiology and pathology gives him remarkable insight—vision really—but he brings no such passion to his dealings with his fellow men and women. His 'distinction of mind' does not 'penetrate his feeling and judgement' about ordinary things: petty things, as he thinks them, beneath his lofty field of vision. Lydgate will become a victim of this 'vulgarity of feeling' (chapter 15), in contrast to Dorothea, whose intellectual passion and moral passion are fused. That fusion of two passions could only take place in art. George Eliot's goal as a novelist was the same as T. H. Huxley's aspiration as a scientist—'severe truthfulness', therefore.[20] But while it made an important contribution to the nineteenth-century quest for a scientific (that is, rational) foundation for social theory, post-Christian ethics, and aesthetics, it also offered an important critique of the limits of science.

Eliot embodies these limits in Lydgate. He is not just a model of the progressive scientist, but a doctor who joins the medical profession because it offers him, as the literary profession offered Eliot, 'the most perfect interchange between science and art' and 'the most direct alliance between intellectual conquest and the social good' (*Middlemarch*, chapter 15). In the late 1820s, the period in which *Middlemarch* is set, medicine has the same uncertain status as fiction has during Eliot's career. Even in 1871, when it began to appear, the novel as a literary form was still frequently accused of being a species of intellectual quackery—the 'mind-and-millinery species' of the silly novels by lady novelists (*Essays*, p. 301)—and still only occasionally a serious intellectual pursuit. Eliot, like Lydgate, was a pioneer in this regard. Yet Lydgate's spot of commonness is also a 'spot of commonness' in science itself: unlike fiction, with its capacity to grasp broadly across disciplines, the growing intellectual exclusivity of the sciences, their specialization and professionalization, leaves them vulnerable, Eliot implies, to limitations: to arrogance. Like Lydgate, Eliot sets about 'enlarging the scientific, rational basis' of the novel (*Middlemarch*, chapter 15), but part of her purpose is also to enlarge science in the process.

CHAPTER 8

RECONTEXTUALIZING GEORGE ELIOT

Eliot after 1900

IN VIRGINIA WOOLF'S *To the Lighthouse* (1927), Minta Doyle, one of the young guests of the Ramsays at their holiday house on the Isle of Skye, is 'terrified' by the domineering head of the family: Mr Ramsay 'was so fearfully clever, . . . the first night when she had sat by him, and he talked about George Eliot, she had been really frightened, for she had left the third volume of *Middlemarch* in the train and she never knew what happened in the end'.[1] Mr Ramsay—in part a portrait of Woolf's father, Sir Leslie Stephen—stands for a generation of liberal intellectuals stranded in the new century and tormented by the unravelling of Victorian certainties: Eliot's generation. Yet as forbidding as they may seem to the impressionable Minta, Eliot and the 'Eliotites', with their stern language of duty and intellectual heaviness, were no longer so intimidating to Woolf and her contemporaries—indeed, they were virtually figures of fun.[2] Once the spell had broken, Woolf recalled in 1919, Eliot 'became one of the butts for youth to laugh at, the convenient symbol of a group of serious people who were all guilty of the same idolatry and could be dismissed with the same scorn'.[3] Eliot's reputation had begun to decline before the early twentieth-century reaction against Victorianism set in, however. There were murmurings of rebellion even in the decade of her death, partly as the inadvertent result of the stuffy, reverential three-volume 'life-and-letters' biography written by her husband, John Walter Cross, in 1885. In its wake, Eliot suffered the fate of Mrs Transome: 'her knowledge and accomplishments [became] as valueless as old-fashioned stucco ornaments, of which the substance was never worth anything, while the form is no longer to the taste of any living mortal'. As early as 1890, W. E. Henley deplored her ' "Death's Head Style" of art': 'her sententiousness revolted while it amused him'.[4] George Saintsbury casually observed in 1895 that she had 'more or less passed out of contemporary critical appreciation',[5] and Arnold Bennett wrote in his journal the following year: 'I dipped into *Adam Bede*, and my impression that George Eliot will never be among the classical writers was made a certainty!'[6] In the aftermath of the First World War, moreover, which brought about a profound collapse in the values of dynastic Europe, Eliot's affinity with German culture seems especially to have marginalized her. Gosse, for example, writing in 1922 (the year of James Joyce's modernist masterpiece, *Ulysses*), remarked that it was 'unfortunate for her genius that after her early enthusiasm for French culture she turned to Germany and became, in measure, like so many powerful minds of her generation, Teutonized. This fostered the very tendencies which it was desirable to eradicate'.[7]

For Virginia Woolf, however, Eliot was a forebear to be reckoned with, her greatness as an artist beyond question.[8] That is precisely why *Middlemarch* casts its shadow over *To the Lighthouse*. Woolf was defining her own art against it, and helping in the process to shape the ways Eliot's fiction was destined to be read in the light of all the traumatic ethical, social, and aesthetic disturbances of the post-Victorian century: totalitarianism, modernism, mass culture, consumer capitalism, postmodernism, feminism, postcolonialism—tremendous upheavals of the known world of the Victorians. That Minta Doyle, with all her unreflective vitality, all her bland modernity, should absent-mindedly misplace the last volume of *Middlemarch* (incidentally, not published in three, but four, volumes) and never know how it ends suggests a great deal about the fate of Eliot's fiction as it made its unfamiliar way into the twentieth century—recontextualized for new generations of readers (and viewers) whose life worlds and experiences were unimaginable even to the most percipient mid-Victorians.

Among those unforeseen conditions was the onset, shortly after Eliot's death, of a 'great divide' between high art and popular mass culture.[9] By the first decades of the twentieth century the 'cultivated' non-professional readership on which Eliot's whole imaginative enterprise depended was almost extinct. In its place was a sharply polarized reading public, created by complex sets of economic, educational, and technological factors: increased wealth, and a new emphasis on spending; compulsory elementary education; and advances in paper production and high-speed printing techniques.

On one side, a small number of 'cultural specialists'—progressive writers and their coteries (such as the Bloomsbury group), and champions of the avant-garde—began producing self-consciously 'literary' works characterized by experimentation and difficulty. On the other side, new markets emerged for commercial popular fiction, ranging from cheap disposable newspaper serials to 'middlebrow' literature to the new 'booming' best-sellers. In this bifurcated cultural field, Eliot's quintessentially Victorian species of 'seriousness' disappeared altogether: abhorrent to the modernists, for whom it signified pomposity and philistinism; indigestible and unmarketable to a mass readership.

The stray volume of *Middlemarch* is therefore an eloquent announcement of the modernist challenge to the Victorian novel of ideas. *To the Lighthouse* emphatically disrupts the fluency of Eliot's fiction, its steady progress towards resolution, its faith in formal coherence and moral absolutes: its poise and reach. Gone is the conviction that selves are unified, consistent, knowable, and securely embedded in their social worlds. Perhaps more particularly for Woolf's project, the lost last volume—while it dramatizes Eliot's famous declaration (in a letter Woolf may well have read in the *Life* (p. 219)) that endings are problematic because of 'the very nature of a conclusion, which is at best a negation' (*Letters*, ii. 324)—also symbolically enacts the modernist rupturing of Victorian closure: can uncertainties be resolved, a work of art fully achieved, the lighthouse reached? Most of all, Woolf rejects the most fundamental Victorian assumptions about art and its function. Eliot was a great aesthetic experimenter—consider the opening of *The Mill on the Floss*, which influenced Proust's narrative technique, or the modernistic self-awareness of *Daniel Deronda*—and her emphasis on psychological analysis set the pattern for modern stream-of-consciousness fiction. But her aesthetic experiments never completely unsettle Eliot's confidence in rationalism—the productive labour of thought and analysis at the heart of her work—which places them firmly in the nineteenth century. For the moderns, moreover, 'seriousness' in art was no longer to be equated with intellectualism, and Eliot's fiction lost favour because of the 'tremendous lot of thinking'[10] that went on in them: 'the excess of reflection', in Henry James's words, and 'absence of free aesthetic life' (*CH*, p. 497)—by which he meant that art ought to be wholly free of the oppressive preponderance of mind, and free from any sense of its own moral *function*. For James these two were interlocked: 'We feel in her, always, that she proceeds from the abstract to the concrete; that her figures and situations are evolved . . . from her moral consciousness, and are only indirectly the products of observations' (*CH*, p. 498). Eliot's own description of her art as 'aesthetic teaching', therefore—a form of teaching which must be 'purely aesthetic', requiring 'the severe effort of trying to make certain ideas thoroughly incarnate, as if they had revealed themselves to me first in the flesh and not in the spirit' (*Letters*, iv. 300)—was anathema to the moderns because it *was* teaching—a 'moralized fable' (*CH*, p. 497) which took no 'pleasure . . . in the fact of representation for itself' (*CH*, p. 499).

After James (himself a highly cerebral writer, of course), novelists were even more vehement in their rejection of the ponderous intellectualism they perceived in Eliot's work. By the end of the twentieth century, 'seriousness' in literature denoted aesthetic experimentation or ethical commitment, but not the vulgar bourgeois display of learning. Perhaps this happened because what changed, in fact, was the whole idea of a serious reading public. Twentieth-century nostalgia for the loss of such a public may be traced back to the end of Victorianism—to a nostalgia, most wistfully and elegantly expressed in G. M. Young's *Victorian England: Portrait of an Age* (1936), for 'a serious and liberal habit of mind' which could disengage itself from partisan interests and range across forms of knowledge. Supplanted, or so Young argued, by the specializing tendencies of the encroaching professional age (novelists do not deal in ideas as philosophers or scientists do) and by the proliferation of cheap amusements (newspapers, sports, cinema), the ideal reader of Eliot's fiction was replaced in the twentieth century by professional academics, students, a sprinkling of amateur lovers of literature, and the tens of thousands of buyers of copies of television tie-in editions, many of which remain, like Minta's *Middlemarch*, unfinished.

Eliot's reputation in the twentieth century was not tied to the fortunes of progressive fiction, however, but precisely to this emergence of new forms of readership. Her critical reputation grew steadily with the growth of professional criticism in universities in English-speaking countries after World War II, and remained ascendant, enriched by the arrival of continental literary theory, the accelerated evolution of academic feminism (see Chapter 5, above), and the 'turn to history' in the academy in the 1970s and 1980s. The process began in the late 1940s with the publication of two crucial books. F. R. Leavis's *The Great Tradition* (1948), based on essays originally published in the journal *Scrutiny*, was a turning point in the re-evaluation of Eliot's fiction. Leavis was disaffected with the dominance of continental aestheticism in the modernist canon— which grew out of the 'disgust or disdain or boredom' that drove Flaubert's quest for formal perfection. He was intent upon resurrecting a distinctively 'English' tradition of fiction. The characteristics of this counter-tradition were not perfection of form but formal innovation in the service of 'an unusually developed interest in life . . . a vital capacity for experience, a kind of reverent openness before life, and a marked moral intensity'.[11] For Leavis—who was frank about what he perceived as Eliot's weaknesses, especially her lapses from the 'impersonality of genius' into idealization or sentimentality[12]—Eliot's moral imagination and formal innovativeness were inseparable, and her intelligence was the intelligence of the genuine artist, not the translator of German abstract philosophy.

Already in *The Great Tradition* the implied 'general reader' is not the intelligent layperson choosing among English novels, but the student. When Leavis wants to point to the conventional wisdom about his authors, he offers as evidence exam papers and undergraduate essays. The importance of the classroom cannot be underestimated, therefore, in the resurgence of Eliot's reputation. In the immediate post-war years, hundreds of thousands of men and women returned to education, and found in English studies a set of critical methodologies congenial to minds wishing to turn inward from the ravages of recent history, and a set of pedagogies suitable for very large class sizes. Anglo-American New Criticism was allied to Leavisism in that it sought the integration of formal and thematic coherence in literary works. Although Leavis was more explicitly and passionately ethical in approach, viewing literary significance in terms of the 'human awareness' great works promote—'awareness of the possibilities of life'—New Criticism also sought to impart an intensified critical attentiveness that was essentially moral in nature. The social contexts impinging on those texts were accordingly set aside as unwieldy superfluities, the business of mere sociologists. A lyric poem (all you needed to bring to class) could be explicated successfully on its own using techniques of close reading. Novels, with their tendency to diffuseness and their cumbersome narrative and descriptive apparatuses, could not be so reliably depended upon to offer the same degree of formal unity, nor be so conducive to purely formalist (that is, non-historical or non-social) explanation. Yet Joan Bennett's *George Eliot: Her Mind and Art* (1948) proved that Eliot's fiction, and especially *Middlemarch*—quickly affirmed by other New Critics as her greatest work—was a rich resource for close reading. The one-time uneasiness of readers with the predominance of Eliot's mind over her art disappeared as a new generation recognized the subtlety of writing that combined formal sophistication, intellectual vigour, and an intensified moral vision.

The New Critics, like the Leavisites—like all critical movements—established a 'canon', a list of works 'sanctified' or given authority by the critical preoccupations of the movement, most immediately at least, but really by the wider prevailing concerns of the historical moment. The Eliot who prospered under the (academic) world-dominance of Leavisism and New Criticism was effectively the author of one and a half authentically great novels: *Middlemarch*; and *Gwendolen Harleth*—the 'good half' of *Daniel Deronda*, so cavalierly retitled by Leavis in *The Great Tradition*. Excluded or demoted were *The Mill on the Floss*, with its disorderly passion and disruptive autobiography, the over-researched *Romola* ('the work of a very gifted mind . . . misusing itself'[13]), the dull *Felix Holt, the Radical* with its schematic political vision (excepting the Mrs Transome sections), the Jewish half of *Daniel Deronda*, and much else besides, including Eliot's poetry. Far-reaching changes in critical fashions since 1970 have seen some (though not all) these other George Eliots brought back into prominence. In part, this occurred because these fresh critical approaches challenged the quality of 'literariness' itself, debunking the very notion of a canon and abandoning the practice of (open) evaluation—deciding which authors and works are great, which 'minor'—at the heart of earlier critical practices. In some cases, too, new aspects of Eliot's work were brought into focus in response to broader changes in cultural mores. *Middlemarch* remains her best-selling title, due in no small part to the popular success of the BBC television serial version (discussed below); *Romola*, considered by many of her contemporaries as her greatest work, is undoubtedly the least read now, along with *Scenes of Clerical Life*. But all the novels, a couple of shorter texts ('The Lifted Veil' and 'Brother Jacob'), selections of critical writings, and even the poems, are still in print today.

This is because Eliot's writing has proved particularly adaptable to critical, and more broadly cultural, shifts over the past thirty years. The major novels in the New Critical canon continued to attract sophisticated formalist readings, most notably by 'Yale School' deconstructionists like J. Hillis Miller in the 1970s and 1980s. Miller is one of the leading American practitioners of deconstruction, a philosophy of language based on the linguistics of Ferdinand de Saussure and developed in France by Jacques Derrida. In brief, deconstruction holds that the meanings of literary works (which it terms 'texts') are ultimately undecidable because language itself is a kind of prison house, which, although it claims to refer to pre-existent things, is the sign that those things are not actually *present*. Words have meanings, but only by virtue of their difference from other words. Hence the overriding tendency of Western culture to think in binary terms (the basis of structuralism), which also has the effect of instituting and maintaining hierarchies and hence social power relations: the meaning of male is *not female*; the meaning of white is *not black*. Literary texts are not, as the New Critics would have it, unified wholes, therefore, but are riven with irreconcilable contradictions: they fail to cohere, to *mean* conclusively. The resolution of textual ironies and ambiguities, at the centre of New Critical practice, is held off indefinitely; and accordingly interpretation, if that denotes settling upon one or more meanings, is impossible.

This would seem to suggest that deconstruction is radically at odds with the claims to objectivity and referentiality of nineteenth-century realism, and that Eliot's fiction would consequently be devalued. In Britain, where critics like Catherine Belsey were influenced by Roland Barthes (mediated through the work of Colin MacCabe in the film journal *Screen*), this is exactly what happened. In *S/Z* (1970), a book on the cusp of structuralism and post-structuralism, Barthes argued for the distinction between 'readerly' texts (those, like the realist novels of Balzac, which tried to shut down the play of language) and 'writerly' texts (such as modernist novels). For Belsey and others, Eliot became the English exemplar of 'classic realism', the author of texts which, in their drive towards 'closure' or the re-establishment of stability, perform the ideological work of reinstating the social order (as in the ending to *Middlemarch*), or providing imaginary solutions to real social conflicts (as in *Felix Holt, the Radical*).[14] The problem with Belsey's argument, as Penny Boumelha has shown, is that 'classic realism' is 'something of a straw figure'. It does not in fact 'correspond to any actual text of the period'—and certainly not to Eliot's texts, which, even when they are most 'realist' (discounting, that is, such profoundly non-realist texts as the epic parts of *Daniel Deronda*, or 'The Lifted Veil'), are characterized by an 'obviousness of *voice* and of a narrator's presence' and a patent textuality in their epigrams and axioms, verse epigraphs, literary models, and self-conscious uses of figural language.[15]

Other deconstructionists, by contrast, picked up on these rhetorical elements in Eliot's texts—particularly their metaphors and other tropes—not to dismantle the meanings of those texts but to demonstrate (in Hillis Miller's words) how they had already dismantled themselves. In his 'Optic and Semiotic in *Middlemarch*', one of the most dynamic and insightful readings of Eliot, Miller examines her presentation 'of certain all-encompassing metaphors' proposed as models for Middlemarch society, which, he begins by saying, is represented as a social totality by the combination of scrupulous specificity and 'generalizing interpretation on the basis of specificity'.[16] Teasing out the implications of Eliot's use of a 'family of intertwined metaphors and motifs—the web, the current, the minutely subdivided entity—[which] make up a single comprehensive model or picture of Middlemarch society',[17] Miller shows how the metaphor of vision deconstructs the totalizing enterprise of realism. Do things really relate or is that just a by-product of our vision? The pier-glass episode at the beginning of chapter 27 would suggest the latter. Can the novel reconcile its claim to be an objective, scientific study of provincial life seen whole, or is that wholeness inevitably perspectival and subjective? Eliot's answer is to practise incessant fine adjustments of vision, as her narrator does, 'using perspective to transcend perspective'.[18]

In his approach Miller was encouraged by Eliot's frank admission of the inherently metaphorical character of language: the fact that we can 'seldom declare what a thing is, except by saying it is something else' (*The Mill on the Floss*, book 2, chapter 1). Yet the mimetic assumptions of realism remained a stumbling block. *Adam*

Bede's narrator, for example, remarks in an apparently proto-deconstructionist moment: 'Nature has her language, and she is not unveracious; but we don't know all the intricacies of her syntax just yet, and in a hasty reading we may happen to extract the very opposite of her real meaning' (chapter 15). Deconstruction works by locating points of insistent opposition in texts, and overturning the hierarchies produced by those oppositions: there are no 'real meanings' in nature. Despite the fact that Eliot's fiction at various points raises issues that problematize processes of narration and interpretation, therefore, its aim is always to play down or disregard those contradictions. This very characteristic, however, is absorbed into the deconstructive act, so that, in D. A. Miller's *Narrative and Its Discontents* (1981), for example, *Middlemarch* oscillates between a magisterial confidence in the validity of its claims and 'an uneasy subversion of [that] habitually assumed validity'. For all its deconstructive insights, what D. A. Miller calls the 'traditional form' of the novel remains largely undisrupted.[19]

As the 1980s progressed, D. A. Miller emerged as one of the leading figures in what came to be called 'new historicism' in the USA, an influential movement in that country against the formalist bias of deconstruction, which new historicists characterized as a supercharged version of New Criticism (that is, it continued to view the literary work as an isolated, self-contained entity). However, as Claire Colebrook remarks, 'It would be naïve to think that new historicism . . . arrived in literary criticism as an "answer" or "overcoming" of post-structuralist relativism', drawing as it does on the work of Lacan, Derrida, and Michel Foucault (in Victorian studies in particular, the influence of Foucault has been pronounced).[20] New historicism, although it follows Fredric Jameson's famous dictum, 'Always historicize!', should also be distinguished from Marxist approaches, even if it may be argued that it draws on the line of Marxist thought influenced by Louis Althusser, whose work in the 1970s showed how literature 'can *produce* individuals in order that the capitalist forces of production may continue': how ideas of 'the self, morality, propriety, and subjectivity are . . . *effects* of literary production'.[21] New historicism rejected Marxist models of social power relations based in the totalizing concepts of class and ideology. It was also symptomatic (along with cultural studies) of the profoundly changed relationship between literature and culture in

Western societies. 'Culture' no longer denoted a few privileged products in the arts and intellectual life of a civilization, but 'the whole range of practices and representations through which a social group's reality (or realities) is constructed and maintained'.[22] The study of literature is accordingly reframed by new historicism as the study of a variety of representational forms which construct and maintain social realities. Literary works—and it is worth observing that new historicism, practised inside American universities where the canon was deeply entrenched, for the most part continued to deal with the big names, including Eliot—are read (closely) in conjunction with legal documents, tracts, scientific books, and so on: documents with more explicit claims to being instruments of social regulation. This deterministic assumption that literature has a fundamentally regulatory function is an important aspect of new historicism. Yet, like deconstruction before it, it typically claims that literature is a contradictory site. It subverts dominant power structures even as it reconfirms them, tending to produce readings of texts that 'can all too adequately be summarized as "kinda hegemonic, kinda subversive"'.[23]

This reorientation of literature as a type of 'discourse' of a piece with other social discourses such as law and politics, household arts, or science, has seen a surge of interest in previously marginal Eliot texts. *Felix Holt, the Radical*, for example—the least critically and commercially successful of all Eliot's novels in her lifetime, and 'hardly ever mentioned' since, as Leavis (who greatly admired parts of it) observed[24]—shifts to the centre of studies of, and courses about, the ideological work of Victorian fiction.[25] 'The Lifted Veil', likewise, which came to prominence in feminist criticism, remains widely read in courses dealing with Victorian literature in its broader cultural contexts—particularly, of course, interactions between literature and science. (It may also be argued that 'The Lifted Veil' is set in preference to *Middlemarch* because of changes in pedagogic practices in response to the growing aliteracy of students.[26])

It should be clear from the above that new historicism is 'new' because it treats 'historical context' in a new way. Literary works are not written against an inert background of historical events or forces. Rather, those works help to *produce* their contexts—in the plural: produce them continually, so that, even in the present (and this is the thrust of 'cultural materialism', more dominant in Britain, which stresses the ongoing political instrumentality of literary works), they play an active role in the production, or reproduction, of social realities. For cultural materialists, therefore, Eliot's novels are not passively 'recontextualized' by finding themselves part of a different, but pre-existing, social and cultural context. Rather, they go on performing the work of constructing those new contexts. To say that *Middlemarch* is recontextualized by the feminist movement, for example, or *Daniel Deronda* by the rise of postcolonialism, would, to a cultural materialist, misrepresent the role of cultural forms in producing those conditions.

In postcolonial studies, this is precisely the thrust of Edward Said's influential thesis about culture and imperialism, first published in 1993. This work, which traced the connections between 'the pursuit of national imperial aims' and cultural works that had little or nothing directly to do with those aims, might have been expected to have had a more significant influence on reappraisals of Eliot's fiction over the past decade. To my knowledge, only one full-length study of the impact of the British empire on Eliot has been undertaken.[27] There have been quite a number of postcolonially inflected essays, but they have tended to concentrate on *Daniel Deronda* and the Jewish question, first raised (controversially) by Said in his *The Question of Palestine* in 1979, when he argued that Eliot 'cannot sustain her admiration of Zionism except by seeing it as a method for transforming the East into the West'. Eliot's Jews, he pointed out, were 'European prototypes so far as colonizing the East is concerned',[28] while the Palestinians and others who actually lived in the future Israel, were virtually non-existent to Westerners. This set the tone for subsequent readings of race and nation in *Daniel Deronda*, some of which charged Eliot with a submerged racism (Deronda's real mission is to lead the Jews *out of* England). There has, however, been little attempt to address, through readings of the novels, the validity of Said's central argument in *Culture and Imperialism* that mid-Victorian British writing which was not directly concerned with imperial matters nevertheless 'nurtured the sentiment, rationale, and above all the imagination of empire'.[29]

Nor might one expect Eliot's high seriousness to be of much interest to cultural studies, which has, since the 1970s, overwhelmingly privileged popular and mass culture in the twentieth century. Earlier work in British cultural studies, however, which had its roots in post-war adult education and the expansion of polytechnics in the 1950s, was very much concerned with the historical relationships between 'culture' and 'society': two interlocked concepts central to Victorian self-understanding. The work of the Marxist humanist Raymond Williams, most notably, was the first to place Eliot's fiction within nineteenth-century traditions of social thought, and, more radically still, to initiate a whole way of looking at society and culture. It is now taken for granted that society 'provides the context in which cultural objects become meaningful, and culture provides one of the means by which social relationships are realized'.[30] This conception of the interdependence of cultural forms such as the novel and the society in which they were produced, and the societies in which they are subsequently *re*produced, in effect opened up work like Eliot's to the social critiques of later generations—Marxism and feminism in the Seventies and Eighties, and new historicism subsequently.

Of late, however, cultural studies has tended to intersect with the high Victorians only when *they* intersect with popular or everyday cultures. Eliot has only very recently, and only momentarily, attracted the kind of mass popularity associated with Dickens and Hardy—let alone that other stellar 'Victorian', Jane Austen.[31] In 1994, tied into the BBC television drama, *Middlemarch* rose to the top of the best-seller lists in Britain for a few weeks. But Eliot has since subsided again into relative obscurity. In part this is because her work has resisted the commodification of literary heritage so much a part of the survival of a few major Victorians in the second half of the twentieth century. This is unusual: Eliot, after all, is not one of the unread Victorians, as we have seen. She is not like other leading figures—Meredith, say, or the Brownings, or Carlyle—who are no longer strongly identified by a wide public, whatever ongoing influence their thought and writing might command. Yet Eliot remains on the fringes of modern popular consciousness, despite the fact that the 'great divide' between high-modernist fiction and mass-market popular fiction has long since given way to a new divide between mass-marketed 'literary fiction' and mass-marketed 'genre fiction'. Assisted by the rise of the new generation 'classic serial' on television, Victorian novels have begun to find new markets. In the book trade, 'classics' were first made available in handsome, cheap, pocket-sized uniform editions (such as 'World's Classics' and

'Everyman' editions) before the First World War; since then, they have been constantly repackaged in paperback editions as fashions and tastes have changed. Gradually, however, classic fiction has become available to two overlapping readerships, one browsing the 'classics' shelves of the large booksellers (where titles have been aggressively discounted since the 1990s); and the other the contemporary 'literary fiction' shelves, where Eliot sits between Umberto Eco and Bret Easton Ellis.

Many of those readers would be likely to have encountered the writing of George Eliot not in her own novels, however, but in other contemporary novels—as quotation. The best known of all Eliot quotations, 'the other side of silence' passage from *Middlemarch*, chapter 20, has become virtually one of the ways of indicating 'literariness' in modern literary fiction. As well as being the title of more than a dozen mass-market fiction and non-fiction books in the past decade,[32] 'the other side of silence' has served as title or epigraph to numerous recent literary novels, including *In the Eye of the Sun* (1992), by the Egyptian-English novelist, Ahdaf Souief, *Unless* (2002) by the American-Canadian novelist and poet Carol Shields, and *The Other Side of Silence* (2002) by the South African novelist and academic André Brink. Removed from its original context, the passage takes on entirely new meanings in these books: no longer a gnomic observation about the nature of subjectivity and sympathy, it has come to express in shorthand the coercive or violent silencing of women, and to act as a point of entry into narratives exploring the different ways in which women respond to this silencing.

If it is fruitless to speculate what Eliot might have thought of, say, Brink's shocking vision of colonial violence in Africa as a destiny for her mild conceit, it is worth noting that there was a time when Eliot's work was represented to many readers exclusively through such excerpted phrases, sentences, and short passages. As Leah Price has shown, Eliot's fiction was 'punctuated with epigraphs and self-contained digressions', and was therefore highly conducive to being repackaged as 'reusable wisdom' in anthologies, calendars, school-books, pocket booklets, and birthday books.[33] Significantly, Eliot herself was involved in that process. In the second half of 1871 a Scottish teacher, Alexander Main, wrote more than twenty gushing fan letters to her, culminating in a request to put together an anthology of excerpts from her work. Lewes, as ever alert to a publishing opportunity, took the proposal to Blackwood, who promptly had Main's *Wise, Witty, and Tender Sayings of George Eliot* ready for the 1871 Christmas market. The book was a commercial success, and went into a number of subsequent editions as new novels produced new sayings, encouraging Blackwood to commission a companion *George Eliot Birthday Book* in 1878. Eliot, although she went along with these anthologies, was extremely dubious about the value (and tastefulness) of such books, and concerned about being associated with them. In a letter to Blackwood she repeated the familiar argument that her books were 'not properly separable into "direct" and "indirect" teaching', and instructed—a little shakily, given her willing involvement in the project—that unless 'my readers are more moved by the ends I seek by my works as wholes than by an assemblage of extracts, my writings are a mistake' (*Letters*, v. 458–9). Yet Eliot did want, more than anything, to move her readers, to influence them. She was acutely aware of 'the quickening spread of all influences' (*Letters*, v. 372) under the impetus of economic and imperial expansion, education, and technological progress. Yet she was troubled by the thought that her own writing might have little influence on the great international reading public opening up before her. She was dismayed, for example, by the commercial failure of the cheap illustrated serial reissues of her novels destined for this new generation of working-class readers, telling Blackwood of 'the strengthening testimonies that have happened to come to me, of people who care about every one of my books and continue to read them—especially young men, who are just the class I care most to influence' (*Letters*, iv. 397). Ironically, Eliot found her great reading public not in the Felix Holt-like young men she cared most to influence, but in a mass market of (mostly) women, where her writing was consumed not as narrative but as 'gems from George Eliot'.

Eliot on Film and Television

The popular appeal of Eliot's sayings proved that her writing could be marketed to a 'middlebrow' twentieth-century readership eager for the cultural capital of the Victorian high bourgeoisie, but disinclined to read long Victorian novels. As the century progressed, however, and the value of Victorian cultural capital plummeted, these collections of potted wisdom, with their anachronistic and demanding vocabulary and syntax, and their dreary intellectualizing and moralizing, contributed to the decline of Eliot's reputation as surely as school editions of *Silas Marner*, the literary equivalent of brimstone and treacle for generations of students. Eliot's writing was something to be endured, not enjoyed; and without the compensating pleasures of consumption that, in the post-World War II decades at least, became such an integral part of the marketing of English literature. Two of the most important forms of consumption were literary tourism and mass entertainment. Significantly, there is no such thing as the 'Eliot country'—not, at least, in the modern sense of a thriving tourist region with picturesque countryside and perfectly preserved, heritage-listed villages and towns. Eliot lovingly depicted the society of her childhood, a society in transition to industrial modernity. Unlike Hardy's Wessex, however—the paradigm of a modernized pastoral (or perhaps a *modernizing* pastoral, since what is preserved and sold as Wessex is a landscape fixed in a perpetual state of transitoriness)—the agricultural landscapes of *Adam Bede*, the cottages of *Silas Marner*, and the gentry society and Georgian townscape of *Middlemarch* have all been modernized and industrialized (or bombed) virtually out of existence. Given, too, that the drabness of the industrializing Midlands was actually integral to Eliot's realist aesthetic, the chances of profitably associating places in the fiction with 'real' originals were slim from the beginning. Even on the back of the success of the BBC television serialization in the 1990s, tourists eager for the 'Middlemarch experience' did not visit Coventry, or any other Midlands town, but Stamford in Lincolnshire, where the serial was filmed.

If there has been no attractive commodity-landscape for readers (and non-readers) to visit in search of an 'Eliot heritage experience', nor has her writing lent itself easily to mass-media reproduction. Whether the dense *written-ness* of the writing—the dominance of the narratorial voice, but also the presence of those epigraphs and long meditative passages so conducive to books of sayings—has made them for some reason less amenable to the image-based media of film and television, is open to question. Yet as Daniel Cottom has remarked, Eliot's fiction 'is a commentary on an art antithetical to her own'[34]—in other words, melodrama—and mainstream cinema (and television drama) *is* that antithetical art. Only twenty film adaptations of Eliot's work have been made in the entire history of cinema—a negligible number when compared, for example, to the total number of adaptations of Dickens's fiction (more than 150, not counting television adaptations, since 1903[35]). It could be countered that Eliot fares rather well beside Hardy, however, a far more popular novelist in the twentieth century.[36] Yet the difference is that, of the twenty Eliot films, fourteen were silent films made before 1930; and most of the rest were made in the 1980s or after, were produced by or in association with television networks, and borrow, in general, from the unadventurous conventions of television adaptation. No Eliot film is particularly remarkable cinematically, as David Lean's *Great Expectations* (1946) is, or Roman Polanski's *Tess* (1979), although some that may well have been masterpieces have been lost (D. W. Griffith's *Silas Marner* adaptation, *A Fair Exchange* (1909), for instance). The most distinguished surviving Eliot film is Henry King's *Romola* (1924). Perhaps surprisingly (or not: see below), *Middlemarch* has never been filmed—yet *Daniel Deronda* has, twice; while *Adam Bede* attracted only two early silent versions. Unsurprisingly, the most popular choices for film-makers have been *Silas Marner* and *The Mill on the Floss*.[37]

Why, then, has Eliot's work attracted so few film-makers overall, and why should it have been so appealing to silent film-makers—just when her critical reputation and popularity among the wider reading public were at their lowest point—but not to film-makers in the sound era? W. C. Brownell observed in 1901 that 'the drama . . . of George Eliot's world is largely an intellectual affair . . . The plot turns on what the characters think', not what they say or do:[38] a singularly unpromising source, one might think, for mainstream cinema, which depends upon conflict externalized as plotted action and dialogue.[39] In addition, as Margaret Harris has suggested, Eliot's narratorial commentary, which conveys so much of the substance of the novels, simply poses 'too great a challenge' to film adaptations.[40] Nor do Eliot's novels—and the later ones particularly—have a clear narrative focus. In defiance of the Aristotelian dictum that plots have a single construction, Eliot's novels (like Dickens's, Thackeray's, or Trollope's) have several narrative lines running in parallel—they are 'large loose baggy monsters' in Henry James's exasperated phrase[41]—which gain their coherence from a combination of converging storylines, thematic correspondences, analogies, echoes, and contrasts. Their very size and unwieldiness makes them difficult to condense into feature-length films—hence the popularity of the more unified *Mill on the Floss* and *Silas Marner*.[42] (Perhaps the cinematic descendants of the multi-plot Victorian novel are the multi-character, multi-storyline films, of which *Grand Hotel* (1932) was probably the original and Robert Altman's *Nashville* (1975) probably the most significant.)

It could be argued that Eliot enjoyed something of a vogue in the silent movie era simply because nineteenth-century novels and plays (and even narrative poems: most famously, Tennyson's *Enoch Arden*) were routinely mined for material. The work of Griffith, in particular, has been seen as a bridge between the aesthetics of Victorian visual and language arts and the aesthetics of cinema, and between an essentially Victorian sensibility (he believed, as Eliot had, that art performed a social and moral function) and the sensibility of the cinema-goer. The historical costume film, in which the melodrama is played out against a background of turbulent historical events and involves historical figures, is as old as cinema. In 1924, Inspiration Pictures (in conjunction with MGM) produced a feature-length version of *Romola*, directed by Henry King (who later directed the musical, *Carousel* (1956)), and starring the Gish sisters, Lillian and Dorothy, as Romola and Tessa, William Powell as Tito, and Ronald Colman as an artist, Carlo Buccellini, whose character was created for the film. Described in the film-trade magazine *Bioscope* as a 'romantic drama', deemed 'suitable, perhaps, for large better-class houses, but . . . not "high-brow" ',[43] *Romola* was shot on location in Florence and Pisa. There are significant plot changes in the film which highlight the challenges of bringing Eliot's fiction to the screen. Stripped of most of the dialogue and narratorial commentary, Tito's protracted slide into corruption cannot be represented at all, since it takes no visible dramatic form, but occurs almost imperceptibly. In the film he must be represented as a villain from the start, whose essential evil is recognized only by Buccellini the artist.

It is also true that, without the encumbrance of spoken dialogue, silent movies were able to strip away the wordy bulk of the novels and focus on the dramatic—and melodramatic—potential of the narrative situations. It is little wonder, then, that the novels with more melodramatic potential, *Silas Marner* and *The Mill on the Floss*, were the most popular choices for silent movie-makers. Indeed, as Harris has commented, the fairy-tale plot of *Silas Marner* (misanthrope redeemed by child) is virtually a Hollywood staple, informing dozens of movies from *Pollyanna* and *Little Lord Fauntleroy* to the Shirley Temple vehicle *Little Miss Marker* (1934).[44] No fewer than six versions of *Silas* itself were made between 1909 and 1922; then nothing for sixty-five years until the BBC and the American Arts and Entertainment Network version, produced as a television film for cinema release by Louis Marks (who also co-wrote the screenplay), directed by Giles Foster, and starring Ben Kingsley as Silas and Jenny Agutter as Nancy Lammeter. Marks later produced *Middlemarch* and *Daniel Deronda* for BBC television, and this version of *Silas* anticipates in many ways the breakthrough classic-serial style of those later adaptations. It never quite loses the feel of a BBC costume drama, although the production values are uniformly high, and it manages to evoke in its muted palette the black wintry desolation of Silas's life yielding to the pastoral idyll, and to convey in its atmospheric music the allegorical character of the original tale. The wonderful performance by Kingsley, whose face in close-up conveys so much of the film's meaning, also lends it a cinematic quality that is largely supported by the rest of the cast, including, among the Rainbow Inn rustics, Jim Broadbent (although Patrick Ryecart as a stiff, slightly comical Godfrey Cass, fails to carry off a difficult role).

In 1994, comedian Steve Martin produced, wrote, and starred in *A Simple Twist of Fate*, an unlikely and unsuccessful modern-dress adaptation of *Silas Marner*, released the year before the most well-known mid-1990s 'updating' of a classic novel, *Clueless* (1995), Amy Heckerling's version of Jane Austen's *Emma*. Set in contemporary small-town Georgia, the Silas Marner character in *Simple Twist* is Michael McCann, who is embittered and reclusive, living and work-ing alone, making fine furniture and spending all his money on collectible gold coins. The plot follows *Silas Marner* closely: McCann discovers an Eppie-figure (whom he names Mathilda) in his cabin one night, and finds her mother dead in the snow outside; the Cass brothers are made over into the Newland brothers—John, the wealthy senator and secret father of the child (Gabriel Byrne) who wants her back to promote his political career, and Tanny, his brother who goes the way of nasty Dunsey Cass. The plot is resolved through a court battle for custody of the child, and the draining of the local pond. Any expectation that the clownish Martin—whose writing credits range from a successful adaptation of the classic French play *Cyrano de Bergerac* in *Roxanne* (1987) to the film of his own play *Picasso at the Lapin Agile* (2003)—would invest the Silas story with his screwball energy are quickly scotched, however. Martin plays Michael McCann with such insipid earnestness that one wonders what he was trying to achieve by choosing this 'serious' role for himself.

For many critics, *Middlemarch* (1994) represented the BBC's triumphant return to costume drama, 'a genre neglected for nearly five years'.[45] In fact the serialization of classic novels had continued virtually uninterrupted on British television for more than forty years when the BBC commissioned its second adaptation of Eliot's novel in 1992 and embarked on filming in the summer of 1993 (the first was in 1968).[46] What set *Middlemarch* apart from its immediate predecessors—*Clarissa* (1991), *Lady Chatterley's Lover* (1993), and *Scarlet and Black* (1993)—was money. For a long time the mainstay of Sunday afternoons and evenings, classic serials were traditionally made with modest budgets and enjoyed by a small, mostly professional middle-class audience. In the post-Thatcherite 1990s, however, the under-funded BBC was compelled to adopt a more commercially oriented (that is, ratings-driven) approach to programming. At the same time, its reputation for producing 'quality' period drama was vulnerable after a string of critical failures.[47] The stakes were high: if the classic serial were to survive, it had to be a commercial hit *and* a critical triumph—indeed, the *Middlemarch* publicity reportedly included vaguely threatening 'pronouncements that its critical success [would] affect the BBC's commitment to the genre'.[48] Under Head of Drama Michael Wearing (who had been responsible for hard-hitting drama series in the 1980s, including Alan Bleasdale's *Boys From the Blackstuff* (1982) and the nuclear thriller, *Edge of Darkness* (1985)), and Louis Marks, the BBC set about repackaging the classic serial as a distinctive 'quality' brand targeted to a broad general audience. Andrew Davies, who had almost three decades' experience writing television plays, original series, and adaptations, was commissioned to write the screenplay.[49] Teams of researchers were sent off to find locations—'intact streets with 1830 and pre-1830 buildings' for the town of Middlemarch, and country houses for the Middlemarch gentry[50]—and filming began on the six-part series in the summer of 1993. Each episode cost a million pounds to make. Scheduled in prime time, *Middlemarch* proved that the BBC was indeed 'sitting on an unexploited asset'.[51] For the first time in its history, it was able to attract a mass audience to a classic serial—5.65 million viewers watched episode one.[52]

The BBC took a risk with *Middlemarch* but it did have an important precedent in the critical success of the classic-serial blockbuster *Brideshead Revisited*, based on Evelyn Waugh's novel and made by Granada for the commercial ITV network more than a decade earlier (1981). *Brideshead* set the parameters of the genre that came to be known as the 'heritage film'—the cinematic representation of the British national past as the Victorian-Edwardian aristocratic elite in decline[53]—and the parameters of what came to be known as 'quality British television'. Its key elements were all once again foregrounded in *Middlemarch*: a narrative of the landed classes in decline, played out through images of them not apparently in decline at all, but gloriously in residence in their great houses (houses that now 'belonged' to the nation); scrupulous attention to the detail of costumes and interiors, landscapes and townscapes; and the breathtaking *costliness* of it all. Serious fiction called for serious money.

There was nothing new about heritage as cultural spectacle in 1994, when *Middlemarch* was shown. As early as the 1970s 'a decline in manufacturing and a growth in the services sector'[54] in Britain had led to an increasing reliance on tourism and leisure. Economic prosperity and social well-being lay not in industrial production, it was predicted, but in the production of images and experiences for sale at home and abroad. English Heritage was established in 1984, just as heritage films were taking off, supplying manufactured images and experiences that functioned in two opposing ways, depending on your political point of view: either to provide a refuge from the desolation of the Thatcherite present; or to celebrate the new national spirit engendered by the Falklands victory in 1982 and capitalized upon by the Conservative party for the 1983 election, fought on 'Victorian values'. But heritage culture was not merely a nostalgic indulgence. The commoditization of the past was big business: manufacturing towns and cities closed down, and industrial heritage museums sprang up in their place. Advertisers sold the (depressed) countryside to commuters or suburban professionals as weekenders and mini-breaks, and supermarket chains packaged processed food as an experience of 'simpler' rural lifestyles and communities. In all these simulations of the past, history was spatialized: turned into a display—a shop window—enticing consumers to spend money. There was little attention to conflicting versions of the past, which was homogenized as the 'heritage experience', whether it took the form of literary tourism—visits to the Brontë country or the Hardy country—or visits to castles, mining museums, Roman ruins, or great houses. Victorian novelists became highly marketable commodities, 'names' that helped to sell a whole range of products aggressively promoted as the 'literary heritage'— tourist experiences, processed foods, lifestyle magazines and television programmes, calendars and greeting cards, and so on.

Before *Middlemarch*, when classic serials claimed to be authentic they were claiming fidelity to the book on which they were based. Yet *Middlemarch* followed heritage films in presenting itself as an authentic version of the historical past—that is, an authentic version of the national past. The idea of 'English literature' as a unified canon of cultural works worth preserving as part of the national heritage took root in the decades of the nationalistic 'New Imperialism' (1870–1900). It was also, however, a response to the rise of imperial competition (with Germany, France, and the USA): 'English literature' was no mere national literature—it was a literature for all civilization. Televised English literature was therefore also a ready-made global product (classic serials had always depended upon sales to the USA, Australia, and elsewhere), offering a spectacle of the English national past as a cultural treasure-house of universal significance. When, in this vein, the director of *Middlemarch*, Anthony Page, described the novel as 'deeply English, and therefore as a result universal',[55] he was also describing the new marketing strategy for BBC serials, which would over the course of the 1990s abandon adaptations of Stendhal and Flaubert for sumptuous repackagings of the great canonical English works.

Looking back, *Middlemarch* was actually a rather risky choice of novel to save a television genre in steep decline. Extremely long, ponderously serious, and most of all neither very promising romantically (Casaubon as pin-up?) nor very cheery in the end, it would require clever marketing to sell. Clearly, the whole *look* of the production was vital. Location and period detail were meticulously attended to, and Eliot's language—at once 'literary' and warmly familiar—was put on display along with the fine houses, gardens, clothes, and accoutrements. '[E]very corner of the screen,' one critic wrote admiringly, 'is filled with scrupulous detailing, down to the Regency-style billiard balls and the red squirrels'. This claim to the authenticity of locations, props, and costumes was integral to the marketing of *Middlemarch* and its successors (most famously the 1995 BBC *Pride and Prejudice*),[56] and it is one of the characteristics that distinguished the new generation of classic serials from their more modest predecessors. In every shot, there is a double focus: on the characters and the drama; and on the setting and objects— landscapes and decor.

As I have already suggested, there are undoubted difficulties with turning Eliot into a heritage commodity, which the makers of the BBC production must have recognized. Coventry and its surround-ings are difficult to market as the 'Eliot country' to package tours, for example, and the representation of 'the past' in Eliot's fiction com-plicates any effort to reconstruct a heritage Midlands. All her novels were set in the past (even the contemporary *Daniel Deronda*, set seven or eight years before its writing), and all of them explore what it means to look backwards to a purportedly simpler rural or semi-rural life. One of *Adam Bede*'s first readers, Jane Welsh Carlyle, even likened her experience of that novel to a weekend break:

Oh yes! It was as good as *going into the country for one's health*, the reading of that Book was!—Like a visit to Scotland *minus* the fatigues of the long journey . . .! I could fancy in reading it, to be seeing and hearing once again a crystal-clear, musical, Scotch stream, such as I long to lie down beside and—*cry* at (!) for gladness and sadness. (*CH*, p. 72)

There is an undeniable nostalgia in Eliot for the rural landscapes of her childhood (even in *Daniel Deronda*) even as there is an intense awareness of the dangers of nostalgia (as in *The Mill on the Floss*). At the same time, the industrial present—the informing condition of Eliot's fiction—is always just out of sight, away from the rural tran-quillity. Perhaps conscious of the danger of blunting the novel's critique of progress and reform, the BBC *Middlemarch* is visually quite muted (compared to the sumptuous landscapes and interiors of *Pride and Prejudice*, for example). Some viewers in 1994 were wary, however. The review of the first episode in *The Times* questioned the 'alarmingly cinematic and profligate opening sequence' which depicts Lydgate's arrival in Middlemarch. In an apparent allusion to the opening of *Felix Holt, the Radical* (itself only filmed once in 1915, and never televised), it begins with a series of establishing shots of a passenger coach passing a team of navvies laying track in a railway cutting with Stevenson's Rocket steaming away at the head of a new tunnel (Lydgate, on top of the coach, announces, rather stagily, ' "The future!" ' as they go by) and makes its way into Middlemarch. The sight of the market square, the reviewer wrote, with 'zillions of extras, horses, leather aprons, acres of fustian, children chasing, poultry clucking, post-horn sounding', called up 'the dread words "Quality Street" and "Muppet Christmas Carol" ': surely, the piece continued, 'the point of classic serials is not the costumes and set-dressing; it's the opportunity to hear meaningful grown-up dialogue in whole, literate sentences delivered by actors who are good at it'.[57]

Which is precisely what the BBC did offer its viewers: a combination of unknown actors (Juliet Aubrey as Dorothea, in her first television role), relative unknowns (Rufus Sewell as Ladislaw), and viewers' favourites (Sir Michael Hordern as Featherstone, Patrick Malahide as Casaubon, Robert Hardy as Brooke) delivering grown-up dialogue in the novel described by Virginia Woolf as 'one of the few English novels written for grown-up people'.[58] Those magic words of Woolf's were, in fact, repeatedly invoked in the publicity for the BBC *Middlemarch* and in virtually every one of its reviews. By marketing it as one of the few television series made for grown-up people, and tacitly suggesting that ordinary television was an infantilizing medium, the BBC made use of the Woolf quote not just to promote *Middlemarch* but to promote the relaunched classic serial as sophisticated television.

Most of what is most grown-up about *Middlemarch*, of course, is transmitted through the voice of the omniscient narrator, which does not, however, translate very successfully to the screen. The Eliotean narrator cannot be turned into a character (as *Tom Jones*'s narrator was, for instance, in that novel's BBC adaptation), representing as it does a sort of consensual voice; nor is voice-over narration sustainable—a couple of minutes of Judi Dench's voice summing things up at the end is all that a television audience will tolerate. Few readers would agree with screenwriter Andrew Davies's remark that what he hated about George Eliot was 'the way she'll write a brilliantly

dramatic and moving scene and then spend the next few pages point-
ing out all the subtleties, just in case we missed them'.[59] Yet few
would wish to have Eliot's subtle commentaries punctuating every
scene. All that remains is to incorporate anything essential from the
narratorial commentaries into dialogue, or attempt to convey
the substance of those commentaries through the direction—in the
choice of shots and edits, or the use of gestures by the actors. The
most obvious example of the former—the bit we are all looking out
for—is the famous 'other side of silence' passage. In the BBC serial
this passage is reassigned to Dorothea, who tells Lydgate:

I sometimes wake very early, go out alone and imagine I can hear the cries
of all the scurrying creatures in the grass. There is so much suffering in
the world. I think of it as a kind of muffled cry on the other side of
silence—if our senses were sharp enough to apprehend it all I think the
pain of it would destroy us. I think we should be glad that we are not too
sensitive and work in any small way we can to help our fellow creatures.

A more complicated example of the transference of narrative commentary into aspects of the direction may be found in the long
disquisition in chapter 15 (which contains almost no dialogue) on
Lydgate's 'spots of commonness', which can only be conveyed in the
television serial in particular emphases in the television screenplay
along with particular directorial choices made over several scenes.

The BBC *Middlemarch* opens with Lydgate, signalling an even-
handedness of treatment which the plot structure of the novel, gradually interweaving the lives of gentry and town, virtually obliges the
television serial to adhere to. Yet the principal BBC publicity still for
the serial (p. 241) shows Patrick Malahide (as Casaubon), Juliet
Aubrey (as Dorothea), and Rufus Sewell (as Ladislaw) as a marooned
love triangle. The married pair look out at the reader/viewer from
the foreground—Casaubon with his careworn expression, clutching
the requisite volume, Dorothea bonneted and self-composed—while
Ladislaw mooches in the background, eyeing them both moodily.
Well might we ask, 'Why always Dorothea?' The PBS 'Mobil
Masterpiece Theater' poster used to publicize the series in the USA,
on the other hand, while it also focused on the melancholy three-
some, depicted them quite differently (p. 241) as part of a stylized
graphic treatment similar to those used for the opening spread of a
serial story in a magazine. The composition of this poster is truer to

the novel. No character is seen whole—and all overlap. Ladislaw is most prominent, Dorothea most central, Casaubon this time looking anxiously at the pair who are not yet a proper couple. The poster also places the principals in the context of Middlemarch—both the townscape, and the rest of the population.

The BBC poster was also used as a television tie-in cover for reissues of the novel in paperback, and Davies's characterization of Casaubon is similarly indicative of the close reciprocal relationship the classic serial maintains between the symbolic values of print culture and television culture. If television tie-in covers sell books which can no longer be read as though they were not themselves media products, classic serials idolize books as precious objects. They are part of the cultural heritage being so sumptuously laid out before the viewer: like great houses, hand-tooled leather books belong to an older world, one now most easily and pleasurably accessible through television. But they are also, of course, the source of the serial's authority, so the character of Casaubon, a man physically and morally withered by a lifetime in the library, presents certain problems. In the media-dominant, image-saturated, unbookish 1990s, there is a risk of undermining the whole enterprise of literary adaptation by undermining the life of the book-scholar. Patrick Malahide's wonderful performance in what must have seemed an unpromising, colourless role produced a Casaubon who was appropriately unattractive to everyone except the myopic Dodo, and really unlikeable; but whose dull eyes and watery smile concealed some great intellectual and moral struggle hardly to be glimpsed by ordinary fellows. So striking was this Casaubon that Mick Imlah, writing in the *Times Literary Supplement*, opined that 'readers of the *TLS* themselves [fellow-scholars, in other words] in particular may feel that the rehabilitation of Casaubon' was overdue. By extending 'real sorrow and sympathy' to the character, Malahide's performance rescued Casaubon, Imlah wrote, from Eliot's 'perplexing hatred of scholarship'(!)—and from his wife's irritating ignorance of scholarship. Here was a man who might well be expected to know when it was the proper time to begin writing his great work, but who was 'magnaminous' enough to 'pity' a woman who could hardly be expected to know better.[60] Is it true that the BBC *Middlemarch* treats Casaubon much better than Eliot's novel does? The narrator's famously brisk expression of sympathy for his failings—'For my part I

BBC publicity still for the 1994 television adaptation of *Middlemarch*

PBS 'Mobil Masterpiece Theater' publicity
poster for *Middlemarch*

am very sorry for him'—has little patience for someone 'present at this great spectacle of life' who will never be 'liberated from a small hungry shivering self'; whose consciousness will never be 'rapturously transformed into the vividness of a thought, the ardour of a passion, the energy of an action' but who will always be 'scholarly and uninspired, ambitious and timid, scrupulous and dim-sighted' (chapter 29). But it is not scholarship that the narrator finds odious in Casaubon, as the later scene with Lydgate in the Yew-Tree Walk makes clear. Casaubon is anxious to let Lydgate know that he has a great work unfinished, and needs to know how much time he has left before his heart gives way. But nothing about Casaubon's 'invariably polite air' changes as he talks, leading the narrator to observe:

To a mind largely instructed in the human destiny hardly anything could be more interesting than the inward conflict implied in his formal measured address, delivered with the usual sing-song and motion of the head. Nay, are there many situations more sublimely tragic than the struggle of the soul with the demand to renounce a work which has been all the significance of its life . . . ? But there was nothing to strike others as sublime about Mr. Casaubon, and Lydgate, who had some contempt at hand for futile scholarship, felt a little amusement mingling with his pity. He was at present too ill acquainted with disaster to enter into the pathos of a lot where everything is below the level of tragedy except the passionate egoism of the sufferer. (chapter 42)

Malahide's Casaubon precisely captures 'the inward conflict' implied in the habitual 'sing-song and motion of the head'—the 'sublimely tragic' struggle of an unendearing man.

   The full complexity of Eliot's treatment of Casaubon is unavailable to the small-screen adaptation largely because the dominant of the novel—*irony*—cannot be conveyed. Shifts in focus (the particular point of view of a character assumed by the camera) can go some way towards it, but one of the purposes of the novel (and the reason the narrator is so important) is to show that we can take no objective standpoint when we are inside our own lives: when we see everything from the centre of our hungry, shivering selves. *Middlemarch* explores the different forms of blindness and insight this entails, showing a range of characters living at the centre of their own lives, from the most *overtly* egoistic (Rosamond, Bulstrode) to the least (Mary Garth). Once these characters are represented alongside one another, and their lives begin to interpenetrate one another, ironical reflections and correspondences are set up.

What, then, is the meaning of the BBC *Middlemarch*? It has been described as 'an intelligent, conservative "reading" of the novel for John Major's Britain',[61] but we could go further and describe it as an audacious defence of the role of television itself—the role of a national television institution, more specifically—in the national cultural life of Major's Britain. From one point of view, it was about television as ceremonial display. 'The meaning of the BBC's latest interpretation is to be found', Chris Baldick suggested in the *New Statesman*, within

the context of attempts by the great institutions shaken by high Thatcherism to re-establish their position in national life by the customary means of pageantry and ritual. Here the BBC seems to be seizing a precious opportunity to upstage the royal family, proving that it can perform the rites of Englishness and stage the heritage with greater dignity.[62]

From another point of view, *Middlemarch* was a celebration of the power of television to commemorate ordinariness. Traditionally, classic serials are reverentially faithful to their literary originals— sure evidence of the old claim that television is completely constituted from other media: the classic serial is a shadowy version of a more substantial printed text; a kind of unadventurous, second-class cinema in which performances are only dignified by the presence of actors and directors borrowed from the theatre. It has been alleged that dozens of archived classic serials from the 1960s and 1970s were destroyed by the BBC before the arrival of VHS video-recording, simply because they were deemed valueless to cultural history. This was not an isolated outbreak of philistinism: television is an inherently ephemeral medium. *Middlemarch*, by contrast, is a monument to the values promoted by the printed text: the permanency of literate culture brings along with it ideas of the centrality of character, unity of voice, clarity, and the rhythms of abstract thought. But the Victorian realist novel is also a monument to mundanity, and one of the aims of the BBC *Middlemarch* was to demonstrate that television culture had something in common with even the loftiest of high-cultural icons. If some critics deplored certain soapy moments in the

BBC production where nothing at all seems to be going in the characters' minds,[63] others were fascinated by the sudden revelation that *Middlemarch* was an ancestor of *Neighbours*: 'a small community beset by in-fighting, gossip, marital breakdown and failing medical services, in which everyone is related to, or owes money to, or is being blackmailed by, everyone else.'[64]

The BBC *Daniel Deronda*, written and produced by the same team, is quite a different case. Heritage issues aside, there was little in *Middlemarch* to suggest explicitly that the national past was always 'above all a *modern* past' being constantly redefined 'around the leading tensions of the contemporary political situation'.[65] It may be argued that *Daniel Deronda*, on the other hand, is an example of the way classic serials may be used to tell 'symbolic stories of class, gender, ethnicity, and identity, clothing them in elegant costumes, and staging them in the most picturesque landscapes and houses of the Old Country'.[66] Shown in late 2002, it reimagines British nationhood during a period of renewed national confidence. Like Eliot's novel, it offers a critique of contemporary culture, but shies away from any explicit comparison between the rootless hedonism of the moneyed classes of the 1860s and cool Britannia. Likewise, it presents a muted version of the visionary Judaism Eliot offers as a renovating force for English culture—and the Zionism that goes with it—instead taking the opportunity to celebrate Britain's growing role in international politics in the aftermath of the World Trade Center attacks in September 2001.

Before considering these issues in more detail, however, it is important to note that *Daniel Deronda* appeared at the end of a decade of—or perhaps I should say a production line of—successful Marks-produced, Davies-written classic serials which followed *Middlemarch*. Interestingly, the pair had begun work on a *Deronda* script intended for cinema release just as *Middlemarch* was going to air, but negotiations with a funding partner fell through, and the project languished until 2000. In its place, they made *Pride and Prejudice* (1995), which quickly overshadowed *Middlemarch* and blunted something of its daring and originality as television. This was partly because, along with the film of *Sense and Sensibility* (1995),[67] it ushered in the Jane Austen phenomenon of the Nineties. But it was also because with *Pride and Prejudice* the BBC managed to tap into a huge, entirely new audience for the classic serial—women readers of popular historical romance. Casting director Jane Fothergill candidly admitted that Colin Firth's Darcy was a Mills and Boon hero: 'the naughty, arrogant, difficult man who under-neath has great charm and sensitivity, and is—oh, yes, most import-ant—rich!'[68] As sexy as Rufus Sewell's Ladislaw might have been, *Middlemarch*'s romantic entanglements looked decidedly con-strained, grown-up affairs next to the smouldering eroticism of *Pride and Prejudice*, which cross-coded sexual desire with the pleasures of heritage consumption, reducing the novel to 300 minutes of unresolved sexual tension amongst sumptuous big houses and parks.

There are plenty of allusions to *Pride and Prejudice* in the BBC *Daniel Deronda*—not least Hugh Bonneville's Grandcourt, described by one reviewer as 'a highly entertaining homage to Colin Firth's Mr Darcy at his most handsomely imperious'[69]—but Davies's rewriting of Eliot's novel resembles his rewriting of Austen's novel in nothing so much as its reductive treatment of the central relationships in *Daniel Deronda* as essentially romantic rela-tionships. Not that sexual tension is absent from Eliot's text, which makes a point of thwarting our readerly expectations concerning the developing intimacy between Daniel and Gwendolen (to say nothing of Gwendolen's expectations). But there are clear problems with making *Daniel Deronda* a love story in the style of the BBC *Pride and Prejudice*. The heroine is unable to love, marries a cruel, cold man out of financial desperation and a desire to master him, and has the most profound relationship of her life with a man she knows almost nothing about, who shocks her by announcing that he is a Jew and heading off to Israel with another woman. To make it work, the television serial (at barely four hours long, virtually a director's-cut movie) has to bring some background figures to the forefront and extract from the novel a series of intersecting love triangles: between Daniel, Grandcourt, and Gwendolen; Daniel, Mirah, and Gwendolen; and Daniel, Hans Meyrick, and Mirah. The website designed for the first episode of the drama accordingly included, among its offerings of *Daniel Deronda* wallpaper and screensavers, a poll asking 'Who should Gwendolen be with?', and inviting viewers to choose Daniel, Henleigh (are we on first-name terms with Grandcourt?), or neither.[70]

The BBC *Daniel Deronda* also makes sense, however, when seen as part of a progressive narrative of landmark BBC classic serials through the late 1990s and into the early 2000s. *Vanity Fair* (1998), *Our Mutual Friend* (1998), and *The Way We Live Now* (2001) all presented a very modern past indeed, providing a kind of costumed commentary on the (so-called) economic boom of the 1990s, with its low interest rates and explosion of consumer credit. *Vanity Fair* may be viewed as an attempt to pick up the mood (and possibly the audience) of the cynical, sophisticated twenty-something British dramas of the 1990s—most notably, *This Life* (1996), whose Natasha Little was cast as Becky Sharp. By the late 1990s, Gen-X hedonism seemed less attractive, however, and the brittle satire of *Vanity Fair* gave way to a darker and more menacing production of *Our Mutual Friend* (1998), another novel about the corrupting power of money. In 2001, finally, the BBC–Davies adaptation of Trollope's cynical, dispirited novel of corruption and greed, *The Way We Live Now* (with David Suchet as the arch-Jewish financier Melmotte), was broadcast in the immediate aftermath of the Enron scandal.

Daniel Deronda, Eliot's version of 'the way we live now', followed *Vanity Fair* in importing the (surprisingly named) Romola Garai from the modish *This Life*-clone, *Attachments* (2000), a slick, world-weary soap about an internet start-up company. But it did not pursue the post-Enron critique shadowed in the Trollope adaptation—although, interestingly, its timing may suggest an effort to balance the figure of the evil Jew Melmotte with the good Jew Mordecai (as Dickens had done in *Our Mutual Friend*, offering in the benign white-bearded Riah, a 'positive' counterpoint to *Oliver Twist*'s Fagin). Traces remain of Eliot's analysis of the rootless cosmopolitanism of the English moderns, but the fetishization of big-house England once more gets in the way. The camera lingers familiarly (and with brilliant intensity of colour) over the lifestyles of the rich and famous: the houses and parks, and trademark ballroom scenes choreographed and photographed from above in elegant slow motion and used to such effect in *Pride and Prejudice* and *Vanity Fair*.

The visual cues to heritage values in *Daniel Deronda* are not drawn principally from the preserved landscapes of the National Trust, however, but from Victorian painting. Because the serial's costumes and interiors reproduce fashions from the 1860s and 1870s, the art direction draws on some key visual styles from the period in popular

William Powell
Frith, *The Fair
Toxophilites*,
1872

William Powell
Frith, *The Salon
d'Or, Homburg*,
1865–75

The BBC *Daniel Deronda* drew on these paintings for two of its scenes.

society paintings: those of Jacques Joseph Tissot, who lived and worked in England between 1871 and 1882; and William Powell Frith, whose huge panoramas of English daily life were sensationally successful in the 1850s, reaching a mass spectatorship through cheap engravings, but who turned to more intimate society pictures in the 1860s. Overall, the BBC *Daniel Deronda* is more indebted in its look and feel to Tissot, who produced a succession of narrative paintings of the privileged classes at play (most of them incorporating portraits of his mistress, Kathleen Newton). The composition and colouring of Tissot's languid ballroom and drawing-room scenes, shipboard and picnic scenes, muted character studies, and riverside scenes are all echoed in the settings, costumes, and colour of the television *Daniel Deronda*. For some of the set-piece scenes, however, specific paintings of Frith's can be identified: the opening scene in the Leubronn casino is based on his *Salon d'Or at Homburg* (1865–75), and the archery contests on *The Fair Toxophilites* (1872: see p. 247). The function of these images is to authenticate and dignify the costume drama, and to code it unambiguously as 'Victorian'. In doing so, however, the BBC *Daniel Deronda* risks reconstructing 'George Eliot' as one more producer of the Victorianism which is already so familiar to us from the conventions of television classic serials and mass-reproduced Victorian images. Eliot's text is not entirely subordinated, however, to the securely generic 'Victorian' text of the classic serial. One of the promotional catchphrases for the BBC *Daniel Deronda* was: 'This is life on the brink of something larger'. If it cannot say precisely what that something larger *was* because we have come a very long way from Eliot's post-Christian ethical humanism, nor can Gwendolen say, and her confused determination to be somehow *better* still strikes a chord with us. Deronda's advice to her—'The refuge you are needing from personal trouble is the higher, the religious life, which holds an enthusiasm for something more than our own appetites and values' (chapter 36)—is likewise timely in a West now under attack for its perceived moral laxity: for the constant gratification of its own appetites and values. The fact that Eliot's fiction is 'stirring up young minds in a promising way' (*Letters*, ii. 423) in its recontextualized form on television suggests it still has important things to say to a society obsessed with material comfort yet increasingly, urgently, aware of its inadequacies. If these dramatizations do not finally do justice to

Eliot's fiction, that is not because they are pale middlebrow entertainments which cannot possibly come up to the level of the original literary work, or because they exclude the voices of those most important of Eliot's characters, her narrators. Rather, it is simply that Eliot's fiction demands to be *read*: demands the active, enthusiastic pursuit of something more than you see there in front of you.

NOTES

CHAPTER 1 The Life of George Eliot

1. Vita Sackville-West, 'George Eliot', in Stuart Hutchinson (ed.), *George Eliot: Critical Assessments*, vol. ii (Mountfield, East Sussex: Helm Information, 1996), 129.
2. Henry James, letter to Henry James, Sen., 10 May 1869, in *Henry James Letters*, ed. Leon Edel, vol. i (London: Macmillan, 1974), 116–17.
3. The cover of this book shows a photograph of Eliot taken by Mayall of Regent St in 1858.
4. *My Literary Life* (London: Hodder and Stoughton, 1899), 97.
5. Ibid. 99.
6. *Nineteenth-Century Studies: Coleridge to Matthew Arnold* (1949; Harmondsworth: Penguin Books, 1973), 215.
7. Gordon S. Haight (ed.), *Selections from George Eliot's Letters* (New Haven: Yale University Press, 1985), 9 (27 Feb. 1840).
8. Charles Bray, *Phases of Opinion and Experience during a Long Life: An Autobiography* (London: Longmans, Green and Co., 1884), 70.
9. Hennell, *An Inquiry Concerning the Origin of Christianity*, 3rd edn. (London: Turner and Co., 1870), pp. v–vi.
10. Ibid., p. vi.
11. F. W. H. Myers, 'George Eliot' (1881), in Hutchinson (ed.), *George Eliot: Critical Assessments*, ii. 637.
12. Peter C. Hodgson, 'Introduction', in David Friedrich Strauss, *The Life of Jesus Critically Examined* (1840), ed. and trans. George Eliot (1846; London: SCM Press, 1973), p. xlviii.
13. *The Real Life of Mary Ann Evans: George Eliot, her Letters and Fiction* (Ithaca, NY: Cornell University Press, 1994), 78.
14. *An Autobiography*, 2 vols., in *The Works of Herbert Spencer*, vols. xx–xxi (Osnabrück: Otto Zeller, 1966), ii. 33.
15. See Gordon S. Haight, *George Eliot and John Chapman. With Chapman's Diaries* (New Haven: Yale University Press, 1940); and N. N. Feltes, *Modes of Production of Victorian Novels* (Chicago: University of Chicago Press, 1986), ch. 3.
16. Rosemary Ashton, *George Eliot: A Life* (Harmondsworth: Penguin Books, 1997), 84–5.
17. Haight, *Eliot and Chapman*, 147.
18. Spencer, *Autobiography*, i. 399.
19. Ibid. 395.
20. David Duncan, *The Life and Letters of Hebert Spencer* (London: Methuen, 1908), 63.
21. Sir Mountstuart Grant Duff (1898), quoted by Haight in 'George Eliot and her Correspondents', *Letters*, vol. i, p. lxix.

22. Rosemary Ashton, *George Henry Lewes: An Unconventional Victorian* (London: Pimlico, 2000), 4–5.

23. George Meredith, *The Letters of George Meredith*, 3 vols. (Oxford: Oxford University Press, 1970), iii. 1460.

24. 'Review of Cross's *George Eliot's Life*', in Hutchinson (ed.), *George Eliot: Critical Assessments*, ii. 526.

25. Including 'Agatha' (published in the *Atlantic Monthly* in Aug. 1869), 'The Legend of Jubal' (finished on 13 Jan. 1870), and 'Armgart' (Aug. 1870).

26. *Felix Holt*, it should be said, still sold almost 5,000 copies in the expensive three-volume edition.

27. Including the Tennysons; Frederic Myers, poet and essayist, school inspector and founder of the Society for Psychical Research; Benjamin Jowett, classicist and master of Balliol, who supported secondary education and university extension; Oscar Browning, schoolmaster, historian, fellow of King's College, Cambridge, and Radical; Emanuel Deutsch, a Hebraist and cataloguer at the British Museum, who first interested her in Jewish nationalism (he contracted cancer and died in December 1872); Henry Sidgwick, Cambridge moral philosopher, Liberal theorist, and agitator for women's admission to the universities; and the physician Thomas Clifford Allbutt.

28. *The Life and Letters of Thomas Henry Huxley*, ed. Leonard Huxley (London: Macmillan, 1903), ii. 19.

29. 'A Woman of Many Names', in George Levine (ed.), *The Cambridge Companion to George Eliot* (Cambridge: Cambridge University Press, 2001), 23. See also Rosemarie Bodenheimer, *The Real Life of Mary Ann Evans*, 57–84 ('Mary Ann Evans's Holy War').

30. The title of ch. 5 of Haight's *George Eliot: A Biography* (Oxford: Oxford University Press, 1968), which follows Chapman's lead in characterizing Marian as a woman who always needed 'some one to lean upon' (the title of ch. 6). This view has been rigorously contested in subsequent biographies.

31. *The Country and the City* (London: Chatto and Windus, 1973), 289.

32. George Levine, 'Introduction: George Eliot and the Art of Realism', in Levine (ed.), *Cambridge Companion to George Eliot*, 14.

33. *Adam Bede*, she wrote on the manuscript of that novel, 'would never have been written but for the happiness [Lewes's] love has conferred on my life'.

CHAPTER 2 The Fabric of Society

1. John Ruskin, the art critic and social critic, was also born in 1819. The first major Victorian cultural figure, Carlyle, had been born in 1795, the same year as Keats. Thomas Hardy was born only three years after Victoria came to the throne, and died only five years before Hitler became chancellor of Germany.

2. Not without cause: virtually continually since 1789 European governments of all persuasions had been convinced that revolution was imminent, and many nineteenth-century social commentators—not least
Marx—believed that Britain would witness the biggest revolution of all.

3. Asa Briggs, *The Age of Improvement 1783–1867* (London: Longmans,
1960), 295.

4. B. R. Mitchell, *European Historical Statistics 1750–1975* (London:
Macmillan, 1980), 34.

5. Ibid. 171.

6. Joseph Fletcher (1847), repr. in Harold Perkin, *The Origins of Modern
English Society* (London: Routledge and Kegan Paul, 1969), 161.

7. Repr. in Richard Altick, *Victorian People and Ideas* (New York: W. W.
Norton, 1973), 75.

8. B. R. Mitchell and Phyllis Deane, *Abstract of British Historical Statistics*
(Cambridge: Cambridge University Press, 1962), 187.

9. *The Expansion of England: Two Courses of Lectures* (London: Macmillan,
1904), 10.

10. Robert Lowe Sherbrooke and John Bright, *Speech on the Representation of
the People Bill and the Redistribution of Seats Bill, May 31st, 1866; Rede
Èuber Die Gesetzesvorlagen Betreffs Volksvertretung Und Die Neuverteilung
Der Parlamentssitze Am 31. Mai 1866* (Wiesbaden: F. Steiner, 1970), 131.

11. Briggs, *Age of Improvement*, 244–5.

12. The Public Libraries Act was ineffectual because Parliament, fearful or
mistrustful of the consequences of working-class education, modified the
Act, restricting the ratepayers' levy to no more than a halfpenny in every
pound of rates, which could not in any case be used to buy books.

13. Altick, *Victorian People and Ideas*, 123.

14. Edwin Chadwick, *Report on the Sanitary Condition of the Labouring Population of Great Britain* (Edinburgh: Edinburgh University Press, 1965), 422.

15. Ibid. 423.

16. E. J. Hobsbawm, *Industry and Empire: From 1750 to the Present Day*, ed.
Chris Wrigley (London: Penguin, 1999), 175.

17. In *Sir Thomas More* (1829); quoted in Asa Briggs, 'The Language of
"Class" in Early Nineteenth-Century England', in Asa Briggs and John
Saville (eds.), *Essays in Labour History* (London: Macmillan, 1960), 45.

18. John Burnett, *The Annals of Labour: Autobiographies of British Working-
Class People, 1820–1920* (Bloomington, Ind.: Indiana University Press,
1974), 19.

19. Geoffrey Crossick, 'Classes and the Masses in Victorian England', *History
Today* (Mar. 1987), 30.

20. Elisabeth Jay, *The Religion of the Heart: Anglican Evangelicalism and the
Nineteenth-Century Novel* (Oxford: Clarendon Press, 1979), 16.

21. *Cassandra and other Selections from Suggestions for Thought*, ed. Mary
Poovey (London: Pickering and Chatto, 1991), 205.

22. John Stuart Mill and Harriet Taylor, *The Subjection of Women* (1869),
ch. 1, in *Collected Works of John Stuart Mill*, ed. John Robson, xxi. *Essays*

on Equality, Law, and Education (Toronto: University of Toronto Press, 1984), 261.

23. Ibid. 276.

24. See, for example, the discussion of Sarah Lewis's *Woman's Mission* (1839), in Chapter 5, below.

CHAPTER 3 Literary and Cultural Contexts

1. Matthew Arnold, *The Letters of Matthew Arnold to Arthur Hugh Clough*, ed. Howard Foster Lowry (London: Oxford University Press, 1968), 99.

2. 'Preface' to 1853 *Poems*, in Matthew Arnold, *The Poetical Works of Matthew Arnold*, ed. Chauncey Brewster Tinker and H. F. Lowry (London: Oxford University Press, 1963).

3. John Tupper, 'The Subject in Art, No. II', *The Germ*, 3 (Mar. 1850), 121.

4. William Powell Frith, *My Autobiography and Reminiscences* (London: Bentley, 1887–8), i. 327.

5. Linda Nochlin, *Realism* (Harmondsworth: Penguin, 1971), 13.

6. Lilian Furst, 'Introduction', *Realism* (London and New York: Longman, 1992), 2.

7. *Westminster Review*, 66 (Apr. 1856), 626.

8. *The Social History of Art* (London: Routledge and Kegan Paul), iii. 104.

9. Walter Houghton, *The Victorian Frame of Mind 1830–1870* (New Haven: Yale University Press, 1957).

10. Rossetti never exhibited at the Royal Academy; he showed *The Girlhood of Mary Virgin* independently in 1849.

11. *The Awakening Conscience* was commissioned by Thomas Fairbairn, an iron and steam engine magnate.

12. On the reciprocal influences of painting and the novel in the modern-life movement, see Tim Dolin and Lucy Dougan, 'Fatal Newness: Modern-Life Art and the Origins of Sensation Fiction', in *Reality's Dark Light: The Transgressive Wilkie Collins* ('Tennessee Studies in Literature', Knoxville: University of Tennessee Press, 2003), 1–33.

13. See e.g. K. M. Newton, *George Eliot: Romantic Humanist* (London: Macmillan, 1981).

14. On the other hand, Eliot was equally attracted to the oracular, 'preacherly' Wordsworth, as Stephen Gill has observed: *Wordsworth and the Victorians* (Oxford: Clarendon Press, 1998), 149.

15. Richard Holt Hutton, quoted in Rosemary Ashton, *The German Idea: Four English Writers and the Reception of German Thought, 1800–1860* (Cambridge: Cambridge University Press, 1980), 169.

16. Eliot wrote a defence of the morality of *Wilhelm Meister's Apprenticeship* for the *Leader* in 1855. As Ashton has shown, it is an important article in the development of Eliot's moral-aesthetic position, and demonstrates Goethe's central place in the formulation of that position (ibid. 166–73).

17. *Sartor Resartus*, bk. 2, ch. 6, in *A Carlyle Reader: Selections from the*

Writings of Thomas Carlyle, ed. G. B. Tennyson (Cambridge: Cambridge University Press, 1984), 233.

18. *George Meredith and English Comedy* (London: Chatto and Windus, 1970), 121–2.

19. The other two were the Whig *Edinburgh Review* and Tory *Quarterly Review*.

20. Walter Houghton, *The Wellesley Index to Victorian Periodicals 1824–1900* (Toronto: University of Toronto Press, 1966–89), iii. 547.

21. In 1847, for example, Lewes and his wife Agnes, whose versatility gave them access to a broad range of venues, published twenty-five articles between them in a wide range of periodicals, from the distinguished quarterlies and monthlies—*Fraser's*, the *Westminster Review*, the *Edinburgh Review*, and the *British Quarterly Review*, which paid between £5. 18s. 6d. for reviews and £19 for articles—to the more middlebrow *Douglas Jerrold's Magazine*, which paid up to £10 per article. Their total earnings from journalism for the year were £347 (*Letters*, vii. 368). In 1856, the year Eliot wrote 'Amos Barton', she also wrote twenty-eight articles and reviews: sixteen for the *Leader*, four for the *Saturday Review*, and eight for the *Westminster* (of which five were the long 'Belles Lettres' review sections). Her total earnings for the year were £254. 3s. 0d. For each of the *Leader* pieces, and most of the *Saturday Review* pieces, she earned £1. 1s. 0d; the *Westminster* paid her between £12 and £20; for 'Amos Barton' alone, she earned £52. 10s. 0d. (*Letters*, vii. 358–9).

22. Peter Shillingsburg, *Pegasus in Harness: Victorian Publishing & W. M. Thackeray* (Charlottesville; Va.: University Press of Virginia, 1992), 78.

23. John Sutherland, *Victorian Novelists and Publishers* (London: Athlone Press, 1976), 133.

24. Circulating libraries were not a Victorian invention. The practice of renting books grew out of bookselling in the early eighteenth century, and by 1801 'there were said to be as many as one thousand circulating libraries in England' (Lee Erickson, *The Economy of Literary Form: English Literature and the Industrialization of Publishing, 1800–1850* (Baltimore: Johns Hopkins University Press, 1996), 127).

25. Sutherland, *Victorian Novelists*, 20–1.

26. Under this system the fiction industry expanded hugely, but its expansion took 'the form of an increase in the number of titles rather than the number of copies' (Terry Lovell, *Consuming Fiction* (London: Verso, 1987), 75).

27. Guinevere Griest, *Mudie's Circulating Library and the Victorian Novel* (London: David and Charles, 1970), 18.

28. Concerning *Scenes of Clerical Life*, for example, Eliot's publisher John Blackwood (Mudie's sworn enemy) wrote to Eliot on 7 January 1858 that he had induced the 'Leviathan Mudie' to take the 350 copies by giving him 'an extra 10 percent discount', something he did very grudgingly to give the novel a start, considering it extremely 'doubtful policy' in general (*Letters*, ii. 417). Six months later Eliot and Lewes were fretting that Mudie had not yet advertised the *Scenes* in his list, and Lewes wrote to

Blackwood: 'As he doesn't know the author it can't be a personal whim—is it to *you?* E. of course takes it as a sign that Mudie doesn't think much of the book' (*Letters*, ii. 467).

29. Mudie's bought three-volume novels with a cover price of 31*s*. 6*d*. for as low as 18*s*.

30. Magazines like the *Cornhill* were 'part of the logic of the increasing growth and power of a nucleus of very large firms' after 1850 (Sutherland, *Victorian Novelists*, 23).

31. Alvar Ellegard, 'The Readership of the Periodical Press in Mid-Victorian Britain', *Victorian Periodicals Newsletter*, 13 (Sept. 1971), 18.

32. Railway novels ranged from 1½*d*. per part in part issue for Chapman and Hall's 'Cheap' edition of Dickens to 1*s*. or 1*s*. 6*d*. per volume for the various 'Railway Library' editions published by Routledge and Bentley.

33. Sutherland, *Victorian Novelists*, 35.

34. Trollope had incurred losses with *He Knew He Was Right*, which appeared in weekly parts in 1869 (*Biography*, 433).

35. Five thousand each of the first two numbers alone.

36. *Autobiography and Letters of Mrs Margaret Oliphant*, ed. Mrs Harry Coghill (Leicester: Leicester University Press, 1974), 5.

37. Richard D. Altick, *The English Common Reader: A Social History of the Mass Reading Public, 1800–1900* (Chicago: University of Chicago Press, 1957), 384; Kenneth S. Lynn, 'Introduction', *Uncle Tom's Cabin or, Life among the Lowly* (Cambridge, Mass.: The Belknap Press of Harvard University Press, 1962), p. xxviii.

38. Altick, *Common Reader*, 385. In 1860 Lewes wrote to his eldest son that *Adam Bede* 'has had greater success than any novel since Scott (except Dickens). I do not mean has *sold* more—for "Uncle Tom's Cabin" and "Les Mystères de Paris" surpass all novels in sale; but in its *influence*, and in obtaining the suffrages of the highest and wisest as well as of the ordinary novel reader, nothing equals "Adam Bede"' (*Letters*, iii. 275).

39. Sutherland, *Victorian Novelists*, 78.

40. See Gaye Tuchman, *Edging Women Out: Victorian Novelists, Publishers and Social Change* (New Haven: Yale University Press, 1989).

41. Ibid. 1 and ff.; and Lovell, *Consuming Fiction*, 73–5.

42. 'I am only just returned to a sense of the real world about me for I have been reading Villette, a still more wonderful book than Jane Eyre. There is something almost preternatural in its power' (*Letters*, ii. 87).

43. Catherine A. Judd, 'Male Pseudonyms and Female Authority in Victorian England', in John O. Jordan and Richard Patten (eds.), *Literature in the Marketplace* (Cambridge: Cambridge University Press, 1999), 250.

44. Eliot, who never introduced herself or signed herself with that name, insisted on its continued use in relation to her writing (she even wrote a letter to the compilers of the *Oxford English Dictionary* insisting they use 'George Eliot' when quoting from her work).

45. Writing to Charles Bray about her damning article on the popular evangel-

ist Dr John Cumming in the *Westminster Review*, she urged him to keep the 'authorship a secret. The article appears to have produced a strong impression, and that impression would be a little counteracted if the author were known to be a *woman*' (*Letters*, ii. 218).

46. 'The Lady Novelists', *Westminster Review*, 58 (July 1852), 131.
47. Ibid. 132.
48. Lewes also advised Sara Hennell, through Eliot, not to sign herself using her first name, but 'S. S. Hennell' (*Letters*, ii. 282).
49. T. J. Wise and J. A. Symington, *The Brontes: Their Lives, Friendships, and Correspondence*, 4 vols. (Oxford: Basil Blackwell, 1932), iii. 31.
50. Miriam Allott (ed.), *The Brontës: The Critical Heritage* (London: Routledge and Kegan Paul, 1974), 161.
51. Ibid. 163, 165.
52. Wise and Symington, *The Brontës*, iii. 68.
53. Ibid. 67.
54. *George Eliot* (Brighton: Harvester Press, 1986), 18.

CHAPTER 4 Eliot and Social and Political Issues

1. John Stuart Mill, *Public and Parliamentary Speeches*, in *Collected Works of John Stuart Mill*, vol. xxix, ed. John M. Robson and Bruce L. Kinzer (Toronto: University of Toronto Press, 1988), 39.
2. Ibid.
3. Terry Eagleton, *Criticism and Ideology: A Study in Marxist Literary Theory* (London: Verso, 1978), 114.
4. Hayden White, 'Afterword', in *Beyond the Cultural Turn: New Directions in the Study of Society and Culture* (Berkeley and Los Angeles: University of California Press, 1999), 316.
5. *Culture and Society 1780–1950*, 2nd edn. (London: Penguin, 1963), 118.
6. Eagleton, *Criticism and Ideology*, 111.
7. *History of the English People* (London: Macmillan, 1908), vii. 333.
8. 'George Eliot', *Critical Miscellanies* (London: Macmillan, 1886), iii. 126–7.
9. See Bernard Semmel, *George Eliot and the Politics of National Inheritance* (Oxford: Oxford University Press, 1994).
10. Ibid. 6.
11. Simon Dentith, *Society and Cultural Forms in Nineteenth Century England* (Social History in Perspective; Basingstoke: Macmillan, 1998), 40, 41.
12. In *Past and Present* (1843).
13. In Disraeli's Tory 'Young England' trilogy, *Coningsby* (1844), *Sybil* (1845), and *Tancred* (1847); Charles Kingsley's 'muscular' Christian Socialist *Yeast, A Problem* (1848) and *Alton Locke* (1850); and Elizabeth Gaskell's *Mary Barton* (1848) and *North and South* (1855).
14. In *Sir Thomas More: or, Colloquies on the Progress and Prospects of Society* (1829), 47.

15. The reasons for this have as much to do with Eliot's intellectual and aesthetic ambitions, which build on the traditions of the English novel of manners from Fielding, Richardson, and Jane Austen, as with her attachment to the settled traditional social formations of the countryside. Hers is an intellectual fiction that requires leisure for what she calls, in *Daniel Deronda*, 'the unproductive labour of questioning' (chapter 17), and her plots need the breathing space of large houses and farmlands, the perspectives afforded by long views, the time to think and talk. Even her most industrious characters, Adam and Felix, are much more likely to be seen engaging in that 'unproductive labour' than in the work they do. For all her admiration for the artisan classes, Eliot is not, like Hardy or even Dickens, a novelist of work.

16. *The Hand of Ethelberta* (1876; London: Penguin, 1996), 312.

17. Geoffrey Crossick, 'Classes and the Masses in Victorian England', *History Today* (Mar. 1987), 30.

18. It is not that the language of class is incapable of drawing the fine discriminations of social difference that held in these counties and towns, nor that it altogether abandons notions of deference or obligation. As Asa Briggs has pointed out, what mattered in mid-Victorian England was not 'the broad contours of class division, but . . . an almost endless series of social gradations', and 'the role of deference even in an industrial society was stressed', for example in the complicated metamorphosis of the idea of the 'gentleman' in Victorian class society. 'The Language of "Class" in Early Nineteenth-Century England', in *Essays in Labour History* (London: Macmillan, 1960), 69. On the aetiology and use of the term 'gentleman' in Victorian society see Philip Mason, *The English Gentleman: The Rise and Fall of an Ideal* (London: Deutsch, 1982).

19. *The Making of the English Working Class* (London: Gollancz, 1963).

20. Eagleton, *Criticism and Ideology*, 119.

21. *Culture and Society 1780–1950*, 114.

22. Ibid. 115.

23. Although fundamentalism is a later, Protestant concept.

24. Nancy Henry, 'George Eliot and Politics', in George Levine (ed.), *The Cambridge Companion to George Eliot* (Cambridge: Cambridge University Press, 2001), 140.

25. As the nineteenth century progressed, enterprises merged to form monopolies in order to control prices and production.

26. *The Works of John Ruskin*, ed. E. T. Cook and Alexander Wedderburn (London: George Allen, 1905), xvii. 55.

27. 'Culture and Anarchy', in *The Complete Prose Works of Matthew Arnold* (Ann Arbor: University of Michigan Press, 1965), v. 210.

28. Ibid. 97.

29. 'Introduction', *Hard Times* (New York: Harper, 1965).

30. *A Carlyle Reader: Selections from the Writings of Thomas Carlyle*, ed. G. B. Tennyson (Cambridge: Cambridge University Press, 1984), 35.

CHAPTER 5 Eliot and the Woman Question

1. Dinah Mulock, *A Woman's Thoughts about Women* (London: Hurst and Blackett, 1858), 14.
2. *The Common Reader* (London: Hogarth Press, 1925), 217.
3. Millett, *Sexual Politics* (New York: Doubleday, 1970), 139.
4. 'The Greening of Sister George', *Nineteenth-Century Fiction*, 35 (1980), 299.
5. 'George Eliot and the Ends of Realism', in Sue Roe (ed.), *Women Reading Women's Writing* (Brighton: Harvester, 1987), 25–6.
6. Ibid. 26.
7. Ibid. 27.
8. *Uneven Developments: The Ideological Work of Gender in Mid-Victorian England* (Chicago: University of Chicago Press, 1988), 11.
9. Lynda Nead, 'The Magdalen in Modern Times: The Mythology of the Fallen Woman in Pre-Raphaelite Painting', *Oxford Art Journal*, 7/1 (1984), 30.
10. *Athenaeum* (6 May 1854), 560.
11. It should be noted that in the 1850s and early 1860s, when respectable society was closed to her, virtually all Eliot's women visitors were radicals and feminists. At this time (after the breach with Cara Bray and Sara Hennell) she met the woman who would become her closest friend: Barbara Leigh Smith Bodichon, the leading figure of the 'Langham Place Circle' of feminist activists, who wrote the influential pamphlet *A Brief Summary of the Laws in England Concerning Women* (1854) and led the campaign for a bill allowing married women rights to their own property after marriage. Through Bodichon and other radical connections, Eliot was a warm friend and sympathetic supporter of a number of leading feminist activists, most notably Bessie Rayner Parkes and Emily Davies, and signed Bodichon's petition for the Married Women's Property Bill in 1856.
12. Sarah Lewis, *Woman's Mission* (1839), quoted in Elizabeth K. Helsinger, Robin Ann Sheets, and William R. Veeder, *The Woman Question: Society and Literature in Britain and America, 1837–1883* (New York: Garland, 1983), 12.
13. Mary Jacobus, 'Men of Maxims and *The Mill on the Floss*', in *Reading Woman: Essays in Feminist Criticism* (New York: Columbia University Press, 1986), 68.
14. Gillian Beer, *George Eliot* (Brighton: Harvester Press, 1986), 211.
15. *Portrait of an Age: Victorian England* (Oxford: Oxford University Press, 1953), 3.

CHAPTER 6 Eliot and Religion

1. 'Outflow', like 'outleap', is a very important word in Eliot's vocabulary.
2. U. C. Knoepflmacher, *Religious Humanism and the Victorian Novel:*

George Eliot, Walter Pater, and Samuel Butler (Princeton: Princeton University Press, 1965), 55.

3. Gordon S. Haight, *A Century of George Eliot Criticism* (London: Methuen, 1966), 199.

4. Valentine Cunningham, *Everywhere Spoken Against: Dissent in the Victorian Novel* (Oxford: Oxford University Press, 1975), 144.

5. In Michael Goodwin (ed.), *Nineteenth-Century Opinion: An Anthology of Extracts from the First Fifty Volumes of* The Nineteenth Century *1877–1901* (Harmondsworth: Penguin, 1951), 140.

6. Quoted in T. R. Wright, *The Religion of Humanity: The Impact of Comtean Positivism on Victorian Britain* (Cambridge: Cambridge University Press, 1986), 179.

7. Basil Willey, *Nineteenth-Century Studies: Coleridge to Matthew Arnold* (1949; Harmondsworth: Penguin, 1973), 231.

8. Ibid. 223.

9. Charles Hennell, *An Inquiry Concerning the Origin of Christianity*, 3rd edn. (London: Turner and Co., 1870), 'Preface to the first Edition', p. vi.

10. Ibid., p. viii.

11. Willey, *Nineteenth-Century Studies*, 230.

12. Ibid.

13. A method derived from Hegel, or perhaps from Schleiermacher, although Rosemary Ashton also argues that Strauss 'obviously follows Kant's great critical method' of 'criticising the work of his predecessors and by means of that criticism arriving at his own conclusion'. Rosemary Ashton, *The German Idea: Four English Writers and the Reception of German Thought 1800–1860* (Cambridge: Cambridge University Press, 1980), 151.

14. Interestingly, the intellectual background in religious radicalism that led Eliot towards ethical humanism also led her away from the more predictable political radicalism that, in Britain and Europe in the 1840s and 1850s, was generally associated with religious heterodoxy. In Germany, the atheistic humanism of Strauss and Feuerbach was a foundation for Marx's revolutionary socialism: 'the criticism of religion is the presupposition of all criticism', he wrote, because religion preserves the illusions of oppressed people about their real condition. In England, too, the rationalism of liberals in the *Westminster Review* circle was the focus of attacks on the Anglican establishment. The Chapman circle paid to have the *Life of Jesus* translated into English in the hope that it would accelerate the progress of radical reform by undermining the Anglican establishment and its control of public opinion. There is no evidence that Eliot undertook her translation with that aim in mind, or that she subscribed to the political radicalism of the *Westminster* circle or the more extreme radicalism of Hunt and Lewes's *Leader* during those years.

15. David Friedrich Strauss, *The Life of Jesus Critically Examined* (1840), ed. Peter C. Hodgson, trans. George Eliot (London: S. C. M. Press, 1973), iii. 396.

16. Peter C. Hodgson, 'Editor's Introduction', ibid. vol. i, p. xvi.

17. Ibid., p. xv.
18. Even Strauss himself acknowledged this difference in national character-istics in Hennell. He was so impressed with the amateur *Inquiry* that he commissioned its immediate translation into German, writing in the Pref-ace that because Hennell was an 'Englishman, a merchant, a man of the world, he possesses, both by nature and by training, the practical insight, the sure tact, which lays hold on realities. The solution of problems over which the German flutters with many circuits of learned formulae, our English author often succeeds in seizing at one spring' (quoted in *Life*, p. 64).
19. Comte's work was first disseminated in England by Lewes (among others): he went on to edit the positivist *Fortnightly Review* when it began in 1865.
20. Quoted in Wright, *Religion of Humanity*, 23.
21. Ludwig Feuerbach, *The Essence of Christianity*, trans. George Eliot (New York: Harper, 1957), 270.
22. Ibid. 83.
23. Ibid. 270.
24. Ibid. 185.
25. Ibid. 14.
26. *German Idea*, 155–9.
27. Feuerbach, *Essence*, 274.
28. Ibid. 273.
29. Ibid.
30. Ibid. 274.
31. Ibid. 270.
32. Wright, *Religion of Humanity*, 27.
33. Haight, *Century of George Eliot Criticism*, 203.
34. Ibid. 204.
35. Ashton, *German Idea*, 157.
36. *The Portable Nietzsche*, ed. Walter Kaufmann (Harmondsworth: Penguin, 1976), 515.

CHAPTER 7 Eliot and Victorian Science

1. Richard R. Yeo, 'Scientific Method and the Rhetoric of Science in Britain, 1830–1917', in John A. Schuster and Richard R. Yeo (eds.), *The Politics and Rhetoric of Scientific Method: Historical Studies* (Australasian Studies in History and Philosophy of Science, Dordrecht: Reidel, 1986), 273.
2. *The Grammar of Science* (Contemporary Science Series, London: Walter Scott, 1892), 10–11.
3. T. H. Huxley, *Essays*, iii. 38–9, quoted in Ed Block, Jr., 'T. H. Huxley's Rhetoric and the Popularization of Victorian Scientific Ideas: 1854–1874', in Patrick Brantlinger (ed.), *Energy and Entropy: Science and Culture in Victorian Britain* (Bloomington, Ind.: Indiana University Press, 1989), 212.

4. Huxley, *Essays* iii. 45, quoted ibid.

5. Huxley, *Essays*, i. 31, quoted ibid. 216.

6. Yeo, 'Scientific Method', 262.

7. Ibid. 272.

8. Ibid. 271.

9. Huxley's attack was not an isolated event. In 1853, Robert Chambers also added a long appendix to the tenth edition of his *Vestiges of the Natural History of Creation* (1844) in which he defended himself from the same criticism: that he was 'anti-scientific' because of his 'lack of practical research, second-hand knowledge, and disregard of proper scientific methods'. Richard Yeo, 'Science and Intellectual Authority in Mid-Nineteenth-Century Britain: Robert Chambers and *Vestiges of the Natural History of Creation*', in Brantlinger (ed.), *Energy and Entropy*, 1.

10. Rosemary Ashton, *George Henry Lewes: An Unconventional Victorian* (London: Pimlico, 2000), 237.

11. Yeo, 'Science and Intellectual Authority', 4–5.

12. Michel Serres, 'Paris 1800', in Serres (ed.), *A History of Scientific Thought: Elements of a History of Science* (Oxford: Blackwell, 1995), 428.

13. George Henry Lewes, *Comte's Philosophy of the Sciences: Being an Exposition of the Principles of the Cours de Philosophie Positive of Auguste Comte* (Bohn's Scientific Library, London: H. G. Bohn, 1853), 234.

14. *On the Origin of Species by Means of Natural Selection, or, The Preservation of Favoured Races in the Struggle for Life* (London: John Murray, 1859), 109.

15. *George Eliot and Nineteenth-Century Science: The Make-Believe of a Beginning* (Cambridge: Cambridge University Press, 1984), 23.

16. *Origin of Species*, 415, quoted in Gillian Beer, *Darwin's Plots: Evolutionary Narrative in Darwin, George Eliot, and Nineteenth-Century Fiction* (London: Routledge and Kegan Paul, 1983), 168.

17. Penny Boumelha, 'Realism and the Ends of Feminism', in Susan Sheridan (ed.), *Grafts: Feminist Cultural Criticism* (London: Verso, 1988), 87.

18. Peter J. Bowler, *The Invention of Progress: Victorians and the Past* (Oxford: Blackwell, 1989), 145.

19. Ibid.

20. Tess Cosslett, *The 'Scientific Movement' and Victorian Literature* (Brighton: Harvester Press, 1982), 14.

CHAPTER 8 Recontextualizing George Eliot

1. *To the Lighthouse* (London: Granada Publishing, 1977), 91.

2. The phrase 'George-Eliotite' comes from George Saintsbury's *Corrected Impressions: Essays on Victorian Writers* (1895), repr. in Gordon S. Haight (ed.), *A Century of George Eliot Criticism* (London: Methuen, 1965), 166.

3. 'George Eliot', in *The Common Reader*, 1st ser. (London: Hogarth Press, 1925), 205.

4. In Haight (ed.), *Century of George Eliot Criticism*, 161.

5. Ibid. 168.

6. Ibid. 169.

7. In Stuart Hutchinson (ed.), *George Eliot: Critical Assessments*, 4 vols. (Mountfield, East Sussex: Helm Information, 1996), ii. 87.

8. 'That greatness is here we can have no doubt. The width of the prospect, the large strong outlines of the principal features, the ruddy light of the early books, the searching power and reflective richness of the later tempt us to linger and expatiate beyond our limits'. Woolf, 'George Eliot,' *Common Reader*, 216.

9. The term 'great divide' comes from Andreas Huyssen's *After the Great Divide: Modernism, Mass Culture, Postmodernism* (Bloomington, Ind.: Indiana University Press, 1986), which argues that it was in fact an imaginary divide, and that all cultural products—even those of high modernism—were subject to market forces.

10. Brownell, in Haight (ed.), *Century of George Eliot Criticism*, 171.

11. *The Great Tradition* (1948; Harmondsworth: Penguin Books, 1962), 17.

12. Ibid. 44.

13. Ibid. 63.

14. *Critical Practice* (London: Methuen, 1980), 69–75.

15. 'George Eliot and the End of Realism', in Sue Roe (ed.), *Women Reading Women's Writing* (Brighton: Harvester Press, 1987), 19–22.

16. 'Optic and Semiotic in *Middlemarch*', in Jerome H. Buckley (ed.), *The Worlds of Victorian Fiction* (Cambridge, Mass.: Harvard University Press, 1975), 128.

17. Ibid. 134–5.

18. Ibid. 142.

19. *Narrative and Its Discontents: Problems of Closure in the Traditional Novel* (Princeton: Princeton University Press, 1981), 107.

20. *New Literary Histories: New Historicism and Contemporary Criticism* (Manchester and New York: Manchester University Press, 1997), 1.

21. Ibid. 18.

22. John Frow, *Cultural Studies and Cultural Value* (Oxford: Clarendon Press, 1995), 3.

23. Eve Sedgwick and Adam Frank, 'Shame in the Cybernetic Fold: Reading Silvan Tomkins', *Critical Inquiry*, 21 (1995), 500.

24. *The Great Tradition: George Eliot, Henry James, Joseph Conrad* (London: Chatto and Windus, 1948), 74.

25. Most notably in Catherine Gallagher's *The Industrial Reformation of English Fiction: Social Discourse and Narrative Form, 1832–1867* (Chicago: University of Chicago Press, 1985).

26. The neologism 'aliterate' is defined in *Chambers' Dictionary* (Edinburgh: Chambers Harrap, 1998) as 'unwilling and disinclined to read', p. 38.

27. Nancy Henry, *George Eliot and the British Empire* (Cambridge: Cambridge University Press, 2002).

28. 'Zionism from the Standpoint of its Victims', *The Question of Palestine* (London: Vintage, 1992), 65.

29. *Culture and Imperialism* (London: Chatto and Windus, 1993), 12.

30. Simon Dentith, *Society and Cultural Forms in Nineteenth-Century England* (Basingstoke: Macmillan, 1998), 13.

31. Even among specialists, Austen sometimes counts as an honorary Victorian. John Kucich and Dianne Sadoff's collection, *Victorian Afterlife* (Minneapolis: University of Minnesota Press, 2000), includes a chapter on Austen: to accommodate it, the book is subtitled *Postmodern Culture Rewrites the Nineteenth Century*.

32. These are not, for the most part, books about George Eliot, but range across topics as diverse as meditation, deafness and sign language, the history of poetry, the history of gay identity, date rape, and postcolonial identity. They include a novel about the British KGB spymaster Kim Philby; a romantic thriller about a plane crash in the Amazon jungle; and a fantasy thriller about computer games (respectively by Ted Allbeury (1981), Helen Reno (2002), and Natasha Mostert (2001)).

33. 'George Eliot and the Production of Consumers', *Novel* (Winter 1997), 145.

34. Daniel Cottom, *Social Figures: George Eliot, Social History and Literary Representation* (Minneapolis: University of Minnesota Press, 1987), 125.

35. Based on Andrew Sanders's estimates (he suggests 'at least 180 film or television adaptations') in the companion volume to this one, *Charles Dickens* (Oxford: World's Classics, 2003), 224.

36. Patricia Ingham lists seventeen film adaptations in the companion volume to this one, *Thomas Hardy* (Oxford: World's Classics, 2003), 253–4.

37. And for theatrical adaptations: see Margaret Harris, 'George Eliot on the Stage', in Geoffrey Little (ed.), *Imperfect Apprehensions: Essays in English Literature in Honour of G. A. Wilkes* (Sydney: Challis Press, 1996), 225–34, and the discussion, in particular, of Helen Edmundson's innovative *The Mill on the Floss* (1994), which attempts to solve some of the problems of adapting Eliot's authorial commentary to the stage.

38. In Haight (ed.), *Century of George Eliot Criticism*, 171.

39. It has been suggested that Eliot's novels do not translate well to film because they contain 'a low proportion of dialogue', Harris, 'George Eliot on Stage and Screen', *Arts: The Journal of the Sydney University Arts Association*, 24 (2002), 28. Cf. producer Louis Marks, who was responsible for the 1985 *Silas Marner*, the 1994 BBC *Middlemarch*, and 2002 *Daniel Deronda*, and who admired Eliot's 'ear for language' which 'allowed her to write dialogue' that was 'closer to natural speaking than any other novelist of her times' (http://www.bbc.co.uk/drama/deronda/production2.shtml).

40. 'George Eliot on Stage and Screen', 28.

41. 'Preface to *The Tragic Muse*', in *The Art of the Novel*, ed. R. P. Blackmur (New York: Scribners, 1934), 84.

42. David Lean's two Dickens successes were also adaptations of novels with relatively unified plot-lines, *Oliver Twist* and *Great Expectations*.

43. *Bioscope* (12 Mar. 1925), 50.

44. 'George Eliot on Stage and Screen', 32.

45. Jenny Rice and Carol Saunders, 'Consuming *Middlemarch*: The Construction and Consumption of Nostalgia in Stamford', in *Pulping Fictions: Consuming Culture across the Literature/Media Divide* (London: Pluto Press, 1996), 85. See also Andrew Higson, who argues that *Middlemarch* revived 'the tradition of the costume drama on the BBC in the 1990s', 'Heritage Cinema and Television', in D. Morley and K. Robins (eds.), *British Cultural Studies: Geography, Nationality, and Identity* (Oxford: Oxford University Press, 2001), 251.

46. The first novel adapted for television by the BBC was Trollope's *The Warden* (1951).

47. '*Middlemarch* is a project of the BBC, which has had a string of failures in the costume drama department lately' (Louis Menand, 'Eliot Without Tears', *New York Review of Books* (12 May 1994), 5), including a 'truly execrable "Lady Chatterley's Lover" and a travesty of Stendhal's "Le Rouge et le Noir"' (Sally Beauman, 'Encounters with George Eliot', *New Yorker* (18 Apr. 1994), 86).

48. Lynne Truss, 'Middlemarch is Definitely Worth a Detour', *The Times* (13 Jan. 1994). Louis Marks, on the *Daniel Deronda* website, also wrote of *Middlemarch*: 'on its success hung a big decision by the BBC to reinstate the classic serial as a key element in its production for the future' (http://www.bbc.co.uk/drama/deronda/production2.shtml).

49. Davies's credits as writer of original series include *A Very Peculiar Practice*, his adaptations include *To Serve Them All My Days*, *House of Cards*, and screenplays for classic serials include *Pride and Prejudice* (1995), *Moll Flanders*, *Emma*, *Vanity Fair*, *Wives and Daughters*, and *Daniel Deronda* (2002). He also co-wrote the screenplay of *Bridget Jones's Diary*.

50. Rice and Saunders, 'Consuming *Middlemarch*', 86.

51. Beauman, 'Encounters with George Eliot', 97.

52. Average audiences for each episode were over five million (Rice and Saunders, 'Consuming *Middlemarch*', 85). It began screening on BBC2 at 9p.m. on Wednesday, 12 June 1994.

53. Also the subject of *A Handful of Dust* (1987), *Maurice* (1987), and *Howards End* (1991).

54. John Hill, *British Cinema in the 1980s: Issues and Themes* (Oxford: Oxford University Press, 1999), 73.

55. Quoted in Chris Baldick, 'Central Television', *New Statesman & Society* (14 Jan. 1994), 34.

56. In cinema historical authenticity was used as a marketing tool in Christine Edzard's *Little Dorrit* (1987).

57. Truss, 'Middlemarch is Definitely Worth a Detour'.

58. 'George Eliot', in *Common Reader*, 213.

59. *Screening Middlemarch: Nineteenth-Century Novel to Nineties Television* (London: British Film Institute/BBC, 1994), 40.

60. 'Let's Hear it for Casaubon', *TLS* (4 Feb. 1994), 17.

61. Harris, 'George Eliot on Stage and Screen', 36.

62. Baldick, 'Central Television', 34.

63. Simon Jenkins, in 'Messing about with George', described Lydgate's passionate proposal to Rosamond thus: 'Lydgate speaks the words and then charges across the room at the sight of Rosamond's tears. To swelling background music she sobs, "I'm so unhappy if you do not care about me". He seizes her in his arms and they subject each other to instant, jaw-crushing mouth-to-mouth resuscitation. *Middlemarch* gets a sudden dose of *Neighbours*.' *Against the Grain: Writings of a Sceptical Optimist* (London: John Murray, 1994), 188.

64. Baldick, 'Central Television', 34.

65. Patrick Wright, *On Living in an Old Country* (London: Verso, 1985), 2.

66. Higson, 'Heritage Cinema and Television', 249.

67. Starring and scripted by Emma Thompson.

68. From the BBC *Pride and Prejudice* website.

69. Andrew Anthony, *Observer* (24 Nov. 2002) (http://www.observer.co.uk/Print/0,3858,4553197,00.html).

70. http://www.bbc.co.uk/drama/deronda/

FURTHER READING

GEORGE ELIOT'S LETTERS, JOURNALS, NOTEBOOKS, AND ESSAYS

Ashton, Rosemary (ed.), *Selected Critical Writings* (Oxford and New York: Oxford University Press, 1992).

Baker, William (ed.), *The Letters of George Henry Lewes, vol. 3, with New George Eliot Letters* ('English Literary Studies' series, Victoria, BC: University of Victoria, 1999).

Byatt, A. S., and Warren, Nicholas (eds.), *George Eliot: Selected Essays, Poems and Other Writings* (Harmondsworth: Penguin, 1990).

Haight, Gordon S. (ed.), *The George Eliot Letters*, 9 vols. (New Haven: Yale University Press, 1954–78).

Harris, Margaret, and Johnston, Judith (eds.), *The Journals of George Eliot* (Cambridge: Cambridge University Press, 1998).

Irwin, Jane, *George Eliot's* Daniel Deronda *Notebooks* (Cambridge: Cambridge University Press, 1996).

Pinney, Thomas (ed.), *Essays of George Eliot* (London: Routledge and Kegan Paul, 1963).

Pratt, John Clark and Neufeldt, Victor (eds.), *George Eliot's* Middlemarch *Notebooks: A Transcript* (Berkeley and Los Angeles: University of California Press, 1979).

Waley, Daniel, *George Eliot's Blotter: A Commonplace Book* (London: British Library, 1980).

Wiesenfarth, Joseph (ed.), *A Writer's Notebook, 1854–1879, and Uncollected Writings* (Charlottesville, Va.: University Press of Virginia, 1981).

GEORGE ELIOT'S LIFE

Ashton, Rosemary, *George Eliot: A Life* (Harmondsworth: Penguin Books, 1997).

Bodenheimer, Rosemarie, *The Real Life of Mary Ann Evans: George Eliot, her Letters and Fiction* (Ithaca, NY: Cornell University Press, 1994).

Cross, J. W., *George Eliot's Life as Related in her Letters and Journals*, 2nd edn. (Edinburgh: Blackwoods, 1885).

Dodd, Valerie, *George Eliot: An Intellectual Life* (London: Macmillan, 1990).

Haight, Gordon S., *George Eliot and John Chapman. With Chapman's Diaries* (New Haven: Yale University Press, 1940).

—— *George Eliot: A Biography* (Oxford: Oxford University Press, 1968).

Hughes, Kathryn, *George Eliot: The Last Victorian* (London: Fourth Estate, 1998).

Karl, Frederick R., *George Eliot: A Biography* (London: Harper Collins, 1995).

Redinger, Ruby, *George Eliot: The Emergent Self* (New York: Knopf, 1975).

BIBLIOGRAPHIES AND PERIODICALS

George Eliot–George Henry Lewes Studies (Northern Illinois University).

Levine, George, *An Annotated Critical Bibliography of George Eliot* (Brighton: Harvester Wheatsheaf, 1988).

Pangallo, Karen L., *George Eliot: A Reference Guide, 1972–1987* (Boston: G. K. Hall and Co., 1990).

LITERARY AND CULTURAL CONTEXTS

Altick, Richard D., *The English Common Reader: A Social History of the Mass Reading Public, 1800–1900* (Chicago: University of Chicago Press, 1957).

Baker, William (ed.), *The George Eliot–George Henry Lewes Library: An Annotated Catalogue of their Books at Dr. Williams's Library, London* (New York: Garland, 1977).

Feltes, N. N., *Modes of Production of Victorian Novels* (Chicago: University of Chicago Press, 1980).

Finkelstein, David, *The House of Blackwood: Author–Publisher Relations in the Victorian Era* (University Park, Pa.: Pennsylvania State University Press, 2002).

Sutherland, John, *Victorian Novelists and Publishers* (London: Athlone Press, 1976).

Witemeyer, Hugh, *George Eliot and the Visual Arts* (New Haven: Yale University Press, 1979).

COMPANIONS AND DICTIONARIES

Levine, George (ed.), *The Cambridge Companion to George Eliot* (Cambridge: Cambridge University Press, 2001).

Rignall, John (ed.), *Oxford Reader's Companion to George Eliot* (Oxford: Oxford University Press, 2000).

COLLECTIONS OF CRITICISM

Carroll, David (ed.), *George Eliot: The Critical Heritage* (London: Routledge and Kegan Paul, 1971).

Haight, Gordon S. *A Century of George Eliot Criticism* (London: Methuen, 1966).

Hutchinson, Stuart (ed.), *George Eliot: Critical Assessments*, 4 vols. (Mountfield, East Sussex: Helm Information, 1996).

GENERAL CRITICISM BEFORE 1950

Bennett, Joan, *George Eliot: Her Mind and her Art* (Cambridge: Cambridge University Press, 1948).

Blind, Mathilde, *George Eliot* (London: W. H. Allen and Co., 1893).

James, Henry, 'The Novels of George Eliot', *Atlantic Monthly*, 18 (1866), 479–92.

—— '*Daniel Deronda*: A Conversation', repr. in Hutchinson (ed.), *George Eliot: Critical Assessments*, vol. i.

Leavis, F. R., *The Great Tradition: George Eliot, Henry James, Joseph Conrad* (London: Chatto and Windus, 1948).

Stephen, Leslie, *George Eliot* (London: Macmillan, 1902).

Willey, Basil, *Nineteenth-Century Studies* (London: Chatto and Windus, 1949; Harmondsworth: Penguin Books, 1973).

Woolf, Virginia, 'George Eliot', *The Common Reader* (London: Hogarth Press, 1925).

GENERAL CRITICISM SINCE 1950

Carroll, David, *George Eliot and the Conflict of Interpretations: A Reading of the Novels* (Cambridge: Cambridge University Press, 1992).

Hardy, Barbara, *The Novels of George Eliot: A Study in Form* (London: Athlone Press, 1959).

Harvey, W. J., *The Art of George Eliot* (London: Chatto and Windus, 1961).

Hertz, Neil, *George Eliot's Pulse* (Stanford, Calif.: Stanford University Press, 2003).

Knoepflmacher, U. C., *George Eliot's Early Novels: The Limits of Realism* (Berkeley and Los Angeles: University of California Press, 1968).

Miller, J. Hillis, *The Form of Victorian Fiction* (Notre Dame, Ill.: University of Notre Dame Press, 1968).

Van Ghent, Dorothy, *The English Novel: Form and Function* (New York: Harper and Row, 1953).

Welsh, Alexander, *George Eliot and Blackmail* (Cambridge, Mass.: Harvard University Press, 1985).

Williams, Raymond, *Culture and Society, 1780–1950* (London: Chatto and Windus, 1958).

—— *The English Novel from Dickens to Lawrence* (Oxford and New York: Oxford University Press, 1970).

ELIOT AND SOCIAL AND POLITICAL ISSUES

Armstrong, Nancy, *Desire and Domestic Fiction: A Political History of the Novel* (Oxford and New York: Oxford University Press, 1987).

Cottom, Daniel, *Social Figures: George Eliot, Social History, and Literary Representation* (Minneapolis: University of Minnesota Press, 1987).

David, Deirdre, *Intellectual Women and Victorian Patriarchy: Harriet Martineau, Elizabeth Barrett Browning, George Eliot* (London: Macmillan, 1987).

Ermarth, Elizabeth Deeds, *Realism and Consensus in the Victorian Novel* (Princeton: Princeton University Press, 1983).

Gallagher, Catherine, *The Industrial Reformation of English Fiction: Social Discourse and Narrative Form, 1832–1867* (Chicago: University of Chicago Press, 1985).

Graver, Suzanne, *George Eliot and Community: A Study in Social Theory and Fictional Form* (Berkeley and Los Angeles: University of California Press, 1984).

Meyer, Susan, *Imperialism at Home: Race and Victorian Women's Fiction* (Ithaca, NY: Cornell University Press, 1996).

Mintz, Alan, *George Eliot and the Novel of Vocation* (Cambridge, Mass.: Harvard University Press, 1978).

Semmel, Bernard, *George Eliot and the Politics of National Inheritance* (Oxford: Oxford University Press, 1994).

Williams, Raymond, *The Country and the City* (London: Chatto and Windus, 1973).

ELIOT AND THE WOMAN QUESTION

Auerbach, Nina, 'The Power of Hunger: Demonism and Maggie Tulliver', *Nineteenth-Century Fiction*, 30 (1975), 150–71.

Beer, Gillian, *George Eliot* ('Key Women Writers' series, Brighton: Harvester Press, 1986).

Gilbert, Sandra M., and Gubar, Susan, *The Madwoman in the Attic: The Woman Writer and the Nineteenth-Century Literary Imagination* (New Haven: Yale University Press, 1979).

Showalter, Elaine, 'The Greening of Sister George', *Nineteenth-Century Fiction*, 35 (1980), 292–311.

ELIOT AND SCIENCE

Beer, Gillian, *Darwin's Plots: Evolutionary Narrative in Darwin, George Eliot, and Nineteenth-Century Fiction* (London: Routledge and Kegan Paul, 1983).

Dale, Peter Allan, *In Pursuit of a Scientific Culture: Science, Art, and*

Society in the Victorian Age (Madison: University of Wisconsin Press, 1989).

Levine, George, *Darwin and the Novelists: Patterns of Science in Victorian Fiction* (Chicago: University of Chicago Press, 1988).

Shuttleworth, Sally, *George Eliot and Nineteenth-Century Science: The Make-Believe of a Beginning* (Cambridge: Cambridge University Press, 1984).

ELIOT AND RELIGION

Cunningham, Valentine, *Everywhere Spoken Against: Dissent in the Victorian Novel* (Oxford: Oxford University Press, 1975).

Knoepflmacher, U. C., *Religious Humanism and the Victorian Novel: George Eliot, Walter Pater, and Samuel Butler* (Princeton: Princeton University Press, 1965).

Qualls, Barry V., *The Secular Pilgrims of Victorian Fiction* (Cambridge: Cambridge University Press, 1982).

Vargish, Thomas, *The Providential Aesthetic in Victorian Fiction* (Charlottesville, Va.: University of Virginia Press, 1985).

Wright, T. R., *The Religion of Humanity: The Impact of Comtean Positivism on Victorian Britain* (Cambridge: Cambridge University Press, 1986).

WEBSITES

http://www.victorianweb.org/ George P. Landow's Victorian Web, a valuable resource for students of Victorian literature.

http://www.lang.nagoya-u.ac.jp/~matsuoka/Eliot.html Mitsuharu Matsuoka's George Eliot site with pictures, links to complete texts of Eliot's works, and extensive links to other, more specialized websites.

http://etext.virginia.edu/english/eliot/middlemarch/ An online study guide to *Middlemarch* created by a group of students in 1997 in association with the Electronic Text Center of the University of Virginia, featuring accounts of its critical reception and publishing history as well as biographical sources and an annotated bibliography of criticism.

http://www.bodley.ox.ac.uk/ilej/ The Internet Library of Early Journals, a digital library of eighteenth- and nineteenth-century journals, including full page images of *Blackwood's Edinburgh Magazine*.

FILM AND TELEVISION ADAPTATIONS
OF ELIOT'S FICTION

Adam Bede (US; director Travers Vale, 1915)
Adam Bede (GB; director Maurice Elvey, 1918)
Adam Bede (GB; director Giles Foster, 1991)

Gwendolyn (US; Biograph Films, 1914)
Daniel Deronda (GB; director Walter Rowden, 1921)
Daniel Deronda (BBC TV, 1970, with Robert Hardy as Grandcourt)
Daniel Deronda (BBC TV, director Tom Hooper, script Andrew Davies, 2002)

Felix Holt (US, director Travers Vale, 1915)

Middlemarch (BBC TV, director Joan Craft, 1968)
Middlemarch (BBC/PBS TV, director Anthony Page, script Andrew Davies, 1994)

The Mill on the Floss (UK; director Charles Calvert, 1913)
The Mill on the Floss (US; director Eugene Moore, 1915)
The Mill on the Floss (GB; director Tim Whelan, script John Drinkwater, 1937; with James Mason as Tom Tulliver)
Odio (*Hate*; based on *The Mill on the Floss*; MX, director William Rowland, 1940)
The Mill on the Floss (BBC TV, director Rex Tucker, 1965)
The Mill on the Floss (BBC TV, director Ronald Wilson, 1978)
The Mill on the Floss (GB; director Graham Theakston, 1997; with Emily Watson as Maggie Tulliver)

Mr Gilfil's Love Story (UK, director A.V. Bramble, 1920)

Romola (IT; director Mario Caserino, 1911)
Romola (US; director Henry King, with Lillian and Dorothy Gish and Ronald Colman, 1924)

A Fair Exchange (based on *Silas Marner*; US; director D. W. Griffith, 1909)
Silas Marner (US; director Theodore Marston, 1911)
Silas Marner (US; director Charles J. Brabin, 1913)
Silas Marner (US; director Ernest Warde, 1916)
Are Children to Blame? (based on *Silas Marner*; aka *The Little Outcasts*; US; director Paul Price, 1920)

Silas Marner (US; director Frank P. Donovan, 1922)

Silas Marner (BBC TV, director Harold Clayton, script Constance Cox, 1964)

Silas Marner (UK/US; director Giles Foster, 1985; with Ben Kingsley as Silas)

A Simple Twist of Fate (based on *Silas Marner*; US; director Gillies MacKinnon, script Steve Martin, 1994; with Steve Martin and Gabriel Byrne)

Les Liens du Cœur (based on *Silas Marner*; FR; director Josee Dayan, 1996)

INDEX

CVCA Royal Library
4687 Wyoga Lake Road
Stow, OH 44224-1011